YES, YOU CAN ADOPT!

YES, YOU CAN ADOPT!

A Comprehensive Guide To Adoption

Richard Mintzer

CARROLL & GRAF PUBLISHERS
NEW YORK

YES, YOU CAN ADOPT!
A Comprehensive Guide to Adoption

Carroll & Graf Publishers
An Imprint of Avalon Publishing Group Inc.
161 William St., 16th Floor
New York, NY 10038

Library of Congress Cataloging-in-Publication Data is available.

ISBN: 0-7867-1035-7

Book design by Simon M. Sullivan

Printed in the United States of America
Distributed by Publishers Group West

Contents

ACKNOWLEDGMENTS

I'd like to thank a lot of wonderful people who helped make this book a reality, starting with editor Philip Turner and author Walter Wager. Also, thank you to social worker Bill Betzen; Aaron Britvan, adoption attorney; Kathy Brodsky of Jewish Child Care Association of New York; Ronny Diamond of Spence-Chapin Adoption Services; Robin Fleischner, adoption attorney; Todd Gallinek of Four Corners Travel; Michael Goldstein, adoption attorney; Leanne Jaffe of Adapting to Adoption; Laurie Kroll, (of *Daybreak International*); Susan Kupferberg of Jewish Child Care Association of New York; Dr. Mark Magnusson of Children's Hospital of Philadelphia; Anne Malave, clinical psychologist; Mark McDermott of the American Academy of Adoption Attorneys; Mary Mooney of The Adoption Guide; Pat O'Brien of You Gotta Believe!; Dawn Smith-Pliner of Friends of Adoption; Susan Soon-Keum Cox of Holt International Children's Services; Wendy Stanley of Children's Hope International; Tim Swanson of Federal Travel & Cruises/Adoption Travel Service; Charlotte Urman of Brookwood Adoption Agency, and the folks at Nolo.com.

I'd like to thank Felix Fornino, Sam Pitkowsky, and all of the knowledgeable people of the Adoptive Parents Committee of New York, New Jersey and Connecticut.

Also, a very special thank you to all of the people who provided their wonderful stories, comments, and suggestions for this very personalized book on adoption. And, finally, thank you, Carol, Rebecca and Eric-my own wonderful family, formed in part through adoption.

Note: This book is designed to offer accurate and reliable information and present a wide range of opinions about the adoption process. The author offers this information with the understanding that he is not rendering professional services and is not affiliated with any service providers listed within the book. If legal or other expert advice or assistance is necessary, the services of a professional in the field or professional agency should be sought.

INTRODUCTION

In 1991, after wrestling for a while with infertility, my wife and I decided to pursue adoption. We began by joining the Adoptive Parents Committee (APC), a local support group in New York City. It was several years before the advent of the information highway, a time when interpersonal exchanges were still the manner in which people learned about adoption and formed networking alliances. Little did we know that within a year we would not only learn about adoption and adopt our daughter, but would also become very involved as volunteers in a group that for over forty years has helped families come together through adoption.

Over a decade later, my wife and I are now copresidents of the New York City chapter of APC. We have led many workshops, teaching people all about adoption. In addition, we have helped plan and organize major adoption conferences. Through these activities, we've learned a great deal from both adoption professionals and from families who have been formed through adoption. A dozen years rooted in the adoption community have provided us with a vast amount of resources and information. In 1997 I also managed to secure enough sponsorship to bring an adoption radio program to the New York City airwaves in hopes of spreading the positive word about adoption. While it lasted only a few months, it was the city's first adoption-focused radio program, and was great fun to do.

Today, while people seek out quick answers and find information at their fingertips, there is still a need for the personalized approach to adoption, involving real people and real families. With that in mind, I've included a number of brief stories from adoptive families to illustrate key aspects of adoption throughout the book. I wanted to write a book that would provide information and include the personal approach. I hope the combination provides a basic understanding of adoption and the many different stories that emerge from this complex process.

I'd like to say that *Yes, You Can Adopt* is the culmination of years of involvement in the community, but it's actually part of an ever-evolving process. The book delves into the state of adoption as it is today. By the time my daughter (adopted in 1992 as a newborn) reaches college, the process may have changed dramatically. However, while the rules, laws, and paperwork will change, the decision to adopt an older child or a child of a different ethnic or cultural background will remain a very personal one. Adoption is more than a "how-to" process of filing papers and signing up with an agency or an attorney. It is an emotional process that allows you to make informed, conscious choices in forming a permanent family. And yet, as is always the case when forming a family, there will be some degree of risk involved, plus a leap of faith.

While most of the stories here are positive, it is fair to say that from the beginning stages of the adoption process through your child's emergence into adulthood, there will be highs and lows, positives and negatives, great joy as well as a sense of loss, associated with this often-ambiguous concept. Nevertheless, despite the shortcomings, adoption is a way of forming permanent loving families. In my opinion that makes it something very special and quite wonderful.

YES,
YOU CAN
ADOPT!

Chapter 1
MAKING THE ADOPTION DECISION

If you're considering adoption, it likely stems from one of a few life situations. You are either growing tired of fertility treatments, were married later in life and want to start a family, have decided that single parenting is something that would be right for you, or would simply like to add to your present family.

While the reasons differ, they have one thing in common; They are all guided by the desire to love and raise a child. It is this common denominator that leads many different people, from many walks of life and ethnic backgrounds into making the decision to adopt.

Making the transition from thinking about adoption into actively pursuing the adoption process requires small steps. It is like a toddler taking those first few baby steps. For some, these steps are easy. Others, however, are like the children who cling to the sofa, fearing they will stumble and fall. Adoption is not a "typical" activity. It is not something that everyone does. It is also not something you will likely know very much about unless your family or close friends have been touched by adoption. Therefore, an added degree of trepidation comes with the need to follow a learning curve.

For most people, adoption is a route that was not in the "planning manual" for life. While it will bring you to your same desired goal—parenting a child—it is an unexpected detour. Thus, like most detours it will be full of surprises. Depending on your temperament, your personality, and your response to change, you can either move along smoothly or kicking and screaming (figure of speech, we hope) as you proceed.

There are always those individuals who experience new endeavors with a wide-eyed sense of adventure, confident they will reach their desired destination, but not knowing exactly how or when. Then there are the rest of us, who experience each and every step of the way with a degree of concern, skeptical of whether we will ever reach our desired goal. It's the old "glass half empty/half full" manner of looking at a new journey.

Keep in mind that today's prospective adoptive parents have a greater say in the adoption process than ever before. No longer are most adoptions a matter of "signing up with an agency" and waiting for "the call" to announce that you are now proud parents. Today couples and singles who adopt are quite savvy, as are birth mothers. Couples and singles pursuing adoption are proactive, whether it means making a portfolio, writing a "dear birth mother" letter, placing adoption advertisements, talking with birth mothers by phone, meeting with birth parents in person or selecting between international adoption programs in various parts of the world. More than 95 percent of adoptions come about through "working" the process. People must accumulate information, do plenty of research, ask questions and let it be known that they are very serious about the desire to become a parent.

Three Key Concerns

It is important to take a look at a few of the factors that come into play when you consider whether or not adoption is for you. There are three commonly found concerns.

Concern #1—Heritage and Lineage. Can I Raise a Child Who Is Not of My Lineage?

One of the paramount concerns for many couples, and singles, entering into adoption is that of "bloodlines," "gene pool," or the "family look." Often this has been found to be a greater concern for men than it is for women. There is no denying that the dream of having a "miniature version of yourself" is subsequently diminished, if not completely eliminated in adoption. With rare exception, your child will simply *not* look just like you. That is the first hurdle to overcome. For many of us, (especially us average-looking folks) this is not a great concern. Nonetheless, it is something to ponder. For some people, it will take time to come to grips with this realization. This is the first issue in which couples need to be sensitive toward each other. They need to understand that one person may be several steps ahead of the other in dealing with this concept. Remember, while a couple is adopting together, they may have very different preconceptions of what their forever family will look like. This needs to be discussed openly and honestly.

Bloodlines and gene pool follow suit. Your son or daughter will not have your inherited abilities in mathematics or your athletic prowess. He or she might be more outgoing or more introverted by nature. She may have musical talent or an artistic flair. On the flipside, a different gene pool means that diseases in your family, the need to wear glasses, male-pattern baldness, your inability to run fast, or your compulsive nature will not be inherited by your son or daughter. Although people do not always see it clearly at first for all of the positive genes that are passed along biologically, many negative ones come along for the ride.

In fact, after spending some time with your relatives, and, or in-laws, the idea of dipping into a different gene pool may look more appealing.

Never underestimate the skills and abilities your son or daughter may develop, some of which you do not possess. Through adoption, your children may excel in areas that you were never able to. You can encourage their abilities and even learn from them.

Too often parents assume that their interests or abilities in a specific area will transfer to their child biologically. The assumption is that if the father has artistic abilities then the child will also love to draw and paint. Frequently this is not the case. Aptitude and interest are two different things. Parents often try to push their own interests and abilities onto their children and are met with a negative reaction. Just because a child has her mother's lovely singing voice, does not mean she will enjoy singing.

Children are obviously very much shaped by their environment. You'll discover that your son enjoys telling jokes because you are a good joke teller, or your daughter likes to dance because you enjoy showing her your own dancing steps. Whether or not a child is innately good at something will take a backseat to their desire to try it. They will have fun participating simply because they enjoy the activity and have learned that enjoyment from their environment. Let's face it: Most people are average at most things. The degree to which someone has an interest and a desire to learn allows them to practice and helps them improve. Your children can learn so much from you—for better and for worse. Often you have no idea how much they are picking up just from being around you.

"Where did you learn the "s" word," asked a mom of her nine-year-old daughter who had just cursed. *"From you,"* her daughter replied casually. *"You say it every time you break something in the kitchen."*

"We discovered his talent for baseball when he was young," says Jon, whose teenage son Gerry has emerged as a major

young pitching talent. *"I was always a big baseball fan and a fairly good player, but I was nowhere near the level that he is on. His mother and I both encouraged him to play and worked with him in whatever way we could."* Through Little League, high school, and finally in college ball, Jerry has excelled as a top pitching prospect, scouted by major-league baseball scouts. *"It's important to recognize what skills your child has and be supportive."* says Jon. *"I read that Mo Vaughn was adopted as a child and encouraged by his adoptive parents to pursue his dreams . . . and look how he turned out."* Vaughn is a major-league baseball star and former American League Most Valuable Player.

Concern # 2—Other People:
What Will Other People Say or Think?

Let's face it: No matter whether we admit it or not, we are all influenced by the perceptions and opinions of others. Adoption will evoke a wide range of responses, some of which may surprise you. Keep in mind that if you are among the first in your family or circle of friends to adopt, you're open for your fair share of questions and comments. It is up to you to be fully prepared with knowledge of adoption and even some well-timed sarcasm, should the questions exceed politeness. Do your homework. Also remember that no one has the right to tell you what is or is not the way to start or expand your family.

Today, more and more families are familiar with adoption. In fact, some 60 percent of American families are touched by adoption in some manner, whether it is directly or through a neighbor, relative, or close friend. It is more common than ever before to know families formed through adoption. It is very likely that there are families that you see all the time that were formed by adoption. However, this still does not mean people are well versed in what adoption is all about.

The concern about what others will say and think is very real. The concern about how you will respond to others, even those with the best of intentions, is equally real and understandable. Many people have only a minimal understanding of how adoption works and much of what they have learned has come from mixed messages in the media.

You will need to discuss adoption with those closest to you. Many will be supportive; others will be skeptical. Be an educator and teach others what adoption is about. You need not fill in all of the details of the adoption process, but you will learn a lot as you proceed, and some of that can be passed on to those people closest to you. Sensitivity to all members of the adoption triad—birth parents, adoptive parents, and especially the children—is one of the basic lessons of Adoption 101. Members of the triad have feelings and deserve the same "political correctness" as other minorities. But it's more than just asking people to use the right phrases, such as "birth mother" instead of "real mother." There needs to be an understanding that adoption is a very real, very permanent way of forming a family and that adoption lasts a lifetime. All of that needs to be included — without lecturing—in your guidance when dealing with other people. Television sound bites, inaccurately reported news stories, and idle gossip have people believing many myths about adoption. Three of the most popular are:

1. Only rich people can adopt;
2. Children adopted from other countries are usually not healthy;
3. A birth mother can just show up and take her child back.

These myths need to be dispelled.

"I had always presumed that we would need to have a lot of

money to adopt," says Connie, of New Jersey, who, along with her husband Peter, is now a parent to three children through domestic adoption. *"I was also nervous that if we adopted domestically, as we wanted to do, that the birth mother would show up one day and want the child back. You hear these horror stories on the news, and they make you worry. It wasn't until we joined a support group that we began to dispel what were obviously a lot of misconceptions about adoption. Like anything else, you just need to know where to find proper information. Once we learned what adoption was really all about, we were very relieved. We had an entirely new perception. I guess you need to learn from people who've been there and done that. After all, once upon a time people used to think the world was flat until Columbus set sail and they learned otherwise."* Connie also added that beyond the learning process is the need to digest the information emotionally and assimilate it into your own mental image of what adoption is all about.

As for strangers, there's always someone who asks, "Where'd you get that kid?" or "Is she yours?" or some such intrusive or inappropriate question. Learn to have a thick skin and a sense of humor even before you adopt. One woman replied when a

Dispelling Myths

1. People of all income levels adopt. Adoptions through state foster-care programs cost almost no money at all, and other adoption fees (for international and domestic independent or through an agency) can cost under $20,000, or less than the price of a standard new car.

2. The vast majority of children adopted from overseas are indeed healthy. Screening today can even include developmental evaluations done by medical specialists, who look at videotapes of children living in orphanages overseas.

3. The incidents of a birth mother ever challenging—much less interrupting—an adoption once the child is in the home of the adoptive parents is less than 1 percent. It is the very, very rare exception and there are usually some extenuating factors in those rare cases you hear about every so often on television.

stranger commented that her daughter did not look anything like her, *"No, but she looks a lot like our postman."*

Concern #3—Health of the Child: Will My Child Have Health Problems?

Health concerns, during the pregnancy of the birth mother or those of a child in an orphanage, are very legitimate concerns. Today, depending on the type of adoption you choose, there are tests that a birth mother can be asked to take. She can refuse, but in most cases, if the tests (such as HIV tests) are not painful or intrusive she will often oblige. You can also get medical records from a birth mother's physician with whom you are working in an independent adoption. An adoption agency should also be able to provide you with health information about the birth mother.

When adopting a child from overseas, there may be a greater health risk, particularly because you will have limited background information about the medical history of the child's biological family. There are doctors who specialize in evaluating children from other countries, first by seeing them on videotape and then through actual examinations. See Chapter 9, "International Adoption." Health issues are a concern that you need to address. You will need to determine, in advance, your level of comfort in accepting some degree of medical problem(s). The best you can do is learn as much as possible about your child's present health and collect whatever data you can on his or her ancestry. There will always be some leap of faith in becoming a parent, even biologically, when a child is diagnosed with an illness that may not have been seen in your family for generations.

Adopting Together

For couples it is very important that the adoption decision be one that you reach together. "I'm doing this because she/he wants to" is not only the precursor of resentment within the relationship, but it also won't help with the adoption home study, in which a social worker evaluates you as prospective parents prior to adoption. See Chapter 4, "Home Studies."

Becoming parents will have an impact on every aspect of your life. While you may not both feel the same level of urgency, or be as vocal about your desire to become a parent, it is in your best interest to sit down and carefully voice your own individual thoughts about adoption before entering into the process. *Accidents notwithstanding, it is in any couple's best interests to discuss family planning.*

One tried-and-true method of determining where you both stand in regard to adoption is to make separate lists in which you each write down your thoughts as to how you feel about adoption. What are the reasons you think adoption would work for you? What are your fears, qualms, or concerns about adopting a child?

Comparing lists will let you discuss the issues that either or both of you may have. Issues regarding adoption often stem from not having a great deal of information about the process. Old movies that show couples walking through an orphanage and picking out a child are instilled in the minds of some of us. News stories and television sound bites also cloud our collective judgment. Your own parents, from a previous generation, may have passed their own antiquated views of adoption on to you. Remember, adoption was cloaked in secrecy for many years, from the orphan trains of the 1920s until the late 1970s when adoption slowly began to emerge from the closet.

If one of you presents an issue about adoption, the other needs to respond by:

1. Clearly hearing and understanding the issue your spouse is addressing;

2. Acknowledging that he or she has the right to have such feelings;
3. Recommending that you both pursue more information on the subject. You may choose to research the topic together; many couples do.

When all is said and done, you should be working together at the adoption process as a couple. Yes, one of you may very likely take the initiative, as with bill paying and all other aspects of a relationship. There's nothing wrong with taking on different responsibilities. However, the idea of adoption being a positive route to pursue should be comfortable for both of you, together.

Single Parent Adoption: Can You Do It Alone?

The short answer is yes. The trick to single parenting is a good support structure and an unwavering belief that you can and will succeed as a parent. Whether it's your parents, friends, neighbors, or a combination of all three, you need people close by who believe in you and understand that you are making a good choice. You then need practical help, including support through the adoption process and eventually with parenting duties.

The reality is that it is more difficult for a single parent to adopt for several reasons:

1. Several countries, such as Korea, do not allow for single parent adoptions. Others make it quite difficult.
2. Birth mothers today are more involved in the adoption placement process. More often a birth mother will choose to place her child with a couple over a single individual.
3. The financial burden is on one person.

4. The time involved in the adoption process falls on the shoulders of one person.
5. Some adoption agencies will not accept single parents.

Studies have shown that single parents of the 1990s and the new century have proven to be as nurturing and effective in the parental role as couples. The biggest concern and drawback is the time factor. One person, one job, one home, and one child, barely leaves time for one to enjoy any other aspects of life. Time management is a skill any single parent needs to master.

Another important factor when considering single parenting is that it is still you against the world. While single moms and dads are more prevalent in cities than rural areas, there are still the "Dan Quayles" out there who are critical of single parents. Quayle, as some of you may recall from the early 1990s, highlighted his nondescript (yet highly amusing) term as vice president by denouncing television character Murphy Brown for being a single mom. Unfortunately, the stigma still exists, fueled by old-fashioned notions.

You need to be prepared. People you do not even know may have their two cents to contribute regarding your personal life. Therefore, it is important that you are self-assured that what you are doing is right for you. If you are confident that single parenting is right for you, then that is all that matters. This also brings us back to supportive friends, neighbors, and family members. They are very important for any single parent, not only one who adopts.

If you are thinking of single parenting, you will need to address the following considerations:

1. Will my job allow me some much-needed flexibility as a parent?
2. Can I explain to my son/daughter when he or she is older, why there is no dad or mom in his or her life?

3. Can I provide a nurturing environment?
4. Can I provide my child with adequate role models of the opposite sex?
5. Do I feel comfortable knowing my dating life and potential for a relationship will be changed significantly?
6. Do I have someone to watch my child(ren) when I'm at work, or can I afford day care?

Some answers to the above questions:

1. You will need to have a job that lets you run to pick up your child at school if necessary without jeopardizing your career.
2. You will need to feel good about yourself as a single parent and be able to explain to your child why other kids have two parents and he or she has one. This will mean explaining that different types of families exist and not denying the child the right to feel badly at times if she wishes she had a father/mother.
3. You will need to be confident that through love and careful planning you will be able to provide the same nurturing environment as a two-parent home.
4. You will need to find time to interact with trusted friends and/or relatives of the opposite sex and help forge a bond between your child and at least one of these people.
5. You will not have as easy a time attracting a potential mate, if you are seeking one. Your child will take up a lot of your "socializing" time. Also, many single and even divorced people are leery of relationships with people who have children—it's a shame, but true nonetheless.

6. It is essential that you figure out your child-care plan in advance and know exactly who will help you and who will not be available. If you need child-care, research the cost, quality and availability of either an accessible facility or of having someone as a full- or part-time baby-sitter.

Chapter 18 covers single parent adoptions in more detail.

Fertility Treatments and Adoption

No, the two are not mutually exclusive. However, you may not want to pursue both fertility treatments and adoption at the same time for financial and emotional reasons. Financially, one in vitro fertilization process can cost you over $15,000 and several can certainly add up. The adoption process can likely cost between $15,000 and $25,000.

From an emotional perspective, infertility is draining. It is a frustrating experience that can often cause a feeling of self-doubt and lack of control over your own life and, for a woman, over her own body. That frustration can be transferred to the adoption process, which is also often out of your control in so many ways. The difference is that the percentage of success with adoption is far greater than that of fertility treatments.

Many couples will continue fertility treatments while they begin to explore adoption. However there is usually a time when the decision to end one process in order to best pursue the other is generally made. Most often couples have gone through a significant time focusing on their own infertility and are emotionally exhausted. They then decided to try adoption. It is important that while adoption may be the second choice, it should not be seen as the second-best choice. This may not fully sink in until your child calls out "mommy!" or "daddy!" in the middle of the night because he's had a nightmare, and you need to be there to make everything all right. At this point you won't be thinking of how he came into your life, only how much he means to you.

Dealing with infertility, adoption, or the transition from one to the other can be easier if you have the opportunity to share your feelings with others. You'd be surprised to learn how similar your story is to that of many other couples. Joining a support group like RESOLVE (a national infertility association, founded in 1974, with nationwide chapters) can make a world of difference (RESOLVE 617-623-0744, www.resolve.org)

Note: With your decision to pursue adoption, you may feel of grief or sadness over the loss of an opportunity to have a biological child. This is more common in women, and you need to allow yourself to experience this feeling. It is a change in your emotional perspective and the closure of a thought process that has been with you for a long time; that of giving birth to a child. It does not mean you are any less worthy of being a parent as anyone else. It means that you are now pursuing a new route to becoming a parent.

Fathers and Adoption

Fatherhood has changed. Today there is a greater awareness of birth-father rights. Likewise, adoptive fathers are also heeding this new trend toward greater paternal involvement. They are far more active than ever before in the long and arduous pre-adoption process as well as in raising their children.

Across the United States, many fathers are taking a more active role in raising their children. A few years ago, a New York City attorney even went so far as to sue a major New York City department store for failing to have changing tables or adequate facilities in the men's rooms.

In the adoption community, many issues are commonly shared

by fathers. Some of these issues begin during infertility, some during the adoption process, and others during the early stages of fatherhood. Additional concerns develop as the child grows up and deal with self-esteem issues, some of which stem from adoption while others are simply part of childhood and adolescence.

Many adoptive fathers are just as active as their wives, if not more so, in adoption support groups. In these groups, men often find new friends to bond with during the adoption process. This makes it easier to talk about subjects that can otherwise seem awkward.

Men traditionally do not express feelings and emotions as openly as women. While this may sound stereotypical and even sexist, after running and observing numerous workshops with adoptive parents and adoptive couples-to-be, I've found that this perception holds true. Infertility is an emotional, and even embarrassing issue to discuss. Virility and the perception of "my boy, heir to my throne" or "chip off the old block" go back centuries and are firmly established in the subconscious of many men. There is the old-fashioned, but still-prevalent idea of one's lineage continuing through a miniature version of oneself. Kathy Brodsky, CSW, Director of Adoptive Services for Jewish Child Care in New York City, says "Men are sometimes more reluctant than women to give up the idea of not having a biological child with their same characteristics, penchant for sports, and so on."

Infertility is hard to accept for both men and women. *"Let's face it,"* says Craig, adoptive father of a six-year-old girl. *"It's not like you want to go around telling everyone you can't get your wife pregnant. You wouldn't go around telling strangers you were impotent, right? Just like the word 'impotent' means not potent, 'infertile' means not fertile, unable to grow or reproduce. They are terms you don't like having to accept, much less, actually go to a doctor and discuss,"* he adds. *"I remember discussing everything from my-age old back problems to the New York Yan-*

kees with the doctor before getting to the issue. What was worse, was I felt like I'd let down my wife. It was like the agreement we made to start a family was falling apart and it was my fault."

Dealing with infertility in a relationship is a two-part problem. Whether the husband or the wife is actually experiencing the infertility, the couple is together in their desire to have a child and together in their disappointment at not having one biologically. It can be a serious strain on the relationship, often an unspoken one. Blame and disappointment with each other will often make matters worse.

"For a long time I thought my wife was disappointed in me. I believed that I had let her down and that she would forever harbor some resentment because our infertility problems centered around me," says Mark, now an adoptive father in his late forties. Mark's concern that his wife had lost faith in him as a husband is not uncommon. One day he wrote his feelings down, looked at them, but did not show his wife. Eventually, Mark confronted her with his concerns and showed her what he had written. Perhaps it was easier than trying to find the right words to express what he felt. When they discussed the issue of infertility, he realized that she still loved him and that her feelings about him had not changed and would not change because of his problems. "I told her that she could probably have done better marrying someone else," Mark added. "I apologized for not being the husband she had hoped for. She was very surprised to hear me actually say this and very sad to hear me talk that way. She reassured me that she never doubted her decision to marry me, and that this issue had not changed her feelings in the slightest. It was simply something we'd have to deal with together as a couple."

When men *do* open up and talk about infertility and the possibility of adoption, the idea of "how to become a father" varies greatly. Workshops devoted to fathers, at conferences held by the Adoptive Parents Committee in New York and New Jersey have seen nearly a fifty-fifty split in men who are comfortable becoming fathers through adoption. Half, simply want to be dads (no matter how that comes about), while half of the men in the workshops had a very hard time getting over the idea of not having a child who will not look just like them.

The moderator of one fathers' panel also points out the differences in how men tend to react to the issue of infertility. "How easily a man deals with the issue depends on who has the infertility in the relationship. If it's the female who has the problem, the males tend to be less cooperative and a little more resentful, but when it's them, they feel they are being denied parenthood and are more willing to try other options."

Reaching the Decision to Adopt

The decision to end infertility treatments, or to explore adoption at the same time, is one that couples grapple with. It is rare that a couple arrives at the decision to adopt at the same time. Often the woman will take the lead and express herself first. If the couple has been undergoing infertility treatments, it is she who has had to deal with the blood tests, shots and procedures.

For some couples, the decision is one that they will wrestle over. For other couples, it's as simple as "How about we try adoption?" "Okay with me."

It can be a very easy transition. *"I never really thought much about how we'd start our family,"* says Todd, who, along with his wife Joan, adopted two children internationally. *"I love my kids, and it didn't matter to me at all that we adopted. When my wife suggested it, I didn't bat an eye . . . I just told her it sounded like a good idea. I didn't know much of anything about adoption, but my only thought was being a family with kids, and I didn't really think it mattered how we got to that point."*

It can be a tough transition. *"My wife dragged me to a support-group meeting. I didn't really believe adoption would work . . . I was kind of like someone from Missouri, saying 'show me.' I think I didn't really believe that we would bond with an adopted child,"* says Craig (mentioned earlier). *"It took a few months, but after we went to meetings and I talked with some of the guys, I realized that there were a lot of people just like us who were trying to start families, and it was okay to adopt, people did it, and they formed families. I still have to say I wasn't totally convinced until I held my daughter. Then I felt like a different person. I became a supporter of adoption and how wonderful it was."*

Sometimes the idea to adopt finds *you*. Francine and her husband Michael had been trying to become parents for five years. *"After about two years, we started exploring fertility treatments. After five years, we began thinking that it wasn't going to happen for us and that maybe we wouldn't have children. We had talked a little about adoption, but never really focused any attention on it. Then, I remember we were at a party and there were kids all over the place and I felt like crying because we did not have children running around and playing like everyone else. We started talking to a (Caucasian) couple in their thirties, about their children. They told us all about their daughter in pre-school and about how she wanted to hear two stories every night before they could get her to go to sleep and more. They weren't being insensitive because they didn't know that we did not have any children there, and if nothing else, I was encouraging them to talk, thinking that I still wanted it to be me one day talking about my kids. Then suddenly her daughter came running over to tell her something . . . and we got to meet Deirdre, a beautiful little Chinese girl. Suddenly it was like a lightbulb went off over our collective heads. Adoption! We knew it worked, and right in front of us was one very happy, very real family. That was how we made the decision to adopt."*

Chapter 2
THREE KEY DECISIONS

You have many choices to make in the adoption process and key decisions that can determine how smoothly you will proceed along the road to adopting your child(ren) and what your forever family will look like. These decisions will overlap greatly. For example, if you decide you want only a newborn baby, you are making two decisions at once. First, you are deciding that you do not want to adopt an older child in the world of adoption, older can mean a few months old; and second, you are making the decision to adopt domestically, since it is nearly impossible to adopt a newborn baby from abroad. Conversely, you will open up several options should you decide that you would be comfortable adopting a child that is eight or nine months of age. In this case international adoption would become possibile. Of course, that opens up yet another question: Will you be comfortable adopting a child of a different ethnic heritage and possibly of a different race? Lots of questions, lots of decisions . . . but you need not make them all at once.

"We attended an adoption conference," says Laurie, who with her husband Fred, are now parents of two children, one adopted domestically and one from overseas. *"It was overwhelming at first. Agencies were asking us if we wanted to adopt a child from Eastern Europe, social workers were talking*

about children from the foster-care system, and one workshop we attended discussed finding a birth mother domestically and adopting a baby here in the United States. We had no idea what manner was the best for us. We knew we wanted a baby in our life, but we weren't ready to make these major decisions." Laurie and Frank took a long weekend at a resort to sort out their many adoption decisions in a relaxing atmosphere.

"A few days away can give you a better perspective," she explains. *"We were able to openly discuss how we envisioned our family. We knew we wanted to adopt soon, but the quickest method did not necessarily mean we'd form a family in a manner that would be comfortable for us. I think people need to picture their family and then make decisions that will help them make that picture a reality. People shouldn't adopt in one manner or another because it's cheaper or faster. They should adopt the way they think they can form the family they really desire."*

Domestic or International Adoption

One of the first decisions you will make is the part of the world in which you will direct your efforts. The two options you are immediately faced with are whether to adopt domestically or internationally. While either method can certainly be a rewarding experience and start you on your way to having a family, both come with their share of risk and plenty of paperwork. They also both require you to be both proactive and patient, as you'll find that you need to ascertain information to make informed decisions and then wait while the process unfolds.

There are practical similarities. Both methods require a home study to be conducted by a social worker, and both methods involve a variety of costs that will be incurred over time. There are, however, significant differences, some of which are more obvious than others. While both domestic and international adoptions are directed at the same goal—forming a family—they present quite different scenarios. Comparing the operational facets of these two methods will only be part of the decision process. More detailed information on the "how to's" of both domestic and international adoption are found later on in this book. First it is important to look at the personal and emotional aspect(s) associated with making this initial decision.

We all have preconceptions—and some misconceptions—about the makeup of our future families. While it is easier to imagine the physical appearance and personalities of biological children, adopted children come in many forms. They may not be infants; they may be of a different race or ethnicity. The fact that your family was formed by adoption may or may not be obvious to the world around you depending on which method of adoption you choose.

The initial step in this decision making process is to turn your attention inward and determine the ideal family situation for yourself. Remember that only you as a couple, or a prospective single parent, can make that determination. Only you can conclude whether or not you are comfortable adopting an older child, a child of a different ethnic heritage, or a child with special needs. No one else is in a position to tell you what you *should* do or from where you *should* adopt. In addition, no one has the right to make you feel guilty about making your personal choice.

Amy C., a single mom of a beautiful little girl, recounts a series of conversations with two close friends who were trying to persuade her to go to China to adopt. *"Being single, I knew that it would be a little more difficult to adopt. China was certainly a good option for single woman at that time* (this is no longer the case), *but my heart was set on trying to adopt a newborn baby. The girls being adopted from China were generally around ten months old, and while they were beautiful children,*

I had always envisioned myself with a newborn baby. I had always thought of myself as married, too, but since that had not yet happened, I felt I should be more prudent about going after what I felt was right for me in my heart. I believed that there would be a newborn baby that was destined to be with me."

Two of Amy's closest friends thought they were being helpful by continually trying to sway her toward adopting from China. *"I knew that it was a viable method and that I could go that route, but I just wanted to follow my own heart. It put a lot of pressure on these friendships and I finally had to sit them down one evening and explain that while I appreciated their good intentions, they had to recognize what my wishes were, even if it meant the process would be more difficult. I couldn't even articulate exactly why this meant so much to me, but it did. From that point on they understood and were supportive."*

A year and a half later, Amy adopted a newborn baby, born in Indiana.

Conversely, Sheila wanted nothing more than to have a child in her life, and sooner than later. *"I knew being a single mom that adopting would be hard, and I just wanted a child very much. I knew there were many little girls in orphanages in China in need of homes, and I wanted to give one a better life."* Sheila adopted her daughter after some eight months in the adoption process. She then joined a New York-based organization of families that had adopted children from China to help her learn about the culture and to provide her daughter with information about her heritage. *"Everyone around me was very supportive of my decision,"* she adds. *"That was important because it made me feel more confident in what I was doing. I had no problem with adopting from overseas. I couldn't love her more than I do,"* says Sheila, who brought her daughter LuAnn home when she was fifteen months old. *"My parents were worried about whether they would bond with a granddaughter born so far away, but as soon as they saw her, they fell in love with her. Now they spoil her."*

Some Comparisons Between Domestic and InternationalAdoption

Domestic	International
Allows you to adopt a newborn baby.	Children are at least four to ten months old.
Adopting a newborn means that developmental delays are less likely.	The older the child, the more likely there may be developmental delays, but these are usually easy to overcome in time.
The process can take upwards of one year and sometimes even two years.	The adoption can be completed in less than a year.
In an independent or agency-identified adoption, the birth mother/birth parents may change their minds at any time prior to the birth of the child or before signing relinquishment papers, thus ending the potential adoption.	The child is generally considered an orphan by the country of birth. Birth parents have already made the decision to relinquish parental care of that child.

Domestic and International Adoption

These are just a few of the many comparisons. Three other significant areas of concern include cost, health issues, and contact with birth parents.

The costs will vary, with international often being less expensive as there are more set fees (i.e., agency fees, orphanage payment, etc.) and fewer variables. However, the travel, including one or more trips to the country, can add up. These costs will often make international and domestic adoption rather comparable from a financial standpoint. Both methods of adoption will generally fall in the $15,000 to $25,000 range unless there are complications (e.g. additional lawyer fees), which can raise the total expenditure.

Medical issues are generally a greater concern when adopting internationally. While some countries, like Colombia, provide detailed health information, many other countries do not have the same information readily available. It is, however, important to note that despite the added concern because of the limited data available, the vast majority of children adopted internationally have few significant medical problems, if any. While there is reason for concern about the health of any child being adopted, the idea that there is a significantly higher incidence of serious illness in international adoption is not accurate.

In fact, there are some valid arguments that present the opposite viewpoint, based on our American lifestyle. Frank and his wife Ann adopted twice, once domestically and once internationally. *"We did an international adoption the second time partly because of our own comfort level . . . we didn't feel comfortable talking with birth mothers, so we went overseas. We adopted from Latin America* (from a country no longer open to international adoption) *and had excellent health information about the prenatal care taken by the birth mother. Having stayed very involved in the adoption community over the past fifteen years, I have realized that often there are more health problems inherent in domestic adoption. Our lifestyle* (as Americans) *is one that can lead to poorer prenatal care than that of some other countries where drugs and alcohol are not as prevalent. I'm not saying that birth mothers as a group abuse drugs or alcohol, only that it is much more common in our society as a whole. Any young person can be in a stressful situation and fall into these bad habits. Even our diet can be rich in junk foods. It is part of our lifestyle in this country and it does affect the prenatal care of a child. In a country such as China, Korea, or some South American countries, a birth mother does not have the same access to all of these things.*

"Often, effects are found much later on in the child's life. We've heard of a number of circumstances where adoptive parents have discovered psychological and physical disorders that are traced back to poor prenatal care by birth mothers here in the United States."

The points raised in Frank's arguments are valid. The American lifestyle can be cause for concern. Today, however, greater communication between birth parents and adoptive parents can help to address such issues. Medical testing can provide greater insight into the prenatal health of the baby. But the birth mother has to be honest with the adoptive parents and amenable to providing such information or undergoing medical tests.

Contact with birth parents is the other key issue that factors into the decision-making process. There is a wide range of theories regarding openness in adoption, or the involvement of birth parents in the adoptive child's (and adoptive parent's) life. The level of "openness" can vary from adoptive and birth families simply having specific contact information in case there is a need (such as medical) to reach each other, to ongoing involvement after the adoption has been finalized. You will find more information on open adoption throughout this book. The point is only brought up here because it is highly unlikely that you will have an open adoption with the birth parents of a child born internationally. Some people will see this as more comforting while others will find this far more distressing.

Let me remind you again, that in adoption, there are no "one-size-fits-all" answers.

Couples and singles must consider when approaching the process whether or not they will feel comfortable interacting with birth mothers at any level. Independent domestic adoption or agency-identified adoptions (two very common methods of domestic adoption) will require that adoptive parents talk with birth mothers to set up an adoption plan. In nearly 60 percent of domestic-adoption scenarios, the adoptive and birth parents meet in person. This is completely opposite in international adoption, where parental rights have been severed and birth parents and adoptive parents do not meet. For some people, meeting birth mothers is a wonderful part of the process but for others it becomes a roadblock.

According to New York/New Jersey-based adoption attorney Robin Fleischner;

> Contact with a birth mother can be a big plus in domestic adoption. It can result in being able to attain important medical records that are valuable in your child's future. It can also be a wonderful experience. Birth parents are not the enemy, they're working on a plan out of love to give the child a better life than they could provide. Once you've talked with them, you'll be able to share more with your child, having gotten to know the birth mother and possibly even the birth father. The fear people have is that they will go through this process with the birth mother, get very emotionally attached and then she'll decide to parent the child herself. This can be difficult emotionally, but it's still worth the risk. Most adoptive parents find that the positives of this relationship with a birth mother outweigh the negatives. Also, psychologists feel the more information parents have the better it is for themselves and for their children.

Risk Factors

There are risks in all aspects of life. Adoption is no exception. The risk of losing money on adoption situations and plans that do not come to fruition is a concern of anyone entering the adoption process. For this reason, doing careful research and double-checking all resources related to your pending adoption is extremely important. Support groups can also be helpful as you can learn from other adoptive parents which agencies, social workers, and other key players in the process are most reputable.

When making the decision between domestic and international adoption, you will find risks that you can minimize and others that are beyond your control. Countries around the world can—and do—change their policies regarding adoption for any number of reasons including the political or economic climate within the country. Obviously, these are risks that are beyond your control. However, they do not preclude you from international adoption, but may simply cause you to change your plans. It may mean changing your focus to a different part of the world.

You can minimize the risks involved in international adoption by selecting countries that provide more accurate health information, and by looking at countries which have run successful adoption programs for several years. Korea and Colombia, for example, have had solid programs in place for a long time and are less risky than countries that are just in the process of establishing adoption programs. While doing research, you will discover that countries such as Japan do not allow international adoption while countries like China, Mexico and Guatemala have rules and regulations in place. (*Note:* These could change before you finish this chapter, so always double-check your research to make sure it is up-to-date.) You will also minimize your adoption risk by having a "contingency or backup plan." Selecting more than one possible country or signing up with an agency that has several well-established programs is advisable.

Many American-based agencies regularly work with several countries, thus reducing the possibility of legal issues, immigration issues, and other such potential risks to a successful adoption.

Domestic Concern

When adopting domestically, one of the most significant concerns is whether or not the birth mother or birth father will challenge the adoption. Media coverage of unique cases have spotlighted birth parents taking cases to court and having adoptions overturned several years after the child was placed in the adoptive family's home. These are the *extremely* rare exceptions. In fact, in most of these, there were early-warning signs that the situation was problematic. Some of these cases were never finalized. The fine print will often show something other than a typical, finalized adoption.

The more common and legitimate concern (or risk) associated with domestic adoption comes prior to the completion of the process when birth mothers can—and do—change their minds and decide not to place a child as initially discussed. Statistics show that this "change of mind" will most often occur within forty-eight hours prior to, or forty-eight hours after—giving birth. While it is hard for someone trying to adopt to understand, it is something that the birth mother feels she must do. Remember, this is a very difficult situation in which she finds herself. One cannot begrudge a birth mother the right to parent her child. She may have found support from family, friends, her church or community. Nonetheless, couples and singles seeking to adopt will feel the pain of such a failed adoption.

"We had an adoption fall through," says Carol F. of New York City, referring to an adoption situation that did not reach fruition. *"The birth mother changed her mind two days before she was due to deliver. My husband and I were devastated. We understood that she had every right to make whatever decision she felt most comfortable making but we were still very disap-*

pointed. We were all ready to be parents and then had to refocus on going back and finding another birth mother and starting again. But within a few weeks we were back in the process, and were not only working with another birth mother, but on our way to adopting our daughter, whom we were holding in our arms just two months later. It's a matter of believing that it will work out in the end and that the child that is meant to be part of your life will be there when the time is right."

Many couples have gone through such an experience, but they all end up adopting if they do not give up on the adoption process. However, this particular emotional roller-coaster ride, is the biggest risk factor that deters couples and singles from attempting domestic adoption. For this reason, it is important to approach independent domestic adoption with the understanding that birth mothers may change their minds until the adoption papers are signed. It is *equally* important to remember that once the child is in your home the odds are more than 99 percent that the adoption will be finalized and your child will be part of your permanent "forever" family.

Adopting domestically through an adoption agency in a traditional format (you sign up and wait until there is a baby available) will minimize this risk. In fact, you will not even know that a birth mother has changed her mind. However, there is a time risk involved, which means you may be waiting a longer period of time before you can adopt. An additional risk with domestic agencies is that you will be rejected by the agency for any number of reasons. More information on all of these forms of adoption will follow throughout this book. Every form of adoption comes with some risks—emotional, financial, time, or all of the above. They all, however, come with a great reward.

Make Your Own Lists

Throughout the adoption process, you may change the

perceptions of your future family on several occasions. Regardless, it is important that you and your spouse (or just you as a future single parent) make a list determining the adoption situations you would be most comfortable pursuing.

You will then evaluate the domestic and international processes and determine which aspects of each process are important to you. You might, for example, decide on adopting from the country of your heritage, providing that country is open for international adoption. If, for example, you are seeking a newborn infant of a similar ethnic background to your own, and are comfortable enough to converse with birth mothers, then you should pursue a domestic adoption. If you are seeking a newborn baby, but uncomfortable about talking with birth mothers then you should seek an agency that handles domestic adoptions in a traditional manner, so that you do not have to talk with birth mothers.

In short, there are many variables that will factor into your decision. There is no right or wrong answer, as this is a personal decision. However, be realistic and paint the entire picture of domestic or international adoption. If, for example you are selecting a country overseas in Eastern Europe from which you can adopt a Caucasian baby because you are a Caucasian couple, do not fool yourselves into believing that this is the same as adopting domestically because the child may look more like you than a child born in Latin America or Asia. This is still a child born in another country with a different cultural heritage and background, and this issue needs to be addressed. Don't try to fool yourselves when making an adoption plan.

Don't Box Yourself Into A Corner

If you start the adoption process with numerous criteria regarding the ideal child you want to adopt, you will prolong the process. You may decide you want an infant and may only feel comfortable with a child of the same race. These decisions are valid. However, if you are only looking to adopt a perfectly healthy newborn biracial baby girl from a certain region of the country, born to birth parents who are exemplary citizens, you may be setting up tremendous restrictions. It is important to keep an open mind because you cannot predict what potential adoption situations will come your way. In fact, many adoptive parents find that their families do not resemble the initial visions they once had of what their families would look like. When asked how they feel about that in adoption surveys and polls, the overwhelming majority would not change a thing.

"It's important to paint a broad picture and not box yourself into a corner" says Andrea of New York City, adoptive mother of two children, one born domestically and one internationally. *"At first, when my husband and I started the process, we envisioned ourselves with two blond-haired blue-eyed newborn babies, a girl and a boy. Over time we realized that we just wanted healthy babies. We perused both domestic and international adoption in an effort to increase our options. We knew we would not get a newborn from overseas, but that was okay with us. When we got into the process, one of the countries we pursued was Croatia, because that's my ancestry. As it turned out we ended up adopting our daughter from right here in the United States. Then, within a few months, we found ourselves working with an agency that handled adoption from Croatia. We adopted our son a short time later. He was seven months old at the time, which meant we went from wanting to start a family to being one with two young children within a few months of each other. As it turns out, our son, who was born thousands of miles away in the country of my heritage, looks like my husband. You cannot plan these things; it's not an exact science. You just try to go for what seems best for your family. But you need to be a little bit flexible."*

As you proceed, you will likely broaden your idea of what your future family photo will look like. By keeping an open mind and not ruling out various possibilities, you allow yourself to increase the opportunity of a successful situation occurring sooner, rather than later. As was the situation with Andrea and her family, you can pursue both domestic and international adoption. Remember that adoption can be stressful, and you may be stretching your emotional, as well as your financial, limits by doing so. Therefore, most couples, and singles, decide between domestic and international adoption, at least for the time being, knowing that it is possible to take the other route later on.

Newborn or Older Child

What constitutes an "older child"? This depends on whom you are talking to. An older child can be a three-month-old, a toddler, or a five-, six-, or even twelve-year-old. Essentially, it is not a newborn baby. If you are adopting from overseas, your decision is made for you since you will not be able to adopt a newborn.

You will also need to consider the age range of a child you would feel comfortable adopting. Even if you are looking to adopt a newborn, you may hear through a support group, or another source, about a five- or six- month-old child in foster care who has become available for adoption. What do you do?

You will need to set up the boundaries within which you feel comfortable. Remember, you are shaping your adoption decisions based on the image you have of your future family. Although, biologically speaking, you would obviously start out with a newborn baby, that is not necessarily where you see yourself as a parent. What is it that you most look forward to about parenting? Holding and bathing an infant? Holding the hand of your toddler as he or she walks clumsily along? Running around playing ball in the backyard with your five-year-old? Reading stories to your young children? Helping your young teen through those adolescent years? What aspects of being a parent are those that you, as a couple, or single, most look forward to? For some people, it is all of them. For others, it is a matter of becoming a parent and picking up the process at the stage where your child is.

It is also important to consider your age in regard to that of a child. It takes a lot of energy to take care of a young child. If you are in your late forties or early fifties, you need to consider how you will manage chasing a toddler around the house. You also need to consider the child when he or she reaches puberty and those "trying" teenage years. How old will you be, and will you be able to provide the parenting guidance and skills necessary? Do you want to be dealing with the woes of a teenager when you're sixty-five? These are areas you need to think carefully about when deciding whether or not you want to adopt an older child. Some psychologists who specialize in adoption strongly suggest that you think of your child as an adolescent even before you adopt.

Keep in mind that from a practical standpoint, it becomes harder to adopt as you move toward—and past—the age of fifty. Someone in their early fifties has to consider that their adoption options are more limited than someone in their thirties or early forties. However, nothing is impossible. It's just more food for thought while making your decision between a newborn, toddler, or three- or even six-year-old.

Emotional Baggage

If you are traveling on a long journey, you bring a lot of suitcases. If it's a weekend trip, you can travel much lighter. Similarly, a newborn baby brings little or no emotional baggage along because his or her journey through life has been brief. As we grow, we all accumulate more emotional baggage. A child in foster care or in an orphanage is not growing up with the same ongoing sense of love and security as a child growing up in a healthy family environment.

Adopting an older child quite simply means the child will have more emotional issues to deal with. He or she is already aware of the outside world and what it has or has not had to offer. Generally speaking, the younger the child, the easier it is to overcome such issues. A one-year-old coming from an orphanage in another country will often have attachment disorders that love and patience can overcome. A four-year-old with behavioral problems will need more than just love. It will take a consistent effort and some work on your part to change negative behavioral problems. In many instances, it will require outside help. An older child (over two) will also ask questions about the transition in his or her life. You need to be prepared and well versed in how to deal with such questions. There is more information on adopting older children in Chapter 8 (adopting from the foster-care system) since children over the age of three or four are usually adopted through state agencies.

For your purposes, it is important to decide how old a child you are comfortable adopting and what you can provide to an older child. It is also important that you realize that an older child presents different issues than a newborn since they have a story that usually includes a degree of instability.

Gary and Fran had adopted three times, through independent domestic placement, each time a newborn baby. Life was hectic for a two-income family with three children plus the obligatory pets, but like most families, they had settled into a steady routine—until they got an unexpected phone call. A friend they had known for several years through an adoption support group in which they had remained quite active, was calling with a most interesting situation. It seemed that she had been called by an adoption agency that was looking to place a domestic-born three-year-old girl. The agency, far more accustomed to dealing with the more common adoption of newborn domestic infants, or international adoptions of young children from orphanages abroad, was in a quandary trying to figure out whether or not they could find a home for this little girl. The child's birth mother did not want her in an institutionalized program such as the foster-care system but instead wanted to find a permanent loving family for her daughter whom she could not take care of.

"Apparently, the birth mother and birth father had split up. She was young and ill prepared to take care of her alone and he was unable to take her with him. They felt that the best thing they could do was place her in a permanent loving home," Gary explains.

"My wife and I had talked about a fourth child, possibly through international adoption, but we had not acted on it in any way. I had just returned to night school, my wife was working, and we had three children, a nine-year-old and two eight-year-olds. We knew it was not going to be easy, but after discussing it, we decided to pursue the situation."

Gary and Fran started off slowly, visiting with young Debbie for a few hours. *"We met with Debbie's birth mother and at first the birth father was not at all in the picture. The first few meetings went well. Finally we had a visit where we brought her out to the house for the day. She had a great time, she was very energetic, and the other kids loved having her around . . . I called it the "new toy syndrome." This was the first of what turned out to be a few visits. Then, when she would leave she would get hysterical and not want to go, which made us feel good that she was having fun but was also troubling because she was leaving with her birth mother."*

As it turned out, Debbie had spent time living with her grandparents in Arizona and with her birth father, who later appeared in the picture. Apparently neither of them was ready for the responsibility of raising a child, so Gary and Fran adopted Debbie. *"It took us a little time to get back into the mind-set of having a three-year-old around. For us it had been some time, and she needed much more constant attention than the older kids."*

There were other issues that Gary and Fran needed to address that they had not dealt with when adopting previously. *"We had psychologists and social workers meet her, and we talked with the board of health to find out about early-intervention programs and see what services she would be eligible for. She had some speech problems, among other things. We went through two or three weeks of evaluations. The psychologists and other people who saw her considered her 'bouncy.' No one wanted to label her as hyper or anything like that, so they kept using the term 'bouncy.' She clearly was not ADHD [Attention Deficit Hyperactivity Disorder] but it was best for her to have a special preschool program and some therapy."*

Gary and Fran did not get much troubling behavior from Debbie. *"We had been forewarned to expect bad behavior from an older child, but we didn't really get any— she was craving stability. The first couple of times she didn't behave, we put her in a time out and that was about it. She did test us a little bit, like if we were at the park she would take off and run out of the park and head down the street. Then she saw that we would always come after her, and she stopped doing it. For the most part she adjusted to everything very well. Our older kids needed time to adjust. The 'new toy syndrome' wore off after a few weeks, and they wondered why she was getting all the attention. It came and went with the two boys, but my older daughter needed a little more time to adjust now that she wasn't the only girl."*

Now a family of six, things are hectic and busy around the house for Gary and Fran. Nonetheless, they have settled into a family routine once again. Gary does recommend that if you are bringing an older child into your home to be ready to deal with the child's life up to that point, which you will learn from him or her. In addition, if you have other children, expect that they, too, will need some time to adjust.

Open or Closed Adoption

"Open adoption" is generally defined as maintaining an open line of communication between the adoptive parents and the birth mother or birth parents after the adoption has been finalized. Nothing is set in stone when determining how much contact or communication constitutes an open adoption.

For many years, nearly all adoptions were done through agencies and were completely closed. Birth parents and adoptive parents had no communication before or after placement. Over the past twenty years, birth mothers have understandably wanted greater involvement in the placement of their children. Today they have a much greater say. Communication between birth parents and prospective adoptive parents prior to placement has become more commonplace with the growth of independent domestic placement. Over the past decade, there has also been an increase in maintaining the lines of communication after placement between birth and adoptive parents—or open adoption.

Before continuing to discuss of how comfortable you are with openness in the adoption process, you can immediately rule out open adoption in nearly any international adoption. The decision is essentially made for you. It is an extremely rare case where there is any kind of ongoing communication between a birth parent and an adoptive parent in an international adoption. Knowing numerous adoptive families, I can say without hesitation that I do not know of any.

The decision of how open your adoption will be, therefore

pertinent to domestic adoption. First you need to consider how comfortable you will feel with the birth mother or birth parents as part of your life, as well as part of the life of your child.

Open-adoption scenarios range from exchanging photos once a year to physically getting together often for meals or just visits. Usually, the birth mother or birth parents will let you know how much involvement, if any, they want in the child's future. You will need to determine in advance what your reaction will be and how comfortable you will be having her—or them—involved in your child's life, not to mention your own.

Proponents of open adoption believe that it is beneficial to children because it gives them a better understanding of their biological roots and history. It gives children a sense of where they come from and what they will look like as adults. It helps paint a realistic picture of the birth parents and helps the adoptee to understand why he or she was placed for adoption, thus filling a void. It is also very helpful for knowledge about their medical history.

Open adoption allows birth parents to see how the child grows up and is raised. It lets them know firsthand how the child's life is turning out. From a birth mothers' perspective, she can also let the child and adoptive parents see her own life progression so that the child can know that the birth mother who was once unable to care for a child is now at a far more enhanced place in her life as well.

The adoptive parents can benefit by having some help in answering the tough adoption questions. They, too, can see what the child will be like when he or she grows up, both physically and emotionally.

On the other side of the open-adoption argument, is the likelihood that a child, as he or she gets older, will not fully understand who mommy and daddy really are. Two sets of parents may be in the picture, yet they may very likely *not* agree on many issues and may have differing lifestyles. Children need a sense of consistency, stability, and one loving family. This can become very cloudy if another party is overly involved. Whereas a nineteen-, twenty- or twenty-one-year-old may be in a far more mature position to understand meeting his or her birth parents, a young child will not necessarily understand the situation. This can cause greater doubt or hurt when confronted often with the person who "gave them up for adoption" (using the words that the child might say). It can also be the root of greater emotional problems.

Note: While many people do say that a child was "given up" for adoption, it is not considered positive adoption language in the adoption community, since giving something up connotes getting rid of or throwing out. Placing a child for adoption or making an adoption plan indicates a well-thought-out choice and is a more positive way of explaining the adoption, particularly around a child.

Often a birth mother is either a teenager or a young woman without much money or emotional support. If she becomes overly dependent on the adoptive family, that, too, can cloud the issue, because you are not adopting her as well. She may feel that by remaining involved she can be a "backseat" parent, and this can become an unhealthy situation for all members of the triad.

In many cases, a birth mother wants to move on with her own life, which means she wants very much to make a clean separation for the sake of her emotional well-being and for the sake of the child and the adoptive parents. Proponents of open adoption often complain that too many adoptive parents are looking to take the child and get away quickly from the birth parents. Often, however, it is the birth mother who is looking to make a clean break. She has just made the toughest decision of her life and needs to separate for her own stability. It may be essential for her to move forward and get on with her life. This may necessitate a comfortable distance.

For adoptive parents, the desire for a closed adoption can help close the door on ambiguity over who is parenting and raising the child. It can help secure the family as a unit, providing a stable and loving environment for the child. This does not mean denying the child's right to know and understand adoption. It just may mean allowing a child to mature and grow in a stable family environment without such complications that he or she may be too young to assimilate into life's big picture.

Since "open adoption" has only grown in popularity in the past ten to fifteen years, there are not many studies that show whether it has or has not been beneficial to the child.

So what is the answer?

First, find a level of openness that is right for the birth parents and for yourselves. Then, make sure that you feel it is in the best interests of the child.

To date, there are generally no contracts upheld by law that will stipulate what your relationship with the birth mother or birth parents should be. In most cases the scenario will play itself out as the adoption process continues and after the child is born. As mentioned earlier, this will usually be set in motion by the birth mother, as she is going through the most trying emotional situation. If she wants to make a clean break and not maintain communication because it's too difficult for her emotionally, then you must respect that, even if you are a strong proponent of open adoption. You can still let her know that you are reachable whenever she feels the time is right.

As with anything that is "new" and innovative, there are open-adoption advocates who take to their soapboxes and preach that it is the only way and that all adoption should be open adoption! The "it's my way or no way" philosophy has no place in adoption. Adoptions, like snowflakes, are all unique.

Your idea of "openness" may not be someone else's. Remember that down the road, you ultimately want what will be best for your child. It is he or she who can benefit or suffer from your decisions. You cannot group all birth mothers, all adoptive parents, or all adoptees. Those who try to do so are misleading you. Both open and closed adoptions have worked wonderfully for numerous families.

Common Level of Openness

Sending occasional photos or letters, if satisfactory to both sides, is a very common degree of openness. Keeping the lines of communication open in the event that contact is needed for a health issue or pressing concern has also become a fairly common arrangement in domestic adoption.

Note: Some states require that you disclose your last names to the birth parents. This immediately means there is the potential for contact. In other states, a "closed" adoption means that the birth mother knows you only by your first names and does not have your last names and address. Either scenario can still lead to a comfortable level of openness. You can exchange mail via your attorneys' office or perhaps through e-mail.

A further discussion on "open adoption" can be found in Chapter 14.

It should be noted that the term "open" may be used to refer to the birth mother's making the choice of a family for her child, as opposed to having an agency make the selection. However, this is not the usual definition of the term "open adoption."

Chapter 3
PREPARING FOR ADOPTION

First, think about the child at the end of the journey. Will he have curly hair? Will she love to splash around in the water? Will she love Barney? Will he like to build with blocks? The child is the light at the end of the adoption journey.

Whether it's the first steps, first grade, first date, or first time borrowing the car, there will be many firsts along the way. You'll get the joy of reliving some of your own firsts, like the first time you went to the circus or the first time you watched *The Wizard of Oz*. Only now you will see it through a new set of eyes, those of your child. These are just some of the many reasons that you are working hard to bring a child into your life . . . the reasons that keep you focused and moving along a different path when an agency rejects your application, a birth mother does not contact your attorney to proceed with the adoption paperwork, or you find out that the country you have selected has a six month moratorium on adoptions.

Preparing for adoption means setting your sights firmly on the child (or children) who will be in your family, and not letting go of that dream or desire.

There is no denying that adoption can be a trying process. You are dealing with a system that in the United States alone, is governed by fifty different sets of laws for fifty states, not including

Washington D.C. In addition, countless rules, regulations, and guidelines regarding adoption law (many of which change often) can be found in nations throughout the world. Adoption is a process in which you are usually working through a typically dispassionate bureaucratic system, with your emotions hung out to dry. Tack on a volume of paperwork, scrutiny, and invasive questions, and you've got the ingredients for significant stress. Then, with the help of lawyers, social workers, agency representatives, and other participants you will try to create a family. Yes, it is an improbable scenario, yet somehow it works.

To prepare for adoption means going into the process with your eyes wide open, prepared to learn and evaluate the various options. It means being ready to work through both practical and emotional issues as you proceed and to understand that you will need both patience and persistence. It means that as much as you want to have a child in your life, you will need to know when to move forward and when to take a step back.

One of the first things you should know is that *many potential adoptive couples and singles lose money pursuing the wrong roads to adoption.* Surveys show that some 50 percent of successful adoptive parents have spent excessive money in the adoptive process. This does not include working with a birth mother who changed her mind prior to signing the adoption papers. Therefore you need to be prepared.

Spending excessive money generally results from one of the following reasons:

1. Not Doing Proper Research.
This could mean signing up with an agency in hopes of adopting a baby only to find out that the agency works primarily with older children. It could mean paying a facilitator to help you locate a child before realizing that you cannot do a facilitated adoption in your state. It could also mean paying an adoption

consultant, but finally finding, working with, and adopting a child through a birth mother without the anticipated help of the consultant. Research will help you avoid these financial pitfalls.

"We started out by buying three books on adoption and then attended a seminar by a local adoption agency," says Craig, who, with his wife Karen, are in their late thirties and currently trying to adopt. *"We then joined a support group which helped us verify what we were reading about and gave us an opportunity to network and talk with other people like ourselves. The Internet can also be helpful, but you have to know where to look. If you type in the search word 'adoption,' you'll get thousands of sites. It's probably better to talk with other people who can help point you to the most helpful web-sites rather than trying to sift through so many. The main thing we are trying to do right now is educate ourselves about the process so we can make informed decisions. I think we'll know when we feel that we've learned enough to move to the next step."*

Conferences

Look for adoption conferences in your area. Several adoption web-sites post upcoming conferences. If you see one in your area, try to attend. While you are there, try not to make any rash decisions. Gather information and pick up as much literature as possible to take home and study carefully.

When assimilating information, it's imperative to double-check what you read. Since adoption is as far from an exact science as you can get, fraught with personal opinions and unique stories, you need to decipher facts from opinions. In addition, you need to make sure you are getting the most updated information, so check the dates of books or postings of web content.

2. Switching Methods

There's nothing wrong with switching from international to domestic adoption, or vice versa if you have decided that you have widened your acceptable parameters. Many people, how-ever, switch methods because they are either uncomfortable or not succeeding at adoption through their original strategy. Since the methods all work, the individuals may be going about them all wrong. Tying this back to reason number one, it is important to have a firm understanding of how each process works so you can decide early on which method will best help you reach your desired goal. This can save you time, anxiety, and stop you from spending excessive amounts of money.

3. Acting Impulsively

It's possible to get swayed by your emotions into spending money without evaluating your options. This happens often. Even the most conscientious, well-organized, well-read individuals can let their emotions get the better of them.

Peter and Denise were taken in by the photos of children displayed by an adoption agency working with Eastern European countries. The agency sent videos of a couple of children to their home even before they signed the application. Denise fell in love with one of the children. The couple signed up with the agency and were sent a follow-up video of their "soon-to-be son," the one from the video. They even paid a pediatrician to look at the videos to determine the developmental growth of the child. But after a few months, contact with the agency began to wane. Calls went unreturned, and they did not hear from the agency. They contacted a support group they belonged to and a member of the group was less than enthusiastic about the international track record of the agency.

Now worried that something was awry, Peter and Denise sought the help of an attorney who followed up on their behalf. As it turned out, the agency did not have the sole rights to placing the child from thevideo whom Denise had fallen for. The child was placed with another couple from another country.

Peter and Denise were heartbroken. They had been lured into an agency that had played on their emotions, showing them a child that they believed would be theirs. With some help from their support group, they received most of their money back from the agency (all but around $1,500, plus the pediatrician and attorney fees). However, they had also endured a very emotionally distressing experience. The agency explained that they would try to place another child with them, but Denise and Peter had no interest in proceeding with this agency.

Denise and Peter adopted a beautiful little boy from Eastern Europe a year later, and are very happy parents today.

This story illustrates what can happen if you follow your emotions—and people try to prey upon them.

Bad Apples

While the vast majority of adoption agencies, attorneys, and social workers are working hard on behalf of their clients and have very reputable credentials, there are those few bad apples you may encounter along the way. The more you learn, the less likely you will be a victim of an individual or agency that is working "around the system," possibly adhering to a loose interpretation of the law. From facilitators who promise a baby for a bundle of cash, to agencies with morally questionable rules and regulations, to birth mothers and even attorneys who are dealing with several couples for the placement of one baby, there are some less-than-reputable characters and businesses looking to take advantage of your emotional state. As is often the case, if you see or hear about a way to get a baby that sounds too good to be true, it is probably not on the level. Of course, as you probably know, baby brokering or baby selling—a process of paying someone to give you a child—are both illegal. Be very careful that the person you are working with is doing everything above board. Agencies and attorneys are licensed, and their licenses can be checked. Beyond that, there are organizations that agencies and attorneys belong to that can verify their ethics and credibility. Talking with other adoptive parents is very helpful.

The last thing you want to do is sign up to work with some high-priced facilitator who tells you, "Don't worry, leave it to me and I'll get you a baby. Just pay me $50,000." He or she very well might place a baby in your arms, but his or her methods may not be ethical or legal. What you don't know can come back to hurt you one day if this individual has worked outside of the legal boundaries. Very stringent laws protect against such illegal dealings and black-market operations. You do not want to be involved in anything of this nature.

For these reasons, you need to exercise caution. This is part of your preparedness for adoption. No, you need not become a cynic and certainly do not want to become paranoid that everyone you meet is out to rip you off—it is certainly not the case—but it is in your best interest to prepare to be part investigator and part researcher and, for lack of a better term, part "savvy consumer" when shopping around for help with the adoption process.

Financial Preparation

To prepare, you need to know that you have access

Tips

1. Don't sign up with an agency or attorney without learning something about them.

2. Read all contracts very carefully. If possible have a lawyer read through them .

3. Compare costs of home studies and agencies—and know exactly what you get for your payments.

4. Make sure agencies, attorneys, and social workers are licensed to do business in your state.

5. Take advice from friends, neighbors, relatives and strangers with a grain of salt, unless you know that they are closely familiar with the adoption process. Too often, well-intentioned individuals give you slightly skewed versions of media stories or sound bites, which are often inaccurate.

to—or can borrow—at least $15,000 without seriously compromising your financial well-being. You also need to prepare a budget, especially for independent adoption, where you will have ongoing monthly costs.

Evaluate your financial situation and decide how you will best manage your funds not only through the adoption but into the high cost of parenting that follows. Chapter 19 covers the financial aspects of adoption.

Emotional Preparation

Emotionally, it is hard to prepare yourself for a potentially bumpy ride. A seat belt helps, but you're still going to bounce around a little. Associating with others who have successfully adopted children and reading about positive adoption stories can provide you with the confidence to believe that at the end of the journey will be a forever family. This confidence is important because if you hold onto it, you will be less likely to make hasty, often poor decisions.

To maintain some sense of emotional stability it is important that the adoption process be *part* of your life—not your whole life. This means talking about other things and maintaining other aspects of your life. Change the subject in conversations to include the rest of your life. It may mean taking a few weekend getaways from adoption. Since much of the process is out of your hands, constant worry, evaluation and re-evaluation of what you could have, should have and might have done becomes counterproductive. Likewise, spending an inordinate amount of time trying to plot and plan every step that lies ahead may also not work to your advantage because there are instances where you will need to change your plans and your course of action as you go. Learn to be flexible and to step away from the process when you are overly stressed.

Carol F., mentioned earlier in chapter 2, comments on her own emotional preparation to adopt. *"This was a very difficult* process. My entire life I grew up expecting to become pregnant and give birth to a baby that would look like me. I felt cheated and angry realizing this was not to be. It was not easy to give up on that idea. I then accepted the loss of a biological child, that may never exist. I remember going with my husband to a support group meeting, and one of the board members asked me to think about what I wanted most to be pregnant or to be a mom. That was a turning point for me because I knew that the most, important thing for me was to be a mom. After I understood what I wanted most, it was easier for me to move forward and turn all my efforts toward reaching our dream."

Prepare Your Support Systems

It is beneficial not only to educate yourself, but to provide those closest to you with some information about the adoption process. The people around you can be most supportive if they have a basic understanding of what adoption is all about. Don't assume they know a great deal about the process.

On the other hand, you may specifically wish to keep some people less informed than others only because you don't want ten people asking every day, "So how's the adoption going?" Often people in the process limit their discussion of adoption around their place of employment because many of the people you work with need not know all about your personal life. Also, your office can be a safe haven where you can go to get away from the adoption process.

Support groups offer you other people in the same place as yourselves and people who have completed the adoption process. This is comforting and also provides a source of relevant information. Getting involved in such a group and networking is to your benefit .

In the eleven years that I've been associated with the Adoptive Parents' Committee of New York City, I've seen many people learn not only from experts speaking at workshops, but from sitting down with other couples and singles and talking about how they adopted.

Two Common Questions

Answers to these two questions will also help you prepare mentally for adoption:

1. Will I bond with an adopted child?

2. Can I love an adopted child as much as a biological child?

The simple answers are "yes" and "yes." However, it is something that you will simply need to discover for yourself. Some parents bond immediately when they adopt their child. For others, it takes a little time. Don't worry, the overwhelming majority of adoptive families have the same strong loving bond as any biological family. In fact, sometimes the bond is greater because the adoptive parents worked so hard to become a family.

Chapter 4
HOME STUDIES

Quick, get out the vacuum, straighten, dust, clean, paint, and let's add on an extra room! The social worker is coming! The social worker is coming! And for goodness' sake, don't act like an idiot while she's here!

No, contrary to popular belief, the home study is not a white-glove test. You need not sound the alarm and do a complete top-to-bottom cleaning of your home. Social workers are not expecting a setting from the pages of *House and Garden,* nor are they expecting the resurrection of Ozzie and Harriet, or any other old sitcom couple that never fought or had a problem that they could not solve in a mere twenty-two minutes.

Home studies are assessments of real people, like you, who wish to become parents. They are a manner of addressing society's justifiable concern for the best interests of a child.

The home study is required for all types of adoption. It is usually one of the earliest steps you will take in the adoption process. A licensed social worker, trained to do adoption home studies, talks with you to evaluate whether or not you would make suitable parents (or a suitable single parent). The social worker then writes up a report of a few pages, which follows guidelines set forth by the state, adoption agency, and/or another country. Then the home study is submitted to the state courts for approval. As daunting as that may sound, only one of the hundreds of adoptive couples I have known did not pass their home study and theirs was an unusual story. A few months later, they, too, passed. The point is that you will probably do just fine on your home study.

Serious Concerns
The most significant reasons why a prospective parent would have cause for concern about passing a home study include a DWI charge, felony charges, or any record of child abuse.

All About Home Studies

Home studies are not new. As far back as the 1890s, Michigan enacted a law requiring that an investigation be conducted by the courts before an adoption. The investigation reviewed the prospective home prior to final placement. Slowly but surely, other states enacted similar adoption home study statutes.

Home studies have changed with the times. The physical home environment has taken a backseat to the mental, emotional, and practical concerns of the people who are looking to adopt. Issues such as working moms, divorce, single parenting, step-parenting and open adoption have become more prevalent in our society since the early days of home studies. Civil rights have also changed. The laws are more stringent regarding the grounds on which someone may be denied eligibility to adopt. Adoption has also come from "in the closet" or a "big family secret" to being discussed openly with adopted children and other family members. Home studies have progressed with the times to address these issues and many others. The social workers who administer home studies today have been trained to be in step with what is acceptable in society legally, ethically, and morally. And yet, despite the changing elements that make up the modern family dynamics and the suitable home environment, the best interests of the child should always remain paramount.

Social Workers

You will need to find a licensed social worker in your state working either independently or through an affiliated home-study agency. Some adoption (placement) agencies have their own lists of social workers in your state. Attorneys also have lists of social workers with whom they frequently work. The social worker you use must be familiar with the state requirements; and if you are working with an agency, the social worker must be familiar with the agency's requirements. He or she must also be approved by that agency. It's crucial that you make sure the adoption agency will accept the home study done by an independent social worker or home-study agency.

One way to waste money is to find an independent social worker to do a home study, only to find out later that the agency you are working with will not accept it. Take five minutes before scheduling the home study to check with the agency that the social worker you have selected is acceptable. If you are adopting internationally, make sure to inquire about the guidelines required by the country you have selected. Countries may require several visits by the social worker over a period of months or even years.

In many cases, social workers who are affiliated with specific agencies also do home studies on their own. It is often to your advantage, even if you are choosing to do an independent domestic adoption (through an attorney), to have a social worker that is *agency affiliated*. This means that the independent social worker has ties to a home-study agency. If, for example you find a child to adopt in a state that requires an agency home study, you will be covered. The social worker will generally charge you a little more money to use the agency letterhead on your behalf.

Support group meetings and adoption conferences are also places where you can find social workers who are licensed to do home studies in your state.

What You Need

It's advisable to get three or more copies of all of the paperwork you will need for the home study, since you will likely need the same paperwork for an agency, the INS (Immigration and Naturalization Service), your attorney, and other purposes. Remember to ask the social worker exactly what paperwork is required before the home study so that you'll be prepared in advance.

Copies of the following documents are typically required for a home study:

1. Birth certificate
2. Marriage license
3. Divorce decree (if applicable)
4. Medical report. This can be a general letter from a doctor who has examined you within the past six to twelve months stating that you are in good health and if there are medical concerns that you are taking medicine or paying the proper attention to such concerns.
5. Income verification (W-2s, income-tax records, and pay stubs)
6. Personal reference letters from friends. Absurd as it sounds, there is a requirement to have letters from three to five people . . . in some cases, more. Some agencies may require that you have a letter from a member of the clergy or from a neighbor. Find these things out in advance. For the most part, these should be people who know you well and will state that you would make marvelous parents.

7. Child abuse/FBI clearance. Different states handle this requirement in different ways. Usually, fingerprints are required from either a police precinct or from Family Court. Fingerprints require separate fees. Before you go, inquire what the fees are and what manner of payment is acceptable. Some states like New York also require what is called "pre-adoption certification," which is essentially the same procedure in which you get fingerprinted. Your attorney or agency will guide you through this simple process.

> ### Too Many Requirements?
>
> *Remember: State requirements or country requirements (in an international adoption) are those that you must meet. Adoption agencies may add their own requirements. If you feel that their requirements are excessive or intrusive, you can choose another agency. Before you sign up with an agency find out their home-study requirements.*

8. Agencies may also require you to write an autobiographical statement about yourselves. Usually the agency will provide a guideline and include questions for you to answer. If you are working with the agency, they may even have a caseworker to assist you. This is essentially a written version of much of the same material, which will be asked by a social worker in a home study. It may shorten the interview process because you are providing data such as where you were born, how many brothers and sisters you have, where you were educated, etc. The more information included in this written version, the less work the social worker has to do. Not that they will lower the fee any, but this may expedite the process since you are doing some of the job.

   (*Note:* Don't make Xerox copies. Go to the proper

state or local records departments and pay for copies of original documents with the raised seals.)

Connie, who with her husband Peter adopted three children (mentioned in chapter 1) did some home-study rehearsals. *"We asked each other a bunch of questions to see how we would respond. Then we taped our answers and played them back. When we did the actual home study, however, we didn't stick to our 'rehearsed' responses. The social worker made us feel at ease, and we talked calmly. The only two things that rehearsing did was taught us not to ramble on and to be comfortable hearing such questions."*

How to Pass a Home Study

Okay, are you ready? Write these down on the palm of your hand. Just kidding.

1. Have all the necessary paperwork ready. (You won't fail if you don't have some papers ready, but the process will be delayed.)
2. Be yourselves.
3. Be honest.
4. Think "child in our life." Then consider how nearly all aspects of your current lifestyle will be affected.
5. Don't turn a simple question into cause to launch into a three-act play. For example, if you are asked to tell a little about your childhood, you need not go into a long diatribe about how a bully harassed you and how that ultimately impeded your social growth for years to come or discuss how your mother's not breast-feeding you resulted in your psychological aversion to milk. It's not a therapy session!

6. Be pleasant toward the social worker. Yes, you may feel that the home study is intrusive, and no, you may not like the fact that you have to answer questions before becoming parents. But this is the process, and the social worker is doing his or her job. Take a deep breath, accept that this is part of the adoption process, and get along with the social worker. Being antagonistic or adamant about an issue is not in your best interests.

The Big Questions

As you read each of the following paragraphs, think of how you would discuss the topics. Remember, there is no set manner in which home studies are conducted. They must only follow the regulations set forth by the individual state. But questions may vary in style, tone, and in the order asked. Agencies often ask their social workers to follow a set of agency guidelines, which may include separate interviews with each family member.

The social worker will ask you about your own upbringing and what your childhood was like. You need to provide a general answer that describes the type of family environment in which you grew up. You may be asked about your relationships with various family members. There is no right or wrong answer. The social worker is trying to get a general idea of how you interact with others and the basic family environment in which you were raised.

There will be questions about your relationship as a couple. Again, no right or wrong answers here. Talk about the basic elements that make your relationship work.

You may be asked about other significant people in your life. This means those individuals with whom you and your soon-to-be family will be in contact with on a regular basis. Particular attention is paid to those individuals who may stay at your home.

You'll be asked about your health. Be honest, but remember, this is not your medical doctor. The social worker wants a general picture. He or she wants to know that you are in overall good health to raise the child. If you have a medical problem, it's important that you are addressing it. Millions of people today are taking prescribed medications to deal with anything from high cholesterol to depression. It's understood that you may not be the perfect picture of physical or mental health. In fact, people with disabilities can and do adopt children. The social worker does not need to know every minor ache and pain you may have or about your every worry.

There will be questions about how you see yourselves raising a child. If you are both working parents, who will stay at home during the day with the baby? Are you considering child care? Will one of your parents take care of your child during the day?

The social worker wants to get a picture of how the child will integrate into your family structure.

You will also be asked about your thoughts on discipline. Yes, you can say you believe in a gentle slap on the wrist for a young child who does something seriously wrong, like lighting matches or throwing the cat across the room. "Time outs" are very popular, although they don't always work. Again, the best answer is one that is well thought out and in the best interests of raising your child.

You'll be asked about your home. No, you need not have a separate bedroom for a baby or child. He or she may share a bedroom with an older sibling, or you might put the baby's crib in your room until you are able to find a bigger apartment. Just have a clear plan. A couple once asked me if they needed to have their house repainted before the home study, and I thought about what a boon this would be for the house-painting business if they could work this into the home-study requirements. The answer is, of course, no, your house need not be repainted.

If the paint job looks shabby, mention that you are planning to have the house repainted soon.

Note: Also mention that you are planning to childproof the house. You might even start the process well in advance if you are looking to adopt a toddler who will be testing your childproofing skills from day one.

You will be asked about your religious beliefs. You need not regularly attend any religious services to pass a home study. Parents are often from different faiths. The question then arises: In which faith will you raise the child? Again, there is no right or wrong answer. Perhaps you'll teach the child about both religions, or perhaps you've already decided in which religion you'd like to raise your son or daughter.

Your employment will come up. You need not be rich. You just need to have a source of steady income that will allow you to support a child. You also need not have a large amount of savings. In fact, people who are paying off debt can still adopt. The point is that you have thought about the added expenses you will incur once you adopt a child and have answers to how you will manage financially.

Questions will arise about your education. MBAs and high-school dropouts have all adopted children. Simply tell it like it is, or was, unless you're still in school (in which case you'll explain how you can fit that into your soon-to-be *busier* schedule).

The subject of infertility treatments will also come up. You may still be involved in ongoing treatments. This will not stop you from passing a home study. You are pursuing adoption now as another means of starting a family and you should be able to explain how and why you were motivated to pursue adoption. *It is very important that you are in this "adoption plan" together as a couple.*

Essentially, what the social worker is trying to do is write up a general report that portrays you as potentially suitable parents who have thought through what it will mean to bring a child into your lives. For example, if you enjoy spontaneously packing your bags and flying off to a different exotic location every other weekend, you will need to accept that your life will be very different and that you may not be jet-setting as often—at least not without a jet-setting nanny in tow.

Some Food for Thought

I would be remiss if I didn't acknowledge what many of you are thinking after reading about all of this personal information that you need to disclose. After all, to put it bluntly, if a couple gets passionate in the back of a Toyota Camry and a pregnancy ensues, no one is questioning their motivation or ability to become parents. So why should *you* have to submit to this inquisition? You have every right to feel that the home-study process is a bit intrusive. However, the difference is that adoption is a process that has legal, ethical, and moral ramifications, which are under the control of the government. In other words, like marriage, for which you get a license, adoption is governed by state and, to some degree, federal laws. Unlike marriage, however, you are not all entering into this agreement as consenting adults understanding all of the implications. One member of the adoption triad needs to be cared for, and *you* are completely responsible for his or her well-being.

There are many people who would like to see some means of government screening for biological parents to protect the best interests of children. It would certainly eliminate much of the need for placing children into the foster-care system, not to mention child abuse caused by parents who were ill prepared for the responsibilities that come with the job. However, this is not practical or within the rights of the government or civil rights laws.

Taking a positive approach, a home study can provide you with your own "readiness check" for parenting. You can think through how you will arrange or rearrange the house, who will watch the baby/child at different times. What will you do regarding discipline? How will you handle dietary concerns? Will you try to adhere strictly to the balanced diet theory, or will you allow your child to have some junk foods? What skills will you bring to parenting that you learned from your own parents?

Preparing for a home study allows you to think in greater detail about your family's future than many biological parents ever have the opportunity to do. Parents are constantly saying, "We'll get around to discussing that." Then they don't do it. Here is your opportunity to make a comprehensive parenting plan.

Kathy Brodsky, of Jewish Child Care Association in New York City, a home-study agency that provides a wide range of adoption education to couples and singles, explains her philosophy on home studies:

> We want to get information, but we also want the home study to be a give-and-take situation. It should be a time where parents can explore the issues of parenting and adoption. We don't expect that someone will have all the answers, but we want to raise the issues that they need to think about. It's important to make the couple, or single person, feel comfortable, or as comfortable as possible given the situation. Even though we are evaluating families, we do not believe in "the perfect family" and don't hold people up to some sort of ideal. Everyone has different ways of doing things, including parenting, and that's okay. We just want to get people to think about adoption and parenting. In fact, we're also there after the adoption for people who wish to come in and ask questions or voice concerns about raising their child.

A few home-study hints:

1. Do not say that you are adopting because he/she wants to. If this is the case, you should not even be at the point of a home study. This can put up a red flag in your home study.

2. Minimize all distractions. Let phone calls go on the answering machine, shut off the television, feed the dog/cat in advance, and try to create a comfortable atmosphere where you can sit calmly and talk with the social worker.

3. Allow each other to talk. One person is usually quieter than the other in any relationship. However, this person will also be a parent, so (s)he needs to speak. Don't try to do all of the talking.

4. Think about home safety and a sense of order. While you don't have to straighten up every corner of your home, you should do a pre-home-study walk-through and pretend your child will come tomorrow. That means you should make sure there are no loose wires hanging from the walls, no chipped paint, and for that matter, you might think about putting the *Playboy* magazines on a higher shelf.

5. Read up on adoption beforehand. You need not be an expert, but it is advantageous to show that you are ready and willing to do your homework. This shows the social worker that you are serious about bringing a child into your life through adoption. In fact, if you know other adoptive families, you may mention that during the home study.

6. Talk with a few social workers or agencies before selecting someone. You want to feel that you will be comfortable with this person. No, a social worker

cannot, by law, reject you because of a personal bias. However, it is comforting and easier to go through this important part of the process with someone with whom you feel comfortable.

7. Don't be afraid to ask a few questions, such as how long it will take until the court receives the home-study report or how you would get an extension should you pass the home study and need more than eighteen months to complete an adoption. On the other hand, don't grill the social worker with a myriad of adoption questions. That's what this book is for, as well as the adoption agency, your attorney, and support group. Remember that the social worker is doing just one important job within the structure of the overall adoption process.

Home studies by the numbers

1. Home studies are good for either one year or eighteen months, depending on the state. They can be updated for an extended amount of time for a fee.

2. Home studies, including the postplacement visit(s), generally cost between $750 and $1,750. It will cost more if it is an agency-affiliated home study. If a situation is already pending and you need it done in a hurry, this may also cost you more. Also, a fee of $2,000 or $3,000 from an agency may include the application fee and other services.

3. The home study can take from three weeks to three or four months depending on documentation necessary, child-abuse clearance required in certain states, and the speed of processing by the courts.

Home Studies for Prospective Single Parents

Karen, an adoptive single mom from Connecticut, says, "*They asked a lot of questions about my support system and plans for day care when I was at work. But all of that is understandable; it's in the best interest of the child.*"

The objective is the same as a home study for a couple: to determine whether or not you are considered to be a suitable parent. The difference, however, is that the questions may seem more intrusive. For one thing, you may be asked why you are still single. You may be asked about whom you date or your social life. Stay calm. Keep smiling. The reality is that this is often part of the job. Of course, in some instances, there may be an attitude or bias evident in the tone and manner of the social worker. This is *not* part of the job. Try to get references from other single parents who have worked with the social worker.

You will need the same documentation as a couple and will have to answer most of the questions mentioned regarding finances, upbringing, education, religion, discipline, and so on. The greater emphasis on a support system is probably the most unique feature of the home study for a prospective single parent.

According to Kathy Brodsky, "When we do home studies for prospective single parents, we look at their support systems. We want to know that there is someone to back them up should they get sick or need assistance. In this situation, or for any home study, we'll also want to meet anyone who is living in the house, including a boarder or other relatives."

Single parents may also be asked to name a legal guardian in the event something happens to them. Chapter 18 has more on single adoption.

Gay and Lesbian Home Studies

The basics are the same. However, attitudes are not the same throughout the country or throughout the world. In fact, gay and lesbian couples can essentially forget about doing most international adoptions as a couple. Some nations even ask social workers working with a single parent to sign an affidavit that an individual is not a homosexual.

Specific additional questions for a gay or lesbian couple might center on role models and how much influence members of the opposite sex (than the couple) the child will have. Also, the couple may be asked how they will explain their lifestyle to the child in contrast to heterosexual couples whom the child will encounter once he or she is old enough to understand various relationships.

It takes more work, but you will need to find a home-study agency that is "lifestyle friendly." Chapter 17 covers gay and lesbian adoption.

Postplacement Follow-up Visits

Like Arnold Schwarzenegger, home studies promise: "I'll be back."

After you have adopted, the social worker will indeed be back. Depending on the state regulations, agency requirements, and those of the country from which you adopted, there may be one, two, or more postplacement visits. These visits are to determine how the child has fit into the family environment and that all is proceeding smoothly. The courts will then get a report from the social worker on the household and the child. Social workers will expect the house to reflect the fact that a child is now living there, which means everything may not

> **Other People**
>
> If someone has moved into the home since the child was placed with the family, the social worker will need to meet with the person and add them to the home-study report.

be in perfect order. "*I was worried,*" said one adoptive parent anonymously. "*The social worker was coming for a follow-up visit and the place was incredibly neat. She might think we gave our son to someone else,*" she quipped. "*We ran around and messed things up a little. I can't help it if we have a neat kid.*"

"Postplacement visits are to see how the entire family is adjusting," says Kathy Brodsky. "It's a way of making sure things are running smoothly and everyone is where they should be. We also let the families know that we're here to help if they have issues they need to discuss."

International postplacement visits are very much to ensure the sending nation that the adoption has proceeded smoothly and the child is doing fine in his or her new home environment. It is important that other nations are confident that by allowing children to come into another country, they are not doing a disservice to the child or to their own nation.

Chapter 5
DOMESTIC AGENCY ADOPTION

For many years the general perception of adoption was that of going to an agency, paying for their services and adopting a child. It was essentially the common manner in which adoptions were handled for many years.

Today, licensed adoption agencies may be either for profit or nonprofit. Despite the fact that the word "nonprofit" may imply a more humanitarian (less business-oriented) approach, there is actually very little difference between the two types of agencies from where you, as the couple or individual, are standing. The fees and the process will be essentially the same. The difference is not that a nonprofit agency is run by volunteers, but in how the money is distributed and in the tax status of the agency.

Most adoption agencies are headed by individuals with long track records in adoption and the placement of children. Social workers and caseworkers are trained to work with birth mothers and adoptive families.

The primary concern for you as prospective adoptive parents is how the agency operates. From the initial application to the fee structure to how you are treated to the contract you are asked to sign, there are a number of areas you will need to address as you prepare to work with an agency. You also need to find out what role the birth mother plays in the process. Does she select the adoptive parents or does the agency make that determination? Many agencies today allow the birth mother to make this important choice.

Bill Betzen, a Dallas-based social worker who has managed child placement for several agencies, says, "You should expect an agency to have the highest standard for child-placement safety." He points to the Child Welfare League of America, which has over 1,100 adoption agencies as members. "One place to start, is with an agency that is a member of the CWLA," adds Betzen. "In addition, you should go to an agency that will tell you up front that they will take the financial risk. An agency should not increase the pressure and nourish the desperation that a family feels by making them responsible for paying all of the birth-mother expenses. They should not make you feel that if you do not spend more money or accept the situation they offer you that you will not be successful. Too many agencies operate on the desperation of people who come to them looking to adopt."

Steve and Mary of Pennsylvania, now proud parents of a gorgeous baby boy from Eastern Europe, paid thousands of dollars in birth-mother expenses to an agency, only to find out that the birth mother changed her mind. They were essentially informed that if they did not pay her expenses, she wouldn't choose them. This is the idea of feeding on a couple's emotional desire to have a child that Betzen is talking about. By disguising birth-mother expenses (which are monitored by the courts in most states) as agency fees, an agency can have you paying excessive amounts of money to house a birth mother, who may not even be the one from whom you are adopting a child.

Betzen's philosophy for adoption is, "The child is the center of the universe, and from there the adoption takes place." He emphasizes that it is all about finding the best home for the child. To do this properly, an agency should have an open and honest rapport with both the birth mother and the adoptive parents. They should get all pertinent information from both sides and be able to work toward a situation that will be best for the entire triad: the adoptive parents, the birth parents and, of course, the child. When an agency is leaning in favor of the birth mother and making adoptive couples jump through hoops or, conversely, is trying to place children in homes by convincing or manipulating a birth mother that adoption is what she "should" do, then they are not serving all members of the triad. Since the baby can neither sign a consent form nor write a check, he or she can sadly get lost among the priorities of some agencies. Fortunately, these agencies are still the exception to the rule. However, it is to your advantage to be aware of how each agency works.

Traditional and Modern Approaches

Agencies vary in their approach. The traditional agency, seen in movies in bygone years, handles a closed adoption. The birth mother signs over her parental rights, and the couple is called and informed that there is a child available for them to adopt. Never do the birth parents and adoptive parents meet. That does not make this a bad, improper, or unethical scenario. If a birth mother implicitly trusts and believes in an agency, based on its reputation, then she may feel that this is the best scenario. She can place her baby in good hands and move on with her life. She may not want to be in the high-pressure position of trying to select the ideal family. Likewise, if a couple or single person has the confidence that the agency will be honest in providing adequate health information about the child, then they, too, may be comfortable with this traditional approach. In addition, for a older couple, for a single parent, or for a family that feels uncomfortable trying to "market" themselves to birth parents through a portfolio, a traditional agency might be more desirable.

In some cases, in these traditional situations, to allow the birth mother time to change her mind, should she choose, the child is placed in foster care for a few days or even several weeks.

Today, because of the growing popularity of independent adoption (legal in most, but not all states), and the opportunity for birth mothers to select from ads placed in newspapers by adoptive parents, many agencies have broadened their policies. Nonetheless, this does not mean that traditional agency adoption is not a viable and suitable method for some people seeking a child.

Many agencies today have programs in which birth mothers and adoptive parents meet each other. A couple, or single parent, who wants to talk with a birth mother and meet her, will select an agency with such a program. A birth mother who wants to be involved in the placement of her baby will go to an agency where she is afforded the opportunity to evaluate the prospective adoptive parents. In some cases she may or may not want contact with them once she has made her selection. In short, there are many types of programs designed to meet the emotional needs of both birth and adoptive parents.

Once the match is made, what happens next?

The prospective adoptive parents wait through the birth mother's pregnancy and go through their own emotional pregnancy. They also deal with agency fees and expenses.

If the agency is willing to charge a couple an up-front fee, but then takes on the financial responsibilities of the birth mother itself from the pool of money brought in from the initial fees, then the adoptive parents are not responsible for paying additional birth-mother expenses. In many instances, a set amount of money is put in escrow to be used for either birth-mother expenses or other such expenses incurred during the adoption process. This amount should be in the $5,000 to $10,000 range.

Remember, in addition to the up-front payment, you will also pay the agency another fee upon placement of the child. Therefore, you do not want to get involved in paying potentially unlimited amounts of birth-mother expenses.

Keep in mind, that agency adoption expense should not exceed $25,000 or perhaps $30,000. Therefore, if you are paying birth-mother expenses, the agency fees should be lower. It should not charge the same fees as an agency that picks up some of this responsibility and then has you pay the birth mother on top of that.

Dawn Smith-Pliner, founder and director of Friends in Adoption, a Vermont-based, and licensed, adoption agency (also licensed in New York, New Jersey, Rhode Island, and Connecticut) stresses that people should educate themselves first about the adoption process. "We run get-acquainted weekends where people can get to know about adoption. Many agencies have some type of orientation" says Smith-Pliner. She also stresses the rapport you establish with the agency. "A lot of adoption in my opinion is based on gut feeling . . . this can be about an agency, an attorney or a birth mother. If an agency is abrupt, or in a hurry, they aren't for you. You need them to be responsive so you can establish a good rapport."

What Do You Want to Know?

Before you consider working with an agency, you want to know as much as possible about the agency. Therefore, you may want to play this game of Twenty Questions.

1. Are you licensed to do adoptions in my state? If their answer is "no", then your response is "Bye".
2. What are your guidelines or restrictions for getting accepted? Don't waste your time on an agency that won't take anyone over the age of forty if you are forty-two years

old. Find out what other criteria they have for rejecting people. Some agencies see the world from their own set of guidelines and perspectives. Inquire also about their home-study process and what is expected. If the guidelines are too restrictive, you may not feel comfortable working with that agency, even if it is likely that it will accept you. Keep in mind that if you are turned down by one agency, you can try others. Agencies can impose their own regulations in an effort to limit the number of waiting families. They can do this as long as they do so in an unbiased manner. By law, they are not allowed to reject someone based on race, religion, etc. If you are turned down by an agency or find out that you will not be accepted, don't take it *too* personally.

3. Do you offer an introductory or orientation session?
4. What is the fee structure and what is included? Some portion of the fee is usually paid once you are accepted by the agency, and the bulk of the fee is paid after placement. There is also usually an application fee of $250 to $500. That is why it is advisable to determine whether you meet the criteria of the agency before spending money to find out you're too old to be accepted. If an agency won't tell you its guidelines regarding acceptability, then move on. Remember, rapport is important.
5. How much is refundable if we find a situation through another means? Will the agency work with an attorney should we locate a birth mother elsewhere through an attorney?
6. Do you provide names of approved social workers or home-study agencies for the home study?
7. Are attorney fees included?
8. How does the agency determine placement? Does the birth mother make the decision or the agency? If it is the birth mother, what does she look at? Profiles? Dear Birth Mother

letters? If it's the agency, what criteria does it use to determine placement?

9. Once a match is made by a birth mother or through the agency, is a caseworker assigned to the individual case?

10. What type of medical information does the agency provide? What do they ask the birth mother to provide? Can you ask for specific testing, such as an HIV test?

11. Do you offer support groups for waiting families?

12. How does the agency attract birth mothers?

13. Is counseling provided for the birth mother? For you?

14. What is the average length of time from acceptance to placement? This should be anywhere in the nine- to eighteen-month range. Of course, this will vary depending on your personal preferences. And remember, you are entitled to have preferences. Just understand that if you specifically seek only a newborn Caucasian baby, the process may take longer a little longer. Children of color are more readily available. *As mentioned earlier, you should not select a child based on how quickly you can bring him or her into your home.*

15. How many placements does your agency do in a given year, and how many people are currently waiting for a placement?

16. How long has the agency been in business, and what are the backgrounds of the principals?

17. Is someone always accessible? Can the agency be reached if something important arises, such as going into labor?

18. What is your policy on "open" adoption? *Listen to this answer closely.* Often an agency defines "open" as communication between birth mother and adoptive families prior to placement. This can be very beneficial. You can get to know the birth mother and she can see if she is comfortable with you as prospective parents. However, once the

child is placed, the agency should not determine the level of openness in your future relationship with the birth mother. After placement, the agency should not have a say in your ongoing relationship with the birth mother—that is a personal agreement between her and you. If the agency insists that you must maintain openness or contact with the birth mother as a prerequisite to working with it, then (whether you want an ongoing relationship with the birth mother or not) walk away. Only in California is openness required, and that means only that both birth parents and adopting parents have identifying information. Remember, adoption agencies should *not* impose their beliefs upon you.

19. What happens if a situation is not right for us? In some agencies, you can be selected by a birth mother and can determine that you do not want to work with her for whatever reasons. (For example, she may need too much money in expenses or have medical problems that make you uncomfortable). Your portfolio or biography should then be readily available to the next birth mother who comes through the door. On the other end of the spectrum is the agency that says if a situation comes up and you don't take it, you go out of the program or to the end of a list. Find out what criteria you can set up (newborn only, biracial okay, but only a girl, and soon) and what happens if you decline a situation.

20. Can you provide references of other families formed by adoption through that agency? Naturally, as is always the case when asking for references, the agency will provide you with people who simply *loved* working with them. Find additional references on your own (through support groups) for a more objective viewpoint. Nonetheless, it's nice to talk to some happy families who just adore the

agency. They won't give you objective information, but may verify some of the good things you've heard about the agency.

Note: Fees vary greatly from agency to agency. Some offer all-inclusive fees while others have menus that let you choose specifically which services you need. For example, one agency will require you to have a home study done by a social worker affiliated with the agency. That will be included in your fee. Another agency will allow you to select a licensed social worker from your home state to do your home study. (Just double-check that this home study will be accepted).

You also want to get a clear idea of how the agency works from the time you sign up until you become adoptive parents—not only from your perspective, but from that of the birth mother. In the case of Friends in Adoption, Dawn Smith-Pliner explains that the agency pairs birth mothers with adoptive couples (and singles) and asks for $5,000 to be put in an escrow account for attorney fees and birth-mother expenses. "Sometimes the situation requires more money and sometimes I am glad to provide a refund," she explains. "Should a situation fall through, we have a fund whereby we can reimburse the family who has lost money in the process. The fund enables us to take some of the financial risk."

Christine and Charles, adoptive parents of two children, worked through an agency that included money for birth-mother expenses in their $18,000 fee. Christine explains, *"If a situation fell through and the birth mother whom you were working with changed her mind, you would lose only another $2,000 on what the agency called a matching fee. This would run the total up to $20,000. The agency would not charge this fee more than once, so if a couple of situations did not end in adoption, you would not be out additional money."*

Jenny and Mark adopted their son through an agency that

had a roll-over policy for expenses. Mark explained, *"A specified part of your initial fee would go toward birth-mother expenses for the birth mother of a couple who were farther along in the process. Then, as you got farther along, another couple who was entering the program would put in the same amount of money, and that money would go toward your birth mother's expenses. Money that was not needed by a birth-mother would go to a fund that was used to cover birth mothers who changed their minds. Therefore, if everyone in the program put in $4,000 toward birth mother expenses and one birth mother only needed $2,000, the additional $2,000 would go into a fund for couples who had a birth mother change her mind, so that the couple would not have to spend an additional $4,000."*

This was considered to be a fair method since no one knew which couples might have a birth mother change her mind. It also prevented the agency from linking families with more money to birth mothers who were in greater need of expense money because everyone was putting in the same amount toward birth mother expenses.

Checking Up

If you are about to trust an agency to help you through something as important as forming your family, you want to make sure it is reputable. Too many people believe that the word "nonprofit" or the idea that an agency is helping you to adopt a child, automatically makes it trustworthy. This is not always the case. Some agencies will feed on your emotions and desire to adopt a child. Therefore, you should check with the Better Business Bureau, the state's licensing bureau, the Interstate Commerce Commission, the Department of Consumer Affairs, or possibly the attorney general's office in the state where the agency is based to determine whether or not there are any complaints or legal actions filed against the agency. Support groups and adoption–based chat rooms are also excellent places to discuss an agency with other adoptive families. However, don't go by rumors since these may be unsubstantiated. Don't allow one person to sway you because he or she had a bad experience. Often a person creates his or her own negative experience. Instead, look for a pattern. If, for example, several people are not happy with the length of time it takes agency representatives to respond to inquiries and provide assistance, then that agency may be lacking in the area of customer service.

Agency-Identified Adoption

With the increased popularity of independent adoption, in which birth mothers and adoptive parents establish a rapport with one and other and work through an attorney to adopt (see the next chapter) came the advent of "agency identified adoption."

This is a method in which agencies help facilitate the adoption process. The agency can provide counseling for either or both parties and guide the prospective parents through the paperwork and home study. Some states insist that an agency be involved in an independent adoption. Therefore, if you are looking to do an independent adoption in such a state, this solves the problem since this method is a compromise between agency and independent adoption.

So how does it work?

Essentially, an agency will have a program whereby it helps assist you through this process. You will do the advertising to locate the birth mother. The agency will help pull together all aspects of the adoption plan. It may or may not provide you with an attorney. Since you are paying for advertising yourself, the agency fee should not equal the cost of a "traditional" agency that is locating the birth mothers by placing its own advertisements. Here you and the birth mother are creating an adoption plan, and the agency is making it happen. Some birth mothers, and adoptive parents will feel more confident with an agency behind them, knowing there are various levels of support and services offered—or at least there should be.

The next step is usually that the birth mother calls the agency, as opposed to calling you directly in an independent adoption. This can work to your advantage with experienced caseworkers answering the phones. It can also work to your disadvantage if the birth mother is less comfortable talking with the agency. There is also the possibility that an agency acting as a go-between can either steer the birth mother to another waiting family or throw other obstacles or restrictions in the path.

It is therefore essential that you know how the entire process works from start to finish and what role the agency will play in the communication between you and the birth mother.

If you want to work with an agency but maintain greater involvement in the process than a "traditional" agency offers, this is a good option. Do your homework. In a perfect world, this might be the ideal compromise between agency and independent adoption. Unfortunately, you are not in a perfect world, and not all agencies handle this type of program as well as they should. Again, get references.

Another definition of agency-identified adoption comes from www.Nolo.com, an on-line legal dictionary:

An identified, or designated, adoption is one in which the adopting parents locate a birthmother (or the other way around), and then ask an adoption agency to take over the rest of the adoption process. In this way, the process is a hybrid of an independent and an agency adoption. Prospective parents are spared the waiting lists of agencies by finding the birthparents themselves, but reap the other benefits of agencies, such as their experience with adoption legalities and their counseling services. Everyone may simply feel more comfortable if an agency is involved. Plus, identified adoptions provide an alternative to parents in states that ban independent adoptions.

This is a nice summation of the identified-adoption process whereby the birth mother and adoptive parents locate each other and then work through the agency.

Why choose agency-identified adoption over working with an attorney?

It's a matter of comfort. It's the same reason that some people choose an independent CPA whom they trust implicitly, and others work with a large, reputable CPA firm. Comfort.

Note: Agency-identified adoption is still relatively new, and some "traditional" agencies have reluctantly taken it upon themselves to join the growing trend. They do not, however, relish giving up their more traditional manner of control and may impose regulations and guidelines that are restrictive. Find out how long the identified program has been in existence, ask about all rules, regulations, stipulations, and guidelines, and find other people who have gone through the program with that agency.

Variations on a Theme

Between "traditional" and "identified" adoption, there are many variations. Agencies today usually let birth mothers select prospective parents after reading their bios, portfolios, or Dear Birth Mother letters. Birth mothers are having a far greater say in the home that will be found for their baby than ever before. How much choice they have in placement and the degree of preadoption communication with the adoptive parents will vary from agency to agency.

In most cases, before the birth mother and adoptive parents

speak to one another, the agency acts as the matchmaker, bringing the birth mother, or birth parents and adoptive couple or single, together and opening the lines of communications.

Christine and Charles, mentioned above, adopted twice through this type of situation. Christine explains, *"The portfolio is very important. The first time, I wrote a Dear Birth Mother letter that was geared to a teenager. Since birth mothers are of all different ages, it didn't go over that well and the process took a year and a half. The second time we adopted, we worked harder on our portfolio. We took longer to put it together and changed it around several times. When we were done, it appealed to a wider range of birth mothers. We were selected very quickly and adopted in just three months."*

Portfolios and Dear Birth Mother letters are common methods of attracting birth parents to prospective adoptive parents. Prepare a couple of written pages about your hobbies, neighborhood, vacations, careers. Include a few pages of photos of yourselves. There is no way of knowing what a birth mother will look for when seeking the best family and home environment for the child. The best you can do is to try hard to make a positive impression, one that radiates warmth and family.

Denise from Connecticut, with her husband Jeff, adopted siblings. They felt that such an agency adoption allowed them to present themselves in such a way that would appeal to a birth mother. Denise discussed their portfolio: *"Our portfolio was about eighteen pages long. That was a little too long, but we knew it was important to convey to a birth mother what you're like, who you are and give her a feel for your personalities. You can't fake it because that won't work. You have to be true to yourself and present yourself in a positive manner. We combined a mix of photos with accompanying text. Photos included us at a nearby beach, some of our home, and a few with family and friends and so on. We wanted them to see us in a variety of family 'settings'. Pets are also a big thing."* Denise points out that you should omit wedding photos, since the birth mother might not be walking down the aisle anytime soon.

It's also advantageous to look at other profiles. Through joining a support group, you may be able to do just that. *"While you don't know what is or is not going to appeal to a birth mother, since every birth mother will have her own likes and dislikes, the best you can do is to present a well rounded family-friendly portfolio."*

Denise also adds that you should sign your names by hand at the end of a typed letter or printed material in the portfolio to add a personal touch.

Competition

Agencies are businesses and they are competitive. If they are trying to impress you with personalized service and an out-pouring of concern for the adoption triad, that's in their favor.

Denise also points out that it's very important to learn how the agency treats the birth mothers. This may come more through networking than through the agency directly. *"You want an agency with whom the birth mother feels comfortable when she's making this very important decision."*

Also keep in mind that if an agency is trying to sell you on the ideas that identified adoption doesn't work, traditional adoption will take you five years, or open adoption is the only type of adoption that works, they are essentially using political smear tactics. Avoid agencies that try to lure you by bad-mouthing other forms of adoption. In addition, if you don't like the tone an agency uses, perhaps you should look elsewhere. For example, a Connecticut-based agency's home page has a long-winded message explaining why they do not handle identified-agency adoptions. Reading between the lines, the text is quite negative.

The fact that adoption laws vary greatly from state to state is a clear indication that many people do not agree on the best methods of adoption. However, children are adopted through agencies in all fifty states, so various methods are working despite what critics will tell you. You only need find the one most suitable for you and stay firmly within the laws and guidelines.

Contracts

Read the contract carefully before signing with an agency. Make sure you read the fine print. You may even ask a contract attorney to review it for you. If an agency is not willing to discuss and explain their contract, then do not sign it. Understand the fees and fee structure, your right to refuse a potential adoption, and other possibilities. Everything should be spelled out

---

Sample Generic Adoption-Agency Guidelines:

- *Couples or singles may apply to adopt through the agency.*

- *Birth mothers are found through outreach and advertising.*

- *The Generic Agency does not ask adoptive parents to take on the financial responsibilities of birth-parent expenses.*

- *An application fee will be charged. Applications are accepted or denied within sixty days. A list of acceptable criteria will be made available free of charge for anyone interested in filling out an application. If accepted into the Generic Agency program, the prospective adoptive parents will be charged an initial fee upon signing.*

- *Couples or singles in the program will be asked to provide two portfolios with photos and text for birth mothers to look through. They will also need to include a "Dear Birth Mother" letter. Generic Agency staff will help with the compilation of this material for no additional fee. Birth mothers will be able to select adoptive parents from these albums. There will be no identifying information made available at this time. If a birth mother chooses, the agency can make the selection process for her.*

- *The Generic Agency does not take a position on the openness of the adoption. Birth parents and prospective adoptive parents can request a meeting,*

clearly. Look for any unusual stipulations, such as you cannot already have a child, you cannot talk to the birth mother from the time you first meet her until she gives birth, you will have continued personal contact with the birth mother at least twice a year, etc. You'd be surprised at what some agencies have slipped into their contracts. Read the contract when you are wide awake and not distracted.

This is just a brief overview to give you an idea of some of the adoption agency guidelines you can look for when selecting an agency.

Ask a lot of questions, read the contract carefully, get references, talk to other people who are familiar with the agency, and do some research to assure their credibility. If all has proceeded smoothly in the selection process and you have been accepted by

which will be facilitated by the Generic Agency. From that point on, they may or may not decide to maintain contact after the adoption and exchange identifying information. The Generic Agency can serve as a go-between for information if both sides wish to have a closed adoption. The Generic Agency has found that in recent years, there has been an increase in the number of open adoptions, and the majority of these situations have been very successful.

- *Couples or singles may specify preferences of ethnicity, age, special needs, or sibling groups.*

- *The Generic Agency requires two preplacement visits by a licensed social worker approved by the agency for completion of the home study. A fee will be paid directly to the licensed social worker or home-study agency through the Generic Agency. The only other fee for the Generic Agency will be at the completion of the adoption.*

- *Birth mothers will be provided with counseling sessions.*

- *Adoptive parents may select from postplacement services (for an additional fee) at their discretion. All adoption-related travel expenses for the adoptive parents are not included in the agency fees and will be paid for by the adoptive parents. There is no further obligation to the Generic Agency after the adoption is completed.*
- *The Generic Agency does not guarantee placement within a set time frame.*

the agency, you will sign the contracts and be on your way. Make sure you know who your contact person (or people) are at the agency for questions and information. Don't panic if they do not respond immediately to your every need—however, expect answers and information to be provided within a reasonable amount of time. Learn from the agency and be proactive, which means double-check that things are getting done, call with a polite reminder if papers you were supposed to receive have yet to arrive. Gary, mentioned earlier, after adopting his three-year-old daughter Debbie in a unique domestic-agency private adoption (she was an older child) noted that after four months he was still waiting for immunization records and other medical information from the agency. *"They call and ask when I'll be sending the final payment, and I ask when they'll be sending the medical information they promised months ago. We kind of go back and forth."* Being that the particular agency does not generally deal with older children, this situation is a bit more complicated than most. In most cases, domestic agencies will provide you with all of the information that they can obtain for you.

Independent adoption, discussed in the next chapter, has caused many adoption agencies to rethink and reevaluate their programs in order to stay in business. This has actually worked favorably, as it has changed the way in which many agencies operate, thus giving birth mothers and adoptive parents far more options. Being forced to rethink a business plan often encourages new ideas and can benefit any business. Domestic agencies today are, in essence, a long-established manner of adoption with many new and progressive policies that benefit all members of the adoption triad.

Chapter 6
DOMESTIC ADOPTION: INDEPENDENT PLACEMENT

Over the past twenty years, the United States has seen the emergence of what is known as independent adoption. It is a means of domestic placement, whereby a couple or single individual adopts a child independently of an adoption agency. There is direct contact between the birth mother or birth parents and prospective adoptive parents. An adoption attorney handles the legal process.

Independent adoption allows the birth mother to have significant involvement in the process. She is, in fact, finding the best home environment for her child. For the adoptive parents, it allows them to not only know something about the birth parents, but to have a direct line of communication. In more than half of independent adoptions, the birth parents and adoptive parents meet in person before the adoption.

Jeanne and Bob adopted their son through independent adoption. They found an attorney, advertised that they were looking to adopt, spoke on the telephone with birth mothers, and eventually made an adoption plan with a woman who would become the birth mother of their son. Five years later, Jeanne spent some time recalling the story of first meeting their son's birth mother:

"The first time we met our son's birth mother was the day

after he was born. The initial call from her came five months prior to his birth. The next time we heard anything from her was a few weeks before he was born. She seemed to want to stay distant and we respected that. We spoke a couple of times during the few weeks before our son was born, usually after she had a doctor's appointment.

We made travel plans to fly cross-country the night our son was born. Once we arrived, we still had about a two-hour trip ahead of us. By the time we got to the hospital, he was a day old. We picked up a beautiful floral arrangement for his birth mom, but she never even said thank you. Although it wasn't a new-baby arrangement, I felt I had probably made a huge mistake getting the flowers. We all held the baby and as I recall it was a little awkward. We didn't know how to act, afraid that she would think we wouldn't make good parents. Later that day she was being discharged, and we were to go back and pick up the baby that evening. When it was time to say goodbye to her, we all cried and at that moment I knew why she had tried to stay so distant. She really loved this baby and wanted the absolute best for him. It was a decision that she knew was right, but that didn't mean she was not filled with emotion. She told us to take care of him, and we promised her we would.

"Mother's Day was just a little more than a month after our son was born and a few days before that Sunday arrived, we got a card from his birth mother that read:

> Thanks for the beautiful flowers and for making the hardest day of my life a little easier. Now that everything is done I realize a few things I never thought to say, so could you please take a moment to read the enclosed letter.

"Here's what she wrote in the letter:

> Here are a few things that have been going through

my head that I never got the chance to say. Please tell him when he grows up—if he ever asks questions, that giving him up for adoption was the hardest thing I've ever had to do. I love him very much and will always love him and think of him often. If he ever wants to look me up I would love to see him. Thank you both for being yourselves and putting me at ease with my decision. I know in my heart that I did the right thing, you make a great couple of parents.

With love, A.

"I thought of her daily for the first year. Every time the baby did something new, I wished I could let her know. As time went on, I thought of her less often, but she is still in my thoughts a lot. She gave us the greatest gift we've ever received and I feel forever bonded to her.

"Although she chose not to have any contact, I write her a note once a year, enclose a picture, and put it away in a drawer. If the day comes that my son contacts her, she'll be able to have a small glimpse of what he was like as a child."

While all adoption stories are unique, independent-adoption stories run the gamut. They are fraught with emotions and range from three-month adoption vignettes to long two-year novellas. Each one, as in the story told by Jeanne, is filled with memories that evoke a wide range of emotions.

The independent-adoption process is not hard to learn. It is, however, one that requires a great deal of attention to detail. It is a hands-on, proactive method of adopting. *You* make the decisions and remain involved every step of the way. Of course, there are risks involved, which will be discussed in this chapter. But in the forty-six states, which allow for independent domestic adoption, the process, despite its instability, does work—and it works well.

The Process

Independent-adoption can place a newborn baby in your arms. It can allow you to learn about the health of the unborn child as you talk with the birth mother during her pregnancy. It is a method of adoption in which the birth mother and adoptive parents can form a strong bond. It can also provide all sides of the adoption triad (birth mother, adoptive parents, and the child) with the most information and communication.

The process involves:

- Hiring an adoption attorney;
- Filing all appropriate preadoption paperwork (which will vary from state to state);
- Having a home study completed by a state certified social worker;
- Advertising, and, or networking to find a birth mother;
- Talking with birth mothers on the phone and possibly meeting some in person;
- Making an adoption plan with a birth mother;
- Traveling to meet and adopt your child;
- Returning home after the birth mother has signed the consent form (and the Interstate Compact has also been signed, if you have adopted from another state);
- Finalizing the adoption through the courts.

Yes, this is a *very* simplified overview, but these are the basic steps.

Finding an Adoption Attorney

Okay, so your brother-in-law is a contract attorney and your nephew is a tax attorney. Why not save some money and let one of them handle an adoption for you? How hard can it be? Well, if you consider that there are fifty-one sets of laws governing each of the fifty states plus Washington D.C., you may get a general idea.

Adoption law is a specialty and adoption attorneys spend their time staying on top of the many changes in adoption law that take place on an almost-weekly basis. There is always something being amended or challenged in some state regarding adoption. Therefore, it is essential that you seek out an adoption attorney if you are choosing independent adoption. An adoption attorney will know and understand how to most effectively and cordially work with birth mothers, who are often frightened or intimidated by the idea of dealing with an attorney.

Your attorney will serve as your guide through the independent-adoption process. He or she will explain the legal process, guide you through the paperwork and advise you. He or she should put you in a position to make the adoption process work best for you.

To find an attorney, you might attend meetings of a local support group and ask for recommendations by others who have completed an independent adoption in your state. It is important to get a word-of-mouth referral. You can also find adoption attorneys at the American Academy of Adoption Attorneys (AAAA) at www.adoptionattorneys.com (202-832-2222) and look under your state for listings. The AAAA started in 1989, and all members must meet specific criteria before being accepted. There are strict standards to which they must adhere. You can also go on-line at www.adoptiondirectory and click on "State Search" to find professionals in your state.

Adoption conferences, seminars, or workshops sponsored by local groups or associations may feature attorneys as speakers or provide places for networking and getting the names of attorneys. Since there are not a great number of adoption attorneys in most

Networking Questions

When talking to others about an attorney, ask the following three questions:

1. Did the attorney respond, or did someone on his or her staff respond to your questions in a timely fashion?

2. Did the attorney provide guidance in an unbiased manner?

3. Was he or she conservative or liberal in advising you how to spend your money on advertising and birth-mother expenses?

You might also inquire about the rapport you had with the attorney. As Dawn Smith Pliner stated earlier, gut feeling and a good rapport are also very important.

cities or towns, chances are that if you network, you will find an adoptive parent who has worked with the attorney and can give you their personal opinion. Remember; Every adoption is different. Therefore, the circumstances and individuals involved in any adoption will differ.

Know the Laws

It is to your advantage to do a little scouting and find out what the laws are governing adoption attorneys in your state. This may sound a little odd. After all, why should you check laws governing an attorney? Shouldn't he or she know the laws?

There are "gray areas" in adoption law in which an unscrupulous attorney can hide and numerous loopholes which he or she can try to climb through on your behalf. "You do not, however, want to be operating on the edge of the envelope," to quote one long-time adoption attorney. Therefore, you need to be confident that you are working with someone who is very reputable.

In some states, adoption attorneys are allowed to act as go-betweens and introduce birth parents to prospective adoptive couples or singles. An attorney may have listings or portfolios of couples or singles looking to adopt, much like an agency might have. Conversely, in other states, such as New York, the attorney cannot act as a go-between in any manner to facilitate the adoption. Make sure you have a general idea of what is and is not allowed in your state.

Can an attorney take money for a birth mother's "expenses" and then claim that she "changed her mind," thus taking the money for himself? Legally he can't, but you'll probably never catch him.

Can an attorney work through an agency in another state to house or support birth mothers because he is working in a state that does not allow him to have such involvement? Legally no, but again, he or she could probably get away with this setup for a while. The point is there are some attorneys who have built their practice right in the middle of the gray area. Fortunately, this is a small percentage.

You should find out what an attorney is and is not allowed to do by law in regard to finding a birth mother, placing ads, or paying birth-mother expenses. Most adoption attorneys are quite reputable, and many chose this particular area of law because they are adoptive parents themselves. They therefore understand the emotional as well as the legal aspects of your adoption.

You can usually double-check basic legal information in your state (regarding independent adoption and attorneys) through the state bar association, at a law library, or on the Internet by looking at a reputable web-site such as The National Adoption Clearinghouse, www.calib.com/naic/ (under Adoption Law).

The Fees

Attorneys can charge either a flat fee or an hourly rate.

Attorneys surveyed from various states around the country quote flat fees from $3,000 to $5,000. You'll find higher and lower amounts. You'll also find hourly rates generally falling in the $150 to $250 range. Of course, if you are agreeing to an hourly rate, you'll need to find out approximately how many hours an adoption should take, assuming there are no significant problems. Therefore, if an attorney quotes you a flat fee of $10,000 or says it should take 200 hours, ask why it will cost so much money or take so many hours. This should raise a red flag.

Note: Attorneys cannot charge contingency fees—meaning, in essence, that if they place a baby with you that you would then owe them "x" dollars. This is not a charge for their services and raises the question of baby buying/selling practices.

Also, make sure you know what additional expenses you will be billed for and at what cost. Some attorneys do not bill you for phone calls while others will bill you for every paper clip they use (at $1.00 per clip!). Get a good idea of all costs up front.

Attorneys may also charge a consultation fee. A veteran might charge for such a meeting, but it may be worthwhile. However, someone who does not charge a consultation fee may be just as qualified. The highest-priced attorney is not necessarily the best. The one with whom you feel comfortable and have confidence in is the best attorney for you.

Establish a Rapport

It is important that you feel comfortable with the attorney you select. This is a much more emotional situation than hiring a contract attorney to review the contracts for an impending business merger. You may even need some hand-holding along the way. Adoption attorneys generally have well-trained staffs who will answer your questions, alleviate your fears, and help guide you through the process.

The adoption attorney you choose may be more conservative or liberal in recommending how you pursue your adoption. Some will suggest that you do an advertising blitz—$2,000 the first month in advertising. This could become a problem in the second, third, or fourth months if the initial blitz does not result in a potential adoption. Other attorneys will suggest that you set a more conservative advertising budget of perhaps $500 or

$700 per month. The same holds true when it comes to paying birth-mother expenses. Some attorneys will urge you to pay whatever is allowed to make the situation work, while other attorneys will strongly recommend that you pay very little or pay expenses only retroactively, after the placement.

According to Mark McDermott, former president of the American Association of Adoption Attorneys, and current legislative chairman, "Attorneys should not impose their views on subjects such as having an open or closed adoption. An adoption attorney should be an expert on the law, an expert on the facts, and he or she should be objective." Since adoption law is unique, McDermott also sees great value in the accumulated experiences of an adoption attorney who may have seen various situations like yours in the past.

Last, you'll need to think about the qualities that make you feel comfortable or uncomfortable about this person. You want a trusting relationship. After all, he or she is going to help guide you through some of the most important decisions you will ever make. Therefore, you should list some questions prior to your first meeting:

- In which states are you licensed to do an adoption?
- How many adoptions have you done in the past year?
- How long have you been in practice?
- What are your fees?
- What do the fees include? Not include? (A retainer, precertification, finalization, and office expenses such as phone calls and photocopies are typical.) What fees are refundable?
- What is the schedule of payment? (Most attorneys do not receive the full fee until the adoption is completed.)
- Will we be working directly with you or with one of

your associates? (Often larger practices employ other people who will help you with many of the details. This is not necessarily a bad thing. It frees up the attorney to focus on the key issues.)

- Will there always be someone reachable in case a birth mother should call or you must be reached in an emergency?

- Will you or your office be able to assist us in placing advertising? (This will often simply mean helping you determine where to advertise, and not actually placing ads for you.)

- How much do you estimate the average cost-of-living expenses for the birth mother should come to? (Many will say that this varies. However, if you can get an approximate cost you'll have an idea whether this attorney finds it perfectly normal to spend $10,000 on birth-mother expenses or a more typical amount such as $2,000 to $5,000.)

Also keep in mind that your attorney, an expert on adoption law, is not an expert on all birth mothers—no one is. Every adoptive situation is unique and every birth mother is different. Your attorney can guide you, but cannot make guarantees. Too often people have unrealistic expectations. Attorneys cannot make a situation work. They cannot—or should not—influence a birth mother. They usually cannot even select the judge before whom you will appear to finalize your adoption. They also cannot answer every question the minute you ask, so, they may need to call you back after doing research. (And remember, if they are doing research on your behalf, they are working for you and should be billing you for their time.) Good attorneys can find the answers to questions about adoption law and use their knowledge to guide you.

If possible, you should try to meet with more than one adoption attorney to compare and contrast the answers.

Note: Word of mouth and personal references are very important when hiring a professional. However, don't go by one person's opinion. There is always one person who hated the same attorney that a dozen other people loved. If you meet that disgruntled client first, you may be swayed away from using a very good attorney. Try to find a few people who know of the attorney.

The Interstate Compact

The details of this interstate legal matter should not concern you directly. It is a bureaucratic matter for the most part, and you need not know all the details about the Interstate Compact. However, to transport the baby from one state to another the Interstate Compact must be signed by the compact administrators in both the sending state (where the baby is born) and the receiving state (the state in which you are currently living). The process, generally governed by the state social-service divisions, usually takes five to seven days. There are some states in which it takes considerably longer. Michael Goldstein, New York-based adoption attorney, and adoptive father, recommends that you ask your attorney about the length of time you will need to stay in a state, waiting for this document to be signed. "There are some states where you will have to stay more than a week before you can bring your baby home. Your attorney should guide you in this respect, as it will help you determine the states in which you choose to place your ads."

While you may enjoy the short "honeymoon" period of vacationing in a hotel with your new baby for a week, you may not wish to be away from your home, the rest of your family, and your job for several weeks. Therefore, inquire about the various states and find out which few states may require you to stick around a little longer until the Interstate Compact is signed.

Finding a Birth Mother

Networking

Independent adoption means that it's up to you to find a baby to adopt. Attorneys can help you in some states, but in many they cannot. There are adoption consultants who, for a fee, will help you in your search, but independent adoption was around long before this new breed of consultants. Thus, they are unnecessary.

You will hear people tell you, and may read elsewhere, that you should tell everyone that you are looking to adopt. Spreading the word in this manner will build up a large network of people who know that you are seeking to adopt. If everyone knows, then someone can help you find your child.

While this may work for some people, I personally disagree with the tell-everyone theory as an effective means of net-working. Adoption is not a desperate cry for help. It is a means of forming a family. You need to be somewhat selective in how and where you spread the word

Think about it. How many times have you run across a birth mother who has told you that she's looking to place her child for adoption? For most people, the answer will be "very few" or "never."

Some reasons *not* to tell everyone that you are looking to adopt:

First, attorneys agree that the vast majority (more than 80 percent) of placements are the result of advertisements placed in newspapers, circulars, or elsewhere. Those situations that resulted from networking were most often calculated net-working within adoption support groups or at adoption-related conferences or gatherings.

Second, you need to ask yourself; Do I really want everyone involved in this process? This includes people who will feel sympathy for you, others who will not understand and may have unintentional hurtful comments, and still others who will be offended if you don't follow their lead. If, for example you are hoping to adopt a newborn Caucasian infant and a friend hears about a young Asian woman who may place her child for adoption, how do you explain to your friend who is trying to help that you are not comfortable with that situation? Your friend may not understand how you could not pursue this situation. Thus you will strain the relationship. Adoption is a very personal issue that you can share only with people you know and trust. It is also an issue that, like borrowing money or starting a business with people you are close to, can come between friends because not everyone feels the same way you do about forming a family.

You also run the risk of a go-between creating an awkward situation. For example, if you and the birth-mother both want a closed adoption, or an open adoption with limited contact, it will be awkward having an ongoing mutual connection through someone you both know. Won't it make you a bit uncomfortable to go to a friend's dinner party and bump into the birth mother? And what if the situation falls through? How many times can the mutual contact apologize?

There are also many people who simply don't know anything about adoption. Rather than being helpful, they will bombard you with either questions about adoption or comments that are not at all what you would call supportive.

Spreading the word to everyone also means you will be wearing your deepest desires—to have a child—on your sleeve, like pinning a scarlet "A" to your sweater. You'll have to answer how the adoption hunt is going to everyone, from your postman to your dry cleaner. Embarrassment, pity, and constant questions are far more likely to become part of your day-to-day routine than is the likelihood of someone calling you up who knows of a pregnant woman who wants to place her baby for adoption. You won't be able to get away from adoption should you want to—or need to from time to time. You also don't want to become the local community project. Unlike looking for a job or a date, which everyone has experienced, this is not a "typical" situation. Think about how many bad blind dates you were set up on, or turned down. Think about how many people called with jobs they saw in the paper that were way off course for you. Now think again about telling *everyone* that you are looking to adopt.

In short, my personal recommendation is to tell those people whom you know and trust that you are looking to adopt, and that you appreciate their support. But this is quite different from trying to involve everyone around you in something that is very personal and fraught with emotion. "I wish we hadn't told everyone" is the frequent cry from someone after hanging up the phone with a neighbor calling nightly to ask, "So did you find a kid yet?"

If you want to spread the word, talk to your obstetrician and inquire whether he or she can keep an ear out should they hear of a woman who is planning to place her child for adoption, or tell your niece who is doing an internship at a teen pregnancy center. Be selective, not secretive.

When you join a support group, let them know where you are in the process. Perhaps another couple in the group turned down a situation for some reason. Perhaps they were not comfortable with a biracial child but you would be fine with such a choice. One couple decided that they were going to pass on a situation because they thought the birth mother was drinking too much. Another couple inquired about that birth mother and asked two doctors to review the her blood-alcohol levels. The doctors found it was not out of the ordinary. The second couple adopted the child and, years later, are very thankful that they did.

Advertising

Placing cards in obstetrician's offices or writing "Dear Birth Mother letters" which describe a little about yourself and giving them to a local priest might fall into the advertising category. Either way, these are among the many methods of spreading the word that you are looking to adopt. But, advertising in newspapers is the strategy that leads to the most independent adoptions.

Ads are generally short and to the point. They express the sentiment that you are looking for a child to adopt. Love, warmth, family, security, a happy home environment, and financial security are usually more eye-catching terms in this type of ad than M.B.A., Ph.D., knowledge of Quark, or well traveled. Your ad needs to be one that will make a positive impression on a birth mother as she reads through several such ads. You do not want to sound pretentious or intimidating. In fact, such ads that show wealth may attract scam artists who are looking for pigeons.

Look at newspaper classified sections and see if adoption ads are placed. Read them and get some ideas of how you might phrase your ad. Remember: Like all advertising, if you are not getting a response, you can alter the ad or change it completely.

Some Advertising Pointers
- Try to think from the perspective of a woman in the difficult position of looking for a better home than she can provide for her unborn child. What will make her feel comfortable and secure in choosing *you* as the parents for that child?
- Mention your professions(s) if they are generally respected or unique and interesting. Teachers or lawyers are popular professions, and a writer, artist, or a professional tennis player may catch someone's attention. A taxidermist or assistant operational plant supervisor may not enhance your ad.
- Use your first names. Even if you are comfortable with the birth parents knowing your last names, you don't need the city of Chicago knowing them. Use

your real names. If you think your name sounds too ethnic or too formal, shorten it. Angelina could be Angie and Alexander can be Alex.

- Since the ads are alphabetized (usually) under the word "adoption," start with the word "A." "A happily married couple . . ." or "A financially secure, loving couple . . ." or "A teacher and a horse trainer . . ."

- You can specify newborn infant, but many newspapers will not allow you to specify ethnicity.

- Since most adoption ads look alike, you might try to add something unique. Remember this should be unique in a family way. The fact that you bowled a 300 game is not as important as the fact that you have a large backyard, which is ideal for playing. Think about the type of environment you can offer a child. Does one of you love to play the piano? Do you enjoy sailing, camping, and the great outdoors? Is your house a couple of blocks away from the zoo?

- Don't volunteer unnecessary opinions. From "big Howard Stern fan" to "opera lovers," these are not necessary. They do not promote kids and family, and even though they are true, such information will only serve to eliminate birth mothers more than attract them. Add nothing that can weed out possible birth mothers.

- If you are over forty, leave your age out of the ad. Not that many couples and singles in their forties don't succeed at independent adoption, but you may be competing against couples in their thirties who may sound more appealing to a young birth mother. Anything you think are not your "strongest selling points" can be brought up later when you talk to the birth mother. This way she can first read what great parents you will make, take a liking to you and get the details later.

- Be honest!
- Leave religion out of the ad. Save it for the phone conversation. Some birth mothers will want a good Christian home; others will not be concerned if you are Jewish or of another faith. This won't change if you mention religion in the ad, so don't bother.
- Keep the ad short—three or four lines maximum.
- While some will disagree, it's not to your advantage to mention that you will pay all expenses. Again, you are announcing that you have money to spend in an advertisement that can be read by the general public.
- Include your phone number as your only contact. Usually the phone number should be a special 1-800 number that you have installed specifically for calls from birth mothers.

  Note: Get an unlisted 1-800 phone number installed before you advertise. Double-check to make sure the line is working, and then don't give out the number to friends, neighbors, or anyone else. This way you will pay only for birth-mother calls and you will always know that when the phone rings that it is in response to the ad and not another telemarketer. This will give you a moment to catch your breath, gather your wits, and prepare for an important phone call.
- Find out about lower rates for running the ad over a period of time. Most newspapers will have a cheaper rate if you run the ad for several days or even weeks. It's to your advantage to have ads running for at least a couple of weeks. Keep in mind that you can try negotiating. Many newspapers classified advertising rates are not set in stone.

Some Sample Ads

A happy, loving couple has plenty of hugs, kisses and love to share with a newborn baby. Please call Jack and Connie at 1-800-xxx-xxxx

A teacher and a dentist, happily married for nine years, are ready to love a newborn baby. We'd be excited to talk with you.

A warm and loving country environment, with plenty of music, smiles, and cheerful times awaits a newborn baby. Please make our dreams come true.

Our loving home longs for a child to love. We will cherish your newborn forever and provide the brightest future.

Adoption creates a loving family . . . just ask our four-year-old son Michael. He'd love a baby brother or sister to show around the house and play with in our large backyard. We'd love to talk with you.

I'm a nurse and my husband is a college professor. Together we enjoy camping, boating, and spending the day at the park or the beach. We'd love to share our joy, fun, education, and all that life has to offer with a baby. Please help us with our quest.

Five cousins, two cats, and four grandparents are all waiting the arrival of a new baby in our home. Help us complete the picture and become parents. We have plenty of love to share.

Family life filled with love, warmth, happiness and financial security to give to a newborn.

Hello! We can't wait to become parents—we have lots to offer including love, financial security, flexible schedules, and very supportive friends and family. Please contact us—we'd love to talk to you.

Where to Advertise

Every town, every city, every community has at least one newspaper, whether it's a daily or a weekly. First you'll need to find out if the state allows independent adoption (most do) and whether or not they allow for advertising for independent adoption. Some states that allow such adoptions do not allow you to advertise, so you'll need to find another way of reaching the people of that state.

These states do not allow independent adoption: Colorado, Connecticut, Delaware and Massachusetts

A few states, such as Wisconsin, allow independent adoption but require you to use the services of an agency—which takes the "independent" out of independent adoption. Wisconsin also insists that the child spend several weeks in foster care before you can take him/her home. Other states have other unique laws that you need to be aware of before advertising in that state. Your attorney should help guide you before you advertise. Discuss where you plan to advertise with your attorney before placing the ads.

Note: For advertising in states that do not allow advertising for independent adoptions, you can locate a birth mother by advertising in an out of state publication that is read in that state, or a national publication like *USA Today* (it's expensive), which will be read in every state.

Your best bet, however, is to aim for local papers that reach large circulations for reasonable rates. Major-market newspapers in New York City, Los Angeles, or Washington, D.C. will be too costly in which to advertise on a regular basis.

Economic conditions, religious beliefs, transient populations, and other factors may make one state a more likely place in which to find a birth mother than another. Sometimes, however, it's just luck.

Often couples (more often men) will want a scientific approach to selecting advertising locations. Most adoption professionals will agree that it is not an exact science. The best place to advertise will be—in hindsight—the state from which you adopted your son or daughter.

You might consider the travel implications of advertising on the other side of the country. Conversely, you may not want to advertise too close to home, to avoid bumping into the birth mother at the supermarket. Even in an open adoption, a little distance is healthy. Remember; the wider your geographic boundaries, the more likely that you will get responses to your ads. Additionally, the more ads you place at one time, the more likely that you will get a response. If, you blitz (place many ads at once), you are more likely to get a number of calls. New York City attorney Aaron Britvan explains, "It's like advertising during the Super Bowl. Companies place ads in the Super Bowl because there is much more exposure. Therefore, if you blitz, you have a much better chance of the ad generating a response. Of course, it is also more costly so you need to be able to afford to do blitz advertising."

Like any other type of advertising, you will be able to gauge how many responses you are getting from each ad you place. A simple ice-breaking part of the conversation with a birth mother may be asking, "So, where did you see our ad?" If you see that one paper is getting responses while another has generated none, then you may take your ad out of the second paper and find another paper to place the ad. Some people recommend pennysavers and store shoppers. These can work, and advertising rates are usually fairly cheap.

I was a big proponent of Sunday papers in towns and cities because the circulation was higher and often they were part of a weeklong package. In addition, many people hold onto Sunday papers or read them more thoroughly. Whatever the reason, we got a lot of calls on Monday afternoons.

You simply need to find papers and contact them for their classified or personal advertising rates. See if they accept adoption ads and, if so, how many ads are usually in the paper at a given time. If there are nine or ten other ads, you may not want to deal with so much competition and may opt for another paper.

If the newspaper requires a letter from your attorney, this should be easily handled by your attorney's office via fax or e-mail. If the newspaper advertising sales representative is too inquisitive, move on. It's not his or her place to make any judgments.

Once you place the ad, then you need to ask for a tear sheet. This is a copy of the page on which the ad is published. You want to see that it ran correctly. It is also an important document to save for legal reasons, in case you ever need to verify how you came into contact with the birth mother.

As for locating newspapers, you will need to utilize either the library or the Internet for access to a national newspaper directory like Gale's, found in most libraries. A website such as N-Net (www.n-net.com) can provide you with a simple state-by-state listing of newspapers and their phone numbers. Call and ask for the classified advertising department. Then find out if they accept adoption ads (most papers do but some will want a letter from your attorney first) and then ask about their rates. There are also newspaper networks, which will place your ad in numerous papers for a single fee.

You might also consider a college newspaper, or a community paper in a college town. A student may be pregnant and not be in a position to raise a child at this point in her life. However, many college papers will not allow adoption ads.

The truth is that birth mothers can come from almost anywhere. If a woman is too young and/or does not have the financial means or is not emotionally at a point in her life where she can raise a child, she may wish to place the child for adoption. Don't start overanalyzing the process.

If you *really* want the phone to ring, try advertising in *USA Today*. However, the newspaper will bring calls from con artists, prisoners, practical jokers, lonely people looking to talk, potential surrogates, salespeople, advertising reps from other newspapers—and yes, even some birth mothers. It's an expensive place to advertise, so be prepared. If it works, terrific. If not, you may be out a few weeks on your advertising budget for a day or two of national advertising.

Mandy and her husband swear by *USA Today*. *"We were reluctant at first . . . it is very expensive, but once we decided to advertise in the national newspaper the phone started to ring. We ran the ad for three days and we did get some crank calls but we also heard from several birth mothers, one of which turned out to be our son's birth mom. I advise people to try USA Today at least once, but be prepared to stay home and answer the phone that day; you may get a lot of calls."*

Adoptive mom Carol F. (mentioned last in Chapter 3) says, *"We tried USA Today and were prepared for a lot of calls, but we only got two calls all day, one from a birth mother in New Hampshire, but she never called our attorney for the paperwork, and the other call was about advertising in another paper. We were disappointed. A lot of other adoptive families we know preferred going with the smaller local papers so that they would have a better idea of which towns they were advertising in."*

Broadcast or "Dear Birth Mother" Letters and Personal Profiles

Somewhere between advertising and networking are broadcast letters and personal profiles. Birth mother letters express your feelings to a birth mother. They define who you are, what you can offer a child, and what will make you wonderful parents.

Of course, the letter should not read like a sales pitch. You want to sound informal, honest, and sincere. You do not want to try and dazzle her with your literary prowess. Chances are that before she heads to a dictionary to look up some five-syllable word, she'll more likely move on to the next Dear Birth Mother letter. It's important to acknowlegde in your letter that you respect her and recognize that she is going through a difficult time. No matter how difficult infertility may be on you, she is also in a very difficult position. In this letter, you can mention your fertility problems, your marriage, jobs, religion, desire for a child, and aspects of your life that would be attractive to a child, such as nearby proximity to a marvelous park. Try to avoid anything that can be misconstrued or voice strong opinions. Three or four paragraphs should suffice. A personal profile will provide much of the same information in a different format. Unlike a letter, this is a biography of you as a couple or single person. If you are a single, you should discuss the all-important network of people around you. The profile is essentially the same as that mentioned in the section on agency adoption.

Attorneys in some states can forward Dear Birth Mother Letters or personal bios. In other states, you will have to rely on some well-calculated contacts. Clergy members, adoption consultants, or people you meet in adoption support groups can forward your birth mother letters, profiles, or personal biographies. There are also web-sites that let you place Dear Birth Mother letters or personal profiles.

Note: Facilitators are go-betweens in adoption, or people who say they will find a situation for you for x dollars. These middle people have no guidelines and are not licensed, except in California. In fact, in many states, it is illegal to adopt through a paid facilitator. Worse than the risk of simply losing a lot of money is the risk that the facilitator will place a child in your arms that you know nothing about. The child may not have come to you through legal channels. Be extremely careful.

Finding a Pediatrician

While it may seem strange finding a pediatrician while you do not yet have a child, it is advantageous to get to know one before you adopt. This will allow you to show the birth mother's medical records and all information about her pregnancy to a doctor to evaluate. Adoptive parents agree that if there is a question about the health of the child, it is best to have a pediatrician communicate with her doctor. Doctors can often get the most accurate information from one another.

"We had two friends who were pediatricians" says Carol F., adoptive mother of a ten-year-old girl, mentioned earlier. *"Our two pediatrician friends looked at the birth mother's health records and then showed them to two other pediatricians. They didn't want to be biased because they were our friends and wanted so much for us to adopt. This way we ended up with four doctors helping us decide to go with the birth mother. Naturally, you need only one doctor's opinion."*

When choosing a pediatrician, you will usually seek out recommendations from others. You will also want to know that the pediatrician will not be thrown by the fact that your child was adopted. Most pediatricians today are comfortable dealing with adoption. However, you may find one who is not or who stumbles over the right words.

Ask the pediatrician:

- Are other patients adopted?
- Is he or she familiar with children who have come from an institutionalized setting (if you are adopting internationally or from the foster-care system)?
- Who is the covering doctor?
- Which hospital is the doctor affiliated with, should you need to go into the ER and have him or her reached?
- How accessible is the doctor when your child is

sick? (Can you walk in or do you still need an appointment?)

- Can he/she review the birth mother's medical records and discuss any concerns with her doctor?

Check to see that any recommended pediatrician is board certified with the American Academy of Pediatrics. The academy also has a Provisional Section on Adoption. You can see if the doctor is a member. In addition, you may want to inquire about the doctor's area(s) of special interest. For example, he or she may specialize in developmental issues, which may be beneficial with children adopted at an older age, or from an institutionalized setting. Last, you'll want to meet, talk, and evaluate not only the bedside manner of your pediatrician, but get a feel for the staff and how well they relate to the children. Some doctors' offices add that special something that makes the visit less stressful for kids while others go through the motions. You need to feel comfortable for yourself and your child(ren).

Red Flags in the Adoption Process

Sometimes a situation is not meant to be. For example, if a birth mother's *mother* is against the adoption, this can be a very bad sign. While she cannot block the adoption legally (unless the birth mother is a minor), she can play a major role in influencing the birth mother's decision. Adoption attorney Aaron Britvan says that he advises moving cautiously whenever a birth mother is at odds with the support group around her.

Adoption attorney Michael Goldstein also notes that other red flags include, "Too much discussion of money, inconsistent stories whereby she is telling you one thing and telling the attorney something else, or there is a birth father who is in and out of the picture."

In addition, there are other situations that present red flags, such as a birth mother who does not see a doctor about her pregnancy. And then there are situations which are simply illegal. For example, Goldstein cites a case whereby a birth mother was married and pregnant with someone else's child. She wanted to place the child for adoption without telling her husband. "This is illegal and one of the responsibilities of an attorney is to apprise you of such legal matters," explains Goldstein.

Adoption attorneys are good at discerning situations that may end with the birth mothers changing her mind. However, they are not perfect in their assessments, nor should you expect them to be. Even the birth mother, with every intention in the world of placing her child with you, can change her mind when that child is born.

Indian Child Welfare Act

Aaron Britvan points out that we would be remiss if we did not mention one other potential red flag in the adoption process. "It's something that you need to be aware of as potential adoptive parents," he says. The Indian Child Welfare Act, passed in 1978, is a federal law which regulates placement proceedings involving Native American children.

The law applies to Native American children who are unmarried and are under the age of eighteen. If the child is a member of a federally recognized tribe or eligible to become a member of the tribe, he or she is required by law to be placed with extended family members or other members of the tribe. Therefore, an adoptive family must obtain consent from the tribe to adopt the child. This is true even if the child is not born on the reservation. According to the ICWA, an Indian parent who allows someone else guardianship of a child can always revoke that guardianship. Therefore, the tribe must sign a revocation which is then binding in federal court.

Says Britvan, "The point is that no one should take the act for granted. Obtain tribal approval. Find out which tribe you need to contact and get in touch with them."

Signed Consent

And finally . . .

When all goes favorably and the adoptive situation is on track, you will reach the point where the baby is born and the birth mother signs a consent form to relinquish the baby.

Consent is obviously significant in every adoption, on the part of the birth mother or the persons or agency entrusted to care for the child. In adoption, consent means "the agreement by a parent, or a person or agency acting in place of a parent, to relinquish the child for adoption and to release all rights and duties with respect to that child." Most states require that the consent is signed before a judge, or other delegated official. The state laws are designed to protect all members of the triad. Birth parents must make an informed decision without any coercion. Adoptive parents must be confident that once the consent is relinquished in a reasonable amount of time, their rights are protected. And finally the best interests of the child must always be taken into concern. The transition should be as smooth as possible and the child must always be in a position of care and safety.

In most states, the birth mother must wait forty-eight or seventy-two hours before she can sign consent forms. In some states there is no minimum time, while in others it can be several days or even weeks. The two- or three-day wait is intended to make sure that the birth mother has had a chance to think through her decision and is not under the influence of any medication which she may have been given while giving birth. Even in a state where she can sign the consent form immediately, for practical and moral reasons, you want to make sure she is fully aware and sure of what she is doing. This is a difficult decision for her to make and one a birth mother must make of her own free will. Let your attorney guide you with details regarding the signing of the consent in each state. The next chapter covers consent more fully.

State-by-state consent and other listings can be found at the National Adoption Information Clearinghouse web-site at www.calib.com. The clearinghouse is a service of the Children's Bureau, Administration on Children, Youth and Families, Administration for Children and Families, and the U.S. Department of Health and Human Services. Click on "Laws" and then "Statutes at a Glance Summaries." You'll find state-by-state listings of consent to adopt, state regulations on adoption expenses, putative father's rights, and parties to an adoption.

You can also get hard copies of these listings from the clearinghouse at:

National Adoption Information Clearinghouse
330 C Street, SW
Washington, DC 20447
(888) 251-0075
E-mail: naic@calib.com
Web site: http://www.calib.com/naic

Keep in mind that some of these statutes may change. Since there are so many gray areas in adoption laws and because every situation is unique, you should review any and all laws or statutes pertaining to the state or states involved in your adoption with your legal counsel.

Chapter 7
INDEPENDENT ADOPTION: BIRTH MOTHERS AND BRINGING HOME BABY

If you continue trying, remain proactive and establish the right rapport with a birth mother, you will succeed in becoming an adoptive parent through independent adoption. You have to know in your heart that it will happen.

There are so many aspects of independent adoption that I use this chapter to round out a few areas that require some thought and preparation, including dealing with birth-mother expenses and bringing your baby home from the hospital. But first, a brief independent-adoption story:

"When I spoke to the birth mother I just knew it was the right situation," says Laura, who, with her husband Robert, adopted two children through independent adoption. *"We had been placing ads for a while and when we got this particular phone call a red flag went up because it was the birth father who called. Apparently she (the birth mother) was afraid to make the phone call so he called for her. He told us that his girl-friend had seen our ad in the newspaper and really wanted to talk to us. Once she got on the phone and we started talking, I knew it was going to work out . . . we really connected. She was*

in her thirties, very bright and well spoken. It turned out that she and her boyfriend had both gone back to school for new careers, and between them they already had three children and did not feel that they could support and raise another child at this time.

"After talking a few times, the birth mother wanted to meet us, so we made a plan to fly nearly 2,000 miles to meet her during what was essentially our summer vacation. She was about five months pregnant at the time. I was afraid to meet her, afraid she wouldn't like us, worried because we were older then she was. She hadn't asked us how old we were so I hadn't mentioned it. Finally we got out there and met them. We spent hours together, met their kids and really hit it off. Finally when the evening was done, I was very relieved . . . everything had gone well and we could finally relax. Then, of course, on the way home we got stuck in an incredible rainstorm. It was scary, the roads were flooded, and we were basically in the middle of nowhere, between towns on deserted roads. After about a half an hour of trying to get through flooding, we had to turn back. We knew no one else in this area, so we went back to the birth parents' house. They were still up and glad we returned. They ended up putting us up for the night.

"Four months later, we were back in their town when she gave birth. When we got to the hospital, she had already delivered the baby. She went into labor a week earlier than her due date and called us when she was already in labor. She was with the baby when we got there, and I was both thrilled and scared . . . there she was holding her baby that was about to be our baby. It's a very strange feeling. She handed us the baby to hold and was very open about expressing her feelings. She told us that this was very hard for her, but she thought it was the best thing to do. She also said she was very happy to be doing something good for us."

About Birth Mothers

It's important that while you are thinking about adopting a child, you take some time to learn a little bit about birth mothers. Some forty years ago, birth mothers were unwed pregnant women who were considered "the shame of their families." They were sent away from home and labeled as disgraces or troubled women. It was thought that such women could not possibly raise a child properly, and they were encouraged to place their babies for adoption. Fortunately, society has come a long way and is far more understanding in regard to unexpected pregnancies. Today such women are respected for making tough decisions when faced with difficult and challenging situations.

The modern birth mother is most often a young woman who for financial, emotional and other personal reasons does not feel that she can provide an adequate environment in which to raise a child at this time in her life. This does not presuppose that she is not intelligent or educated. She is in a precarious position in which she has chosen not to have an abortion and not to mother a child. Therefore, she wants to find a good home for her baby.

Birth mothers are not all teenagers either; many are in their twenties or thirties.

Some are still living at home with their families, but many are on their own and few are in steady relationships with partners who are willing to be involved in parenting a child.

Most birth mothers do not have a great deal of emotional support from the birth fathers, who are often completely out of the picture. In many cases, a birth mother does not have much support from her parents either.

However, situations change and birth mothers grow. Many of these women will go on to finish college, enjoy successful careers, get married, and have families. They do continue to grow and years later are not the same people who found themselves in this difficult predicament. It is important to understand this because many adoptive parents see the birth mother only at that one significant juncture of her life and take a mental snapshot of her. Unlike a snapshot, a birth mother's life is multidimensional and does not freeze in that moment in time. Rest assured that she will also have a snapshot of herself in that time period that will always stay with her as she moves on with her life. Open adoption can make her life easier or harder depending on the individual, her temperament, her personality and how she copes with the situation. Some birth mothers want to move on and not look back while others want to maintain an active role in the adoption triad. Neither situation should be viewed as right or wrong.

Note: Keep in mind that a birth mother should never feel either coerced or pressured by you or by an agency into giving up a baby for adoption. You would not want a child to come into your life by such means. Unfortunately, there are some agencies, lawyers, facilitators, and families who pressure birth mothers. You should always remember that when working with a birth mother, it is not a "you vs. them" scenario, but one in which you are working together for the best interests of the child.

Talking with Birth Mothers

This is the part of independent adoption that scares some people away. Adoptive mother Ann, mentioned earlier in Chapter Two with her husband Frank, says, *"I simply knew I was not going to be able to talk with birth mothers on the phone. We did two adoptions, one through a domestic agency and one internationally. Independent adoption works wonderfully for many people, but it wasn't for me for that one reason."*

While you need not be a phone person, you do need some level of comfort on what are very difficult phone calls. *"Too much was riding on these calls,"* said one anonymous adoptive mom who found that rehearsing with friends was helpful. *"I had a few of my friends call before we did any advertising to see if I could handle such a call. It was bogus, but it was a way of getting used to speaking with someone on the phone about such an emotional issue."*

If you think you're nervous, imagine the birth mother on the other end of the phone. This is an incredibly difficult call for her to make. So there you are, on opposites sides of one of the most important issues in both of your lives. You want a child and she is placing one for adoption. You are ready and willing to parent a new baby at this juncture in your life, and she is not ready to parent a child at this juncture in hers. Your one common denominator is that you both want what is best for the unborn child.

Needless to say, birth mothers are far more comfortable talking to women than to men. However, if the husband is home and the wife is not, it's better that he take the call than risk missing it—very often birth mothers do not leave answering-machine messages. It's simply too important. What he can do is explain that his wife would want very much to talk with her. Ask for a number where she could be reached. If she doesn't have one or doesn't want to give it out, pick a time for her to call back and say, "I know she'll look forward to talking with you."

My wife used to first acknowledge that it was a difficult conversation for both parties and then say, "Why don't you tell me a little about your situation, (or yourself)?"

The birth mother would usually open up, explaining why she was calling and what her situation was all about.

The conversation with a birth mother is supposed to fulfill three purposes. First, you want her to feel comfortable talking with you. Second, you need to gather some information to make a decision if this is a viable situation and one that might be right for you. Third, you want to get her to contact your lawyer to receive some paperwork.

It's important that you do not grill a birth mother with questions. You want to get information, but you need to be both tactful and respectful. Remember, she is making a very difficult, very emotional phone call. The last thing she needs is for you to intimidate her by firing questions at her. Through polite conversation, you can try to get important information. You want to know:

- How pregnant is she? (If it's only a few weeks, she might not be pregnant at all. She may also lose the pregnancy in the early weeks.)
- Has she seen a doctor yet?
- Who else knows she is pregnant? (States require parental consent if she's under a certain age—this can range from sixteen to eighteen depending on the state.)
- Is the birth father in her life? (This may be a touchy subject so handle with kid gloves. It is important because if the birth father is identified, then his consent is also required for the adoption.)

You will need to have the birth mother contact your attorney so that he or she can send paperwork. There is nothing in this paperwork that legally binds the birth mother to you in any manner. She will never be obligated to relinquish the baby to you until after giving birth and then signing the release forms. When you mention that she should call your attorney, let her know that the paperwork is just for gathering information, and that she is not obligated to do anything.

The relationship you establish with the birth mother is the most important part of that initial phone call. *"I hardly got any information, other than the fact that she was four months pregnant and had not seen a doctor yet,"* explained Connie G., who with her husband Peter, adopted two young boys.

"My husband or I must have talked to about twenty birth mothers before one situation worked out. When we talked to our first son's birth mother, we had a good rapport and I felt comfortable on the phone with her. The first phone call was only about five minutes, but we promised to talk the next day. After a sleepless night of anticipation, we talked again at greater length about ourselves and I learned all about her without having to ask a ton of questions. Over the next three months until she gave birth we talked maybe once or twice a week. She updated me on her doctor visits and much of the conversation was just small talk but we had a cordial rapport. We finally met her when she was two days before her due date. We flew out and it was awkward, but we just continued with the same casual rapport. I didn't want to do or say anything wrong, and she probably felt the same way. I realized afterwards that birth mothers are also worried about making a good impression, thinking you might also choose someone else. In fact, she called three times to confirm that we were coming out to meet her."

Birth mothers will also want to learn about you. It's important that you be honest regarding such facts as your age or religion. You do not want the word "fraud" ever coming up in regard to your adoption. As for opinions, if the birth mother loves country music, you need not tell her you hate it. Keep opinions to yourself unless you can be agreeable. You'd hate to lose an adoption because she loves skiing and you disdain the sport.

Often you won't know which answer is going to help the situation and which might prove harmful. Our birth mother asked us if we had other children. We had to say that we didn't. For a few moments, we did not know what her response was going to be. Would she be disappointed because she wanted the baby adopted into a family with other kids? Would she be pleased that this would be our first child? As it turned out, her response was "Oh, good, I really want her to be special."

Caution

If the birth mother brings up the subject of money frequently, during the first several conversations, be wary. Too much talk of money and too little talk of baby are not a good sign. Someone may be trying to get you to send money with no intention of placing a baby with you. You and your attorney will have to assess each situation.

There's no telling how the conversation will go. You have your forever family pictured in your imagination, and she has the home in which she'd like to place her baby pictured in hers. You cannot make these images blend successfully any more than you can make a relationship work if you are both coming from different places with different needs and desires. Simply, try to be honest and establish a positive line of communication.

Also keep in mind that if the boyfriend, husband, father, mother, sister, brother, neighbor, or a close friend of the birth mother calls, while you may enjoy talking with them, you still need to talk with the birth mother. Only she can make the final decision and therefore initiate the process and the paperwork. You may find yourself talking to other people close to her as you establish a rapport. However, other than the birth father, this is not all that common. The more involved they are in her life, the less likely she will place the baby for adoption. The greater her support system, the greater chance that they will be there for her to help her with the baby. The same often holds true for a birth mother whom you find out is very involved with a church or religious group. Such a religious group may pitch in to help her.

The Relationship

There is no right or wrong relationship that you are expected to have with a birth mother. You need not speak to her once a week or three times a week. You need not pour out your feelings or hold them inside. My wife and I had only a few conversations with our daughter's birth mother, and several of them were brief. We would have been more than happy to have carried on longer conversations, but she didn't seem to want to talk at great length. She specifically wanted *not* to become too attached to us, only to feel confident that we would make good parents.

Other families that we know had long and detailed conversations with birth parents. In fact, many adoptive families meet with birth parents. Mark McDermott of the American Association of Adoption Attorneys recommends to his clients that they go out and meet the birth mother or birth parents. "I tell people that they should have a meeting. It's very powerful to meet face to face with someone," he says.

"We spent nearly two weeks in the birth mother's town waiting until she delivered," says Denise and Jeff, whom we met in the last chapter. *"All the time, you are very conscious of not saying or doing the wrong thing. You want to make a good impression."*

As is the case with many couples, Denise and Jeff found that the more time you spend together the better the bond will be established. While you certainly do not need to spend every hour of every day together, you can get to know one and other and have much more later on to tell your child about his or her birth parents from the experience.

"We felt that if she changed her mind and didn't place the baby with us, we would have been okay with that," adds Denise. *"It would have hurt, and we would have needed some time to get over it, but we got to know her and could understand and respect such a decision if that's what happened."* Ultimately, Denise and Jeff did adopt and headed home. *"It was very hard for us to say goodbye at that point,"* she adds.

While they do not have a completely open adoption, Denise and Jeff have access to, and have talked with, the birth mother since the adoption. They also send photos and a note about their son a few times a year. Through the agency, the birth mother can contact them as well. *"We have a little distance, but we know they* (the birth parents) *are there and they know where we are, which is important,"* adds Denise.

Denise also admits now to driving by the hospital one night while in the birth mother's hometown while they were staying at a hotel, waiting for her to deliver. She claimed that she was getting worried when she couldn't reach the birth mother, that perhaps she'd gone into labor and wasn't going to contact them *"When we didn't see their car in the hospital parking lot, I was very relieved,"* she admits. *"You get so nervous and don't know how to deal with it."* Stressful times have made many adoptive couples act in similar odd ways that they look back on years later with a smile.

During the early stages of your relationship with the birth mother, she needs to get in contact with your attorney for any possibility of an adoption plan to progress. In most states, *she* must make the first call to your attorney's office so it does not appear that the attorney is soliciting the birth mother. If the birth mother does *not* contact your attorney, then you do not yet have a working adoption situation. This is an important step. It allows the attorney to send a background information form and medical consent form to the birth mother. She is in no way obligated to fill anything out and can walk away whenever she chooses. Furthermore, once she fills out the forms, she is also not bound legally in any way to place the baby with you for adoption. This is simply a way in which you can gather information about her and her background—especially her health background and that of the birth father. Don't try to push a birth mother to contact your attorney. If and when she wants to move forward with the adoption plan, she will.

A Seldom-Talked-About Issue

It's worth mentioning that while most adoptive families don't focus much attention on the issue, there is also a concern on the part of many birth mothers that once you are working with them, you may change your mind. Adoptive parents may be working with more than one birth mother.

It's possible that as prospective adoptive parents, you may discover something in the medical records of the birth mother that makes you uncomfortable and you change your mind about working with her. All of this is understandable, but such decisions should be made as early on in the process as possible. A birth mother is often just as fearful that you may not be there to adopt the baby, as you are that she will change her mind about the adoption. Consider the situation from both sides.

Birth Mother Expenses

Birth mothers can ask for you to cover any expenses they choose. However, you and your attorney will have to decide which expenses are legitimate and which are not. You will also need to determine how much you can afford to pay in expenses knowing that a situation might not end up as a successful adoption. All money paid must go through your attorney's office.

Naturally, medical expenses related to the pregnancy are legitimate expenses. Some birth mothers are covered by state medical-health insurance plans like Medicaid. If they are, that's to your advantage, as the cost of the delivery and hospital stay can exceed $10,000. Doctor visits and costs related to specific maternity-related needs are all considered birth-mother expenses that you may be asked to pay for. A new van to get to and from the doctor's office is not such a necessary expense. Most birth mothers are focused primarily on finding the best home for the child and not on money. However, there are exceptions. Also, the idea by either party that by placing a baby for adoption the birth mother is worthy of being given money as a reward or as a way of saying "thank you" is not accepted in the courts.

Usually, any financial involvement should be during the last trimester. In some states, the law allows for paying such expenses only at this time. The courts in each state will regulate expenses given to birth mothers. You still need to exercise sound judgment and determine whether you (and your attorney) believe that this is a situation that will likely lead to an adoption plan. You need to realize that paying expenses in advance of the birth is always a risk you are taking, because even the birth mother who fully intends to place the baby with you can change her mind before or after giving birth. She is not responsible for paying you back any money that you have given her for expenses. This is a calculated risk some people can afford to take. However, the problem with paying expenses (and advertising that you will pay all expenses) is that there are con artists out there looking for your money with either no intention of placing a baby, or potentially no pregnancy at all. Unfortunately, good con artists do exist. Often they have very elaborate well-scripted stories with instant answers to all of the key questions. In fact, if a birth mother seems too sure of herself and has the best response to every question, she might be working from a script. Remember, in reality a woman who is really pregnant and considering placing her child for adoption is usually a bit nervous and may not have all the answers at her fingertips.

It is important to obtain good medical records from the birth mother's doctor. This is not only to verify that she is indeed pregnant, but to find out about the health of the mother and unborn child.

Tips on birth-mother expenses:

- There's nothing wrong with honestly stating that you'd love to pay her $1,000 a week for food expenses, but the courts review everything and won't allow it. You're sorry, but you hope she'll understand. Often you'll settle on a more realistic figure. My wife and I had to do just that when a birth mother asked for a very high weekly amount for food expenses. It's simply being honest and letting her know that it's not strictly your decision.

- Pay expenses for the last trimester only, and possibly postplacement counseling if she requests it. This way you are limiting the time you will spend paying expenses. In fact, you may try, as some attorneys suggest, paying expenses retroactively, following placement. While you do want to help a prospective birth mother, you do not want to fall into a bidding war in which you are making a better offer than another couple. This is not how you want to start your family.

- Avoid situations in which an attorney has you paying for birth-mother expenses as part of his or her so-called adoption program. Some attorneys and agencies have you and other prospective adoptive families pay to house or take care of a birth mother (not necessarily the one you are working with) as standard procedure. Since many agencies and attorneys do not follow this practice, it does not *have* to be done in this manner. Therefore, why should you bother with this type of program? You could spend $10,000 on birth-mother expenses, when in reality the birth mother that you worked with actually needed only $4,000.

- DO NOT PAY A BIRTH MOTHER FOR PLACING HER BABY WITH YOU. Yes, it might be a nice gesture, if as a token of your gratitude (and if you had the money), to give her a check for $10,000 and say, "do whatever you like with it." You can't. Baby buying is illegal and anything the courts believe falls into such a category will jeopardize your adoption and your forever family. Stay within the legal boundaries and do not use money or gifts as bribery or an enticement.

- If money is the preeminent theme of the conversations, walk away. Try to maintain your objective thinking so that you'll know when to walk away from a situation if necessary.

The Birth Mother's Attorney

Paying for the costs of the birth mother's attorney is standard practice in independent adoption. In most states your attorney cannot serve as counsel for both parties; it is considered a conflict of interest. Therefore, your attorney will usually help you locate an attorney for the birth mother. If not, you can contact the American Association of Adoption Attorneys to find an attorney in her state. You will pay her attorney's fees. Know these fees in advance and inquire about any additional costs such as expenses for phone calls or photocopies for the birth mother.

Stay on top of this situation as well. Often it is one area that the adoptive parents do not focus on and simply pay whatever is asked. Costs for the birth mother's attorney should usually total $2,000 to $3,500. Get a list of what any additional costs are for. One couple talked about a birth mother's attorney running up over $1,000 in such miscellaneous expenses in a matter of one week. This should not happen.

In some cases, the birth mother may have found her own attorney. She may even have a friend who is an attorney who will help for very little money. While the gesture is a good one and could save you some money, it is not in your best interest to use someone who does not specialize in adoption. Suggest that you let your attorney help find an adoption attorney in her area.

If she has found an adoption attorney, you can then have your attorney talk with her attorney.

General Expense Warnings

Keep in mind that whether it's paying attorney fees, adoption agency fees, birth-mother expenses or anything else adoption related is that *you do not want to pay too much money prior to placement*. The costs associated with an adoption—including everything—should usually run between $15,000 and $25,000 once the process is completed. However, if you've spent $20,000 and are not proud parents (yet) you may be on the road to a financial disaster. You should not be spending large sums of money up front for an attorney or for agency fees.

Know all upcoming fees, costs, and approximate amount for expenses ahead of time so that there are no sudden surprises when you are finished. It is very common that a couple, or single, will suddenly be hit with a larger bill than expected after placement and pay it because, after all, they are now proud parents, and they are in a happy, spending mood. *Don't be suckered into paying "extra" now that you are parents.*

One couple doing an international adoption without the help of an agency, hired an attorney and an interpreter in the country where the baby was born. They had no idea of the costs of either of these two individuals. The adoptive parents said, "Whatever it is, we'll deal with it afterwards. Right now we just want to get our baby." This was essentially the same as handing these two individuals (thousands of miles away) blank checks. In simple terms, *don't do this*. This goes back to doing your homework. Know what is commonly spent for services and check up on the agency or attorney. Try to locate others who have worked with them to get an idea of their reputation, especially regarding their fees and additional expenses.

Bringing Home Baby

When the moment arrives and the birth mother is due to deliver, it's time for you to:

A. Prepare to be parents.
B. Prepare not to be parents.

First, let's focus on part B. The fact is, birth mothers do change their mind about signing the papers and relinquishing their parental rights. This most often happens within a span of ninety-six hours; forty-eight hours before giving birth and forty-eight hours afterward. It's impossible to be fully prepared for this type of disappointment. The best you can do is to simply know that it can happen and brace yourselves—it is the one significant drawback of the independent adoption process. Keep in mind that if one adoption-situation does not work out, another will come along. This is only mildly comforting to any couple that have been through such disappointment; believe me, I know firsthand.

As for A, preparing to be parents, it means that when it's time to fly or drive to where the birth mother is giving birth, you have to begin thinking in terms of a family and the responsibility that goes with it. Make a list of items to take along since your emotions will be running on high. Gather the practical items that you will need, such as something in which to carry the baby, a car seat, and baby essentials including clothes. You'll want to travel rather lightly since you'll need free hands for holding the new family member. In addition, you'll want to ask for bulkhead seats on the plane—should you be traveling by plane—since they are roomier. Chapter 11 has more on travel.

Remember; Unless you're going to a very remote location, you can buy things like diapers and formula when you get there.

You also need to take some time to mentally prepare yourself to be a parent (or at least make an attempt). Your life is certainly about to change. No matter how much you mentally prepare yourself by reiterating that statement, you can never fully prepare for the feeling you will have when you first hold your child and realize that you are indeed a parent, responsible for another human being. You need not panic that an infant will completely take over your life. In many successful transitions from couple to family, parents report that they smoothly incorporated having a baby into their way of life without having to turn their world completely around. Sure you'll be up for midnight feedings and may not see four-star restaurants very often, but you'll find that lightweight strollers and a variety of carriers allow you to bring a baby with you to a lot of places.

Being in the Delivery Room

For the reasons noted above, regarding birth mothers changing their minds, some attorneys advise against being in the delivery room with the birth mother. Other attorneys, however, think it is a very positive step. Michael Goldstein says, "It is a wonderful experience, and if she lets you into the delivery room, say yes, you'll be there. If the birth mother wants you to be a part of this important moment, it is far less likely that she is going to change her mind about placing the child. It's happened only once in the twenty years I've been practicing."

Some birth mothers will want you there and others will not. Only you can determine your level of comfort based on the specifics of the situation. Remember; each situation is unique. Think about it ahead of time, and then see if the birth mother asks you to be there. If not, you can suggest it, but do not press the issue.

Hospitals

In some cases, the birth mother will deliver in a specific hospital because her medical insurance mandates her to do so. If she has a choice or does not have medical insurance, you may, with the assistance of her attorney (who should be familiar with the hospitals in the area) find a hospital that is "adoption friendly." The majority of hospitals will treat you well as adoptive parents since adoption is more and more part of the norm. However, there are hospitals where you will not be welcomed.

"I was treated very well by everyone in the hospital," says Amy C., single adoptive mom mentioned in Chapter 2. *"I brought my mom with me for support. I really didn't know what to expect because I'd heard stories where some adoptive parents weren't treated very well by the hospital staff. One woman I talked to said she was not allowed up into the nursery to see her baby. When the child was released to her, the social worker had to bring the baby out of the hospital. The hospital claimed it was their `policy'. So, naturally I was worried walking into this hospital some 1,000 miles from home. Since I was both adopting and a single woman, I was prepared that they might not want me around. Thank goodness I was wrong. The nurses welcomed me and one of them told me that she herself was an adult adoptee. I fed my daughter the first day. I spent time with the birth mother . . . it was a very pleasant experience. My only regret was that she didn't want me in the delivery room. I think she wasn't sure how she was going to feel once the baby was born, and my presence might make her feel that she had to give me the baby. When I knew she was giving birth, I just sat in the hotel lobby with my mom and the birth mom's lawyer and waited for the cell phone to ring. I was too nervous to even stay in my hotel room and much to nervous to wait in the small hospital waiting room. It was not a long labor, but it felt like I was sitting there for days. Finally the social*

worker at the hospital called and said she wants us to come to the hospital. It was only about four blocks away . . . I don't even remember walking those four blocks, I probably ran."

Be pleasant but proactive in the hospital. The hospital staff has policies, which they (and you) must adhere to. However, you can differentiate policies from attitude and explain your situation politely. Talk with hospital administrators if necessary. *"The hospital treated us very well,"* says Laura, mentioned earlier in the chapter. *"They gave us the baby care class that they give new parents and were very accommodating. It was a small hospital and the people were friendly, which was good because the whole experience is very nerve-wracking."* It's important that you are flexible and don't let your emotions get the better of you when you are in the hospital.

Remember, you are on their turf. Fortunately, the majority of hospitals today are adoption friendly and supportive of birth mothers' decisions and adoptive parents' rights.

The last stage of your journey will be the long-awaited trip home with your son or daughter. Try to travel as light as possible to have free hands for baby and all of those "baby items" you will need to bring when going places with your newest family member.

As mentioned previously, Chapter 11 has more information on travel.

Chapter 8
PUBLIC AGENCIES AND THE FOSTER-CARE SYSTEM

In every state there are public agencies which operate through state social services. These agencies are legally responsible for the welfare of thousands of children, some of whom come from family environments that are abusive or unhealthy. "Waiting children" is the collective name given to the many children awaiting permanent homes through these agencies. The children come from all racial and ethnic groups, although the majority are African-American. In all cases, a happy home life and the involvement of loving and caring parents can make all the difference in a child's ability to grow and develop. The agencies place these children with foster-care families which provides them some degree of stability, but not the permanency of adoption. Some of the children then become freed for adoption, while many others, unfortunately, do not. The state laws determine how parental rights may be terminated, which is either voluntarily or, in some cases, by court order.

Biological parents are required to sign termination papers allowing the child to be placed for adoption. In some instances, birth parents go through rehabilitation or substance-abuse programs, and the courts then determine what progress has been made in the home environment. In many situations, however, this never happens, and the child is caught up in the bureaucratic red tape of the system, stuck between a family that cannot adequately take care of the child and a legal system that cannot place the child in a permanent loving home until parental rights are terminated.

When children are available for adoption through the state foster-care system, they are usually classified as "older" children. They could be as young as two or three years or as old as seventeen.

Needless to say, children in the foster-care system often carry a lot of emotional baggage. Many of these children have physical or emotional problems and or other special needs.

Since the state is responsible for the children, they can be adopted through public agencies and there is little or no cost to the adoptive parents. In fact, there may be government funding or subsidies provided to help the adoptive parents support the child. While the wheels of bureaucracy grind slowly, you may be able to bring a child into your home as foster parents, with the intent of adoption once the child is freed for adoption within that state. (Every state works differently in its termination of birth-parents rights.) Foster parenting is covered in detail in this chapter.

For someone looking to adopt, adopting a child from a public agency is the quickest, least costly manner in which to bring a child into your life. However, do not choose this method based on those two facts. You need to seriously consider all that comes with adopting a child in this manner. Agencies often provide guidance, counseling, and support to help with what is often a difficult transition for the parents and the child.

From the perspective of adoptive parents, you are asked to work harder to make the transition and subsequent family life as smooth as possible for the child. Unlike a toddler who may be developmentally behind his or her age mates after spending the first several months of life in an orphanage overseas, a child adopted from the foster-care system through a public agency has experienced a lot of the harsh realities of life at a time when he or she should be enjoying the innocence of childhood. A seven-year-old from an abusive home may have seen more violence firsthand than the adults looking to adopt him. He or she may have heard a lot of fighting, and seen the effects of drugs and alcohol on the people who were supposed to be those that could most be trusted for security, love, and guidance. Children are shaped, molded, and guided by those people closest to them and the environment in which they are raised, and they need a nurturing environment in which to develop their physical, emotional, and cognitive skills. This is what is sought in these circumstances, through permanency, education, guidance, and love.

Emotional Baggage Handler

"Parenting 101" is not enough when it comes to taking on the responsibly of adopting a child from the foster-care system. You need to handle the emotional baggage, or issues that are almost always prevalent. Most public agencies provide training and guidance before you are permitted to adopt the child. This can include ten, twenty, or even forty hours of classes or seminars. These classes are designed for you to learn about the realities of bringing an older child with previous life experiences into your family. In addition, the home-study process will be more rigorous as the social worker tries to evaluate how you will handle potentially difficult situations. Children adopted from public agencies face multiple separation issues, having been separated from their birth families and possibly from other foster families. They may also have behavior or self-control issues that need to be addressed and worked on. The early environment from which the child has been removed may have resulted in the child's being aggressive, defiant, impulsive, having low self-esteem, or having learning disabilities. Children are very frequently stuck in levels of behavior that they were unable to progress through in the same manner as children in homes that provided proper love, nurturing, and guidance.

When therapists work with families formed through the foster-care system, they try to assess the developmental needs of the child. They evaluate the child's emotional needs, review the cognitive learning experiences the child has mastered, and look at maladaptive behavioral patterns that need to be addressed. Then they work with the family to structure a day-to-day program. Developmental delays are common in pre-school or early-school-age children. Children have delays in language skill development and may have serious issues with a sense of playing together or working in a group setting. There is often a sense of mistrust of others, and a child may not play age-appropriate activities in the manner of a child from a stable, nurturing home environment. The level at which the child is currently functioning is first addressed so the child is not put into a situation whereby he or she is supposed to act a certain age or reach a certain grade level in his or her developmental skills. Don't be surprised or fooled by children from this type of environment who are uneven in their levels of development. A child may do very well in one area but have fallen behind in another. Since all families and situations are different, there is no boilerplate program to follow for parents adopting from the foster-care system.

Leanne Jaffe, M.S.W., and founder of Adapting to Adoption, a New York-based adoption counseling and consulting service says

> Be as educated as you can be and be an advocate for
> yourself. The foster-care system is difficult because
> of bureaucracy and you need to speak up to get the

information you need from the agency and from case-workers. There is a lot of turnaround with the staff in many of these agencies, so you have to stay on top of everything that is supposed to transpire. It is also important to learn about the circumstances of the birth parents and be able to deal with the anger or disappointment the child may feel. Most of these kids have a long history with their birth families.

The parents who take on these responsibilities will feel great rewards once they have made progressive steps in the development of the child. It can be done, and there are children from the foster-care system who have gone on to marvelous achievements. However, it will mean patience, consistency, set routines, love, discipline, and guidance on the part of the adopting parents.

Special Needs

The term "special needs" is used frequently in public placement and the foster-care system. It is a term used to define children who are harder for the agency to place in a permanent home. This may be simply an issue of age, as a child can become harder to place as he or she gets older. It may also mean mental or physical problems, which can sometimes be serious. Therefore, the phrase "special needs" covers a very wide range.

As in all types of adoption, you need to try to get all available information about the child. In the case of a child classified as having special needs, you need to find out exactly why the specific child has this classification. Sometimes "special needs" refers to two or more siblings who could and should be placed together. While siblings are often split up by well-meaning public-placement agencies (nearly 75 percent of children in the foster-care system have at least one sibling, but less than 25 percent are adopted as siblings because it is harder for many people to take on the responsibility of adopting more than one child at a time), this often has a negative effect on the children as they grow. Often a brother or sister is the last bastion of security and family that a child has. The bond has been proven in studies to be very strong, and breaking it can be more painful for children than even the loss of the parents. Therefore, it is in the best interest of most sibling groups to remain together.

Older Children

Older children entering your home (not babies or toddlers) may be quick to test your abilities as parents. You need to be ready to stand up to the challenges and no matter how you work though them, the child must know that you are not going to give up and go away. An older child will touch your things, break some, possibly take some, and challenge your authority more than a younger child, because he or she will have a greater awareness of what he or she is doing and how you might or might not react.

You may also need to advocate for your child in school and make sure that teachers and others involved with your child on a daily basis understand where he or she is coming from. You do not want your child to be singled out or to be the recipient of pity. On the other hand, you do not need educators exacerbating the situation by failing to understand that a child simply might have issues other than being disruptive in class or falling behind in the classwork. Counselors from the adoption facility with which you worked should be able to help you address how to advocate for your child to see that he or she is treated in a fair manner. You need to build and maintain a solid rapport with the heads of any learning facility your child is attending—this should hold true for all parents, but is especially true for parents adopting children who have been in the foster care system.

Earl's Three Sons

Earl is a single adoptive father of three boys from the New York State foster-care system. In New York, as in many other states, there is a legal requirement that you become a foster parent before you can adopt from the foster-care system. Earl took the assigned classes, became a foster parent, and adopted the first of his sons in 1993. He received as much information as the agency could provide and started the process slowly, getting to know his boys gradually.

"As a social worker, I had some experience with how the system worked. I became a licensed foster-care provider, being fingerprinted, going through the home study and so on. I was a foster parent for six months, but that particular situation didn't work out, which is unusual because 85 percent of the children adopted in foster care are adopted by the foster parents. Anyway, I knew I wanted to be a parent and adopt, so I inquired with an agency and was introduced to a young boy whom I started visiting weekly for about four months at his foster mother's house. It was a gradual process, but we hit it off. I was always a little freaked out at the idea of just bringing a child

home, so the process of spending time together and gradually getting to know each other worked well for me.

"My first child turned four right after he moved in, and after a court hearing, he was officially adopted. He had been in and out of homes since his mother had died, but he adjusted pretty quickly to his new home. The agency gave me as much information as they had about him, which included the fact that he was one of ten children. He has two sisters that he has met, but he doesn't mention them or ask about his family very often. He has very minor recollection of the foster parents, but rarely speaks of them either.

"Five years later I thought I'd like to adopt again. This time I worked with a different agency. They updated my home study and I was introduced to two boys, brothers, whom I gingerly met. At first I was worried about handling three children, but I started visiting and connected with them immediately. They were good kids. Working as a therapist I had a good knowledge of where there might be potential problems, especially between them and my son at home. I started to talk to my first son about it to see how he felt. He was nine at the time, and I asked him if he thought we should do this. I told him that I wouldn't if he didn't want to, since it would mean two other boys in the house. He seemed okay with it and they joined us.

"There were disagreements and some fighting at first but then they started to get along. The two brothers had a good, strong relationship. The brothers stuck together quite a bit and I told them that they would have to open up and accept the third boy as their brother too. I think it's very important for siblings to stay together if at all possible. These two boys had gained great strength from being together. Their relationship with each other was the only long-term relationship they'd ever known. They had been in a foster home with a sixty-year-old woman. At first she was going to adopt them, but then when

I came along, she thought I'd be better with them since I was a bit younger than she was."

Earl put his youngest child into an inclusion program as he had developmental issues. The program was designed to help children fit in emotionally and scholastically with other children in a school environment. He tried to keep them all out of special education classes and worked with outside help where necessary. There were some issues with the brothers but not many. The first child presented more challenges, but that, too, was within his grasp. *"All in all, I had three pretty positive experiences,"* adds Earl, who also comments on the system.

"It's not a middle-class system, some foster parents do it for the money, and there is a great deal of poor judgment exercised by the system. For a while in New York, the government was going overboard to protect the [birth] parents' rights and children were not getting adopted until they were seven, eight, or nine years old because they couldn't get freed for adoption. Now, at least in New York, they are trying to move them through the system faster so they don't have to move from foster home to foster home and they can be freed for adoption. There are some risks doing this, but it worked for me. I just think people should not write off these kids or this way of adopting. There are plenty of good kids out there who need homes."

You'll find another story on adoption from the foster-care system by a single dad in Chapter 18 which deals with single-parent adoptions.

Foster Parenting

Foster parents adopt the majority of children who are adopted from the foster-care system. However, becoming foster parents is a mixed blessing. It brings a child into your home, but it does not assure that you will be able to adopt this child. Therefore, foster parents need to accept this reality from the beginning.

The foster-care system gets a lot of negative press because of how it is run, with children often bouncing from one home to another and the inability to get children freed for adoption in a timely manner. Paperwork and bureaucracy can tie a child up in "the system" for an extended period of time. The problem is that the child doesn't stop growing older and doesn't stop needing a permanent loving family while papers wait to be processed and signed.

Foster-parent agencies can be found in every state. The laws and regulations governing foster parenting are regulated by the individual states. As prospective parents, once you visit a public agency, you will learn the ropes of the system and be walked through the paperwork. You will also be required to complete a home study, pass child-abuse clearance and provide references and significant background information. In addition, you will need to take classes to learn about foster parenting.

Foster parenting is a form of "parenting" and, in some ways, a form of "baby-sitting." There is an attachment formed by having a child in your home. However, there is a fear on the part of both parties that this situation can come to an abrupt end for any number of reasons. Birth parents may return to the picture, sometimes for better and sometimes for worse. This will depend on the situation and why the child was taken out of the birth parents' home. It will depend on what the birth parents have to offer. Unlike adoption, which is permanent, foster parenting is not.

On the positive side of foster care, your home is most likely a better environment than a group home is. You can provide greater stability and a consistent, personalized routine for a child. By helping to shape and mold a child, you will feel very rewarded.

You can also use foster parenting as a possible route to adoption. Many foster-parenting situations do lead to permanent placement; however, the public child-welfare agencies are also committed to trying to return children to their birth families. Foster parents are often asked to work with the birth families, which often means that the foster families help children to visit with their birth parents. This begins with supervised visitation at first, then overnight and weekend visitation to help transition children safely back to their birth parents. If the treatment plan for the birth family does not work out, the foster parents are then asked whether they would be interested in adopting and are available to adopt the child. This is so that the child does not move again, since every move is traumatizing to a child.

Only when the birth parents cannot safely have the child(ren) returned to them and there are no relatives available for kinship placement are foster parents usually asked if they will adopt the child. This can put foster parents in the very awkward position of helping a child return to his or her birth family while at the same time hoping they can adopt the child. However, often it becomes clear that the child cannot be returned to his or her birth family.

Foster Parents and Adoptive Parents

Foster parents provide supportive and loving, caring homes for children who are temporarily separated from their parents. Adoptive parents provide supportive, loving, caring and permanent families for children whose relationship with their biological family has been severed permanently. Both are very important for waiting children.

Note: Foster parents are given a monthly stipend to care for children in agency custody, along with money to cover a child's medical expenses.

Know Your Limitations

Not unlike any adoptive parenting situation, you will need to determine what age child you want to bring into your home and what you can and cannot comfortably handle practically and emotionally. You will need to determine whether or not you are comfortable with an older child, special-needs child or a child of a different race or ethnic background than your own. There are also various levels of need and care that must be addressed. These personal considerations require some deep thought.

If you start as a foster parent, you do not want to go into it with a "we'll see how it goes" attitude. The same holds true for adopting a child from the foster-care system. Pat O'Brien, executive director of New York City's You Gotta Believe! agency, which places children age ten and older for adoption, explains, "These kids have been rejected many times. The worst thing parents can do is take a child on a conditional basis. For this reason, before placing children for adoption, we make sure that prospective parents go through a learning experience and are educated for eight weeks. We want them to understand how unconditional this commitment is. We teach about behavior management, grief and loss, and provide valuable information. This is important material for any parents to learn."

Parents making the decision to adopt through O'Brien's agency need to understand what adopting an older child will be like. Similarly, foster parents need to understand the same principles and not use the lack of permanency as a convenient way out. "Well, he's not behaving as we thought he would, so perhaps it's not working out" is not how foster parenting, or adoptive parenting should begin.

Note: It helps to be well organized and have a sense of structure. These children are often from unstructured environments, so set routines are important. In addition, you will generally have to work meetings with social workers, therapists, doctors, and even birth parents into your busy schedule.

As noted earlier, in Chapter 2, Gary and Fran adopted a three-year-old, and although she was not adopted from the foster-care system, they immediately went into the process with their eyes wide open, determined that the situation was going to work out for them. They educated themselves about their daughter's background as best they could. They then had her evaluated by psychologists and met with the board of health to investigate early-intervention programs. Leanne Jaffe, mentioned above, also pointed out that you need to be proactive and find out what you can do to help an older child. "Evaluation and taking the necessary steps are your responsibilities," she adds.

Good and Bad News About Photo Listings

Recent federal legislation, called the Adoption and Safe Families Act, requires that workers, agencies, and courts work together to find permanent families in a timely manner. The act also places an emphasis on eliminating the bureaucratic and jurisdictional barriers that prevent the placement of children. This has resulted in an increase in the number of children listed on photo listing services, many of which can be found on-line. There have also been increased efforts to place children who have been waiting for adoptive placement for long periods of time.

Among the web-sites featuring waiting children are Faces of Adoption (http://www.adopt.org) and Adopt America Network (www.adoptamericanetwork.org). Both include informative listings of children from all over the United States.

Approach photo listings with some caution. Listings may be outdated, meaning that the child has already been placed or the child may not yet be freed for adoption. There may also be emotional or physical needs that have not yet been addressed before allowing the child to be listed. In addition, some agencies have reportedly taken to using models for the children pictured, while others have been known to show one child and then place another with you. Finally, some agencies do not provide all the relative information for the child listed. In short, be careful—many children are available, but others are not, or the information about the children is not available.

Chapter 9
INTERNATIONAL ADOPTION

Look up in the sky. They're tense, they're excited and they're carrying plenty of paperwork! Yes, they are a couple on their way to adopt a child from another country.

Legal adoption, including adoption from other countries, has taken place in the United States since as far back as the 1850's. However, it was not until one hundred years later, in the 1950s, that Korean adoptions began to shed national attention on international adoption, as children were brought home following the Korean War. These adoptions of Korean-born children into the United States ushered in the modern era of international adoption. Many of the Korean-born adoptees of the late 1950s were those with Korean mothers and GI fathers. Over time, as the American military moved out of Korea, this changed and the children were born to Korean birth parents, many of whom were living in poverty. They saw adoption as a means of giving a child a better life.

Oregon farmer Harry Holt and his wife Bertha, were at the forefront of this new adoption revolution. They adopted eight of the many orphans from South Korea following the war and later went on to start Holt International Children's Services, an adoption agency which, to this day, has placed over 80,000 children in loving homes—not only children born in Korea, but from all over the world. In fact, Susan Soon-Keum Cox, currently the Vice President of Public Policy and External Affairs for Holt International, was one of the first 200 children adopted from Korea back in the 1950s. She has since traveled the globe to help initiate adoption programs and discuss numerous international adoption issues with representatives of other governments.

Over the past fifty years, more than 200,000 Korean-born children have been placed for adoption, not only in the United States, but in Europe. The Korean adoption system has been a model program for other countries. It has been run smoothly and efficiently. Unfortunately, few—if any—other nations have modeled their legal adoption process after the Koreans.

Only in 1988 did Korean adoption run into criticism and the program was jeopardized. The Olympics were held in Korea and both journalists and commentators such as Bryant Gumbel focused attention on the fact the Korea's primary export was babies. South Korea was embarrassed by these accusations and put a halt to adoptions in the months surrounding the Olympics. In the following years, the number of adoptions was also monitored and dropped, but the number of orphans in need of a better home remained the same. What Gumbel failed to realize was that while Korea was indeed a leading "sending" country of children, these children were still in need of secure, loving homes, no matter what the numbers were.

Following the Olympics, Korea actually made plans to end adoption policies completely in 1996. However, as the time approached and the nation's economy took a downturn, adoptions were allowed to continue and the country is, once again, a very viable place for adoptive parents to turn if they are seeking to adopt internationally.

"We chose Korea because we wanted a young baby and babies were coming from Korea at three months old," says Trisha, who with her husband Jim, adopted two children from Korea.

"We weren't interested in doing a domestic adoption . . . it would be okay if our kids looked different and didn't match. I was interested in Asian culture and had been to other Asian countries, so I felt comfortable with this plan. I knew Korea had a very successful adoption program and that the birth mothers got good prenatal care and the children were in foster homes. I also felt so depleted from infertility that I didn't have the strength to market myself, make a book, a portfolio, etc. as you need to do for domestic adoption. It wasn't important to us to have a Caucasian child . . . we sort of liked the randomness of it, that for whatever reason that child would be our baby. I didn't want to be "choosing a baby" and didn't like the idea of not being picked by birth mothers.

"The agency we worked with held workshops, did fingerprints, the home study, etc. We got a referral with a photo and medical information. It's strange because you have a picture of the baby, and say, "this is my baby, but he's in Korea." Then you wait for a few months for the baby to get the visa to come to America. Our son was coming when he was five months old; most kids were coming at three months. It was hard waiting, and my husband and I even asked about going to Korea to pick him up, but we were told that it would not speed up the process any and might make us look like pushy Americans.

"They had someone from the agency who met us at the airport, and we had to sign papers with her in the airport waiting area. Then a woman with our son came off the plane. She brought him over in exchange for the free airfare so she could visit her own children in the United States. It was very unceremonious. She walked off the plane and handed us our baby at the gate. The escort gave us a package of stuff including some baby formula, pictures of his life with the foster family, a Korean flag, some photos, and so on. It was a little frustrating because she didn't speak English, and we couldn't find out much more about him. She was trying to tell us he had a little cold. We went to a pediatrician the next day whom we had interviewed previously and found out he had an ear infection. I remember being a little frightened by all of this. . . . We were first time parents, so we're asking things like "What's an ear infection?" It took us some time to adjust to suddenly being parents."

Since Korean adoptions are not completed overseas, Trisha and Jim had to complete the adoption process domestically. The process was relatively simple, except they had to wait two years before the first adoption was finalized. They had chosen a New York City-based agency and because the finalization would take place in a Manhattan court, the courts were backed up and the wait was extremely long. "When we adopted for the second time, we chose an agency in our own state and the finalization was four months later. Also, because we did the first adoption in another state, we needed a lawyer. The second time we didn't need one and handled the paperwork ourselves."

Today Trisha and Jim are parents of a five-year-old and a two-year-old. They want to provide both children with their Korean culture:

"For our daughter, we got even more things from the foster parents in Korea, including a hanbok, which is the traditional silk costume for celebrating birthdays, etc. For cultural reasons, we also decided that we would settle in a diverse city and have them go to public schools, where they would be exposed to a wider range of cultures and ethnic backgrounds. This way they will both go to school with Asian kids, adopted kids, etc."

International Adoption Today

Today, nearly 20,000 international adoptions annually bring children into American families. Children are available for adoption in many countries in all corners of the globe. These children are classified as orphans, or freed for adoption, in their home countries, which does not always mean their parents are dead. In many cases, it means that birth parents have relinquished their parental rights or had such rights terminated by abandonment. The children have been placed in orphanages or in foster care, depending on the policies of the country or of the province within a country.

Not unlike the United States, with fifty-one sets of adoption laws (including Washington D.C.) the nations of the world are similarly divided by their many different laws, regulations, restrictions, and eligibility requirements. In fact, in many countries, such as Mexico, laws differ from state to state. To confuse matters even more, political, economic, and social conditions within a country often cause the government to change its adoption policies. It is not uncommon for a country to be "open" to international adoption one month and suddenly closed the next. Korea, China, Mexico, the nations of the former Soviet Union, Colombia, Guatemala, Romania, Thailand, Vietnam, and Cambodia are among the leading countries from which children have been adopted into the United States in recent years. This doesn't mean they will remain open to international adoption next month or even next week. The Hague Convention on International Adoption is looking to standardize adoption requirements around the world by means of a treaty. This would create a global process whereby countries would work within an international framework to standardize adoptions. Over sixty countries have already ratified this multilateral treaty, which,

Adopting from the USA?

Few people realize that the United States has been a country from which other nations, including Canada, Great Britain, and France have adopted children. There are few statistics available on this little-known fact, but the United States is also a "sending country."

when completed, will eliminate much of the "gray area" that allows unethical facilitators, agencies, and others to reap benefits from unsuspecting couples and singles.

International vs. Domestic Adoption

From your perspective, the international adoption process can work wonderfully and can help you start or build your family in a matter of months. Clearly, there are children waiting for loving, permanent families worldwide. Agencies that might not open their doors to you—much less accept your application for domestic adoption—are all smiles and handshakes when you start talking about adopting a child from overseas. *Funny, how when there are children available, you suddenly become ideal parenting material in the eyes of some agencies.* Nonetheless, you will need to follow a process that begins with selecting a country (or countries) from which you would like to adopt, working with an agency (there are also attorneys who handle international adoptions), and filling out paperwork and more paperwork to file with the agency and with the INS (Immigration and Naturalization Service). There is a home study and usually travel, which often includes two trips abroad.

A few points of comparison:

- The process of adopting internationally can often be completed more quickly than adopting domestically.
- The cost for an international adoption will most often be about the same as domestic adoption, sometimes slightly less. A range of $20,000 to $25,000 including travel expenses is common. Your costs may be more clearly defined in international adoption than in domestic independent adoption,

where you will have more variables because of advertising and birth-mother expenses.

- The children will generally be under two years of age, but will not be newborn infants, as they may be when you adopt domestically.
- A birth mother changing her mind just prior to or after giving birth will almost never arise. The child will (or should) already be free for adoption placement when you travel to the country.
- Developmental delays are more common in international adoption because the children are usually living in institutionalized settings, as opposed to domestic adoption in the United States, where babies are most often adopted as newborns and brought home from the hospital by the adoptive parents. Children with developmental delays generally catch up in a matter of months or a couple of years.
- The love for your child will be the same whether you adopt domestically or internationally—unconditional!

Before exploring the process, it's also worth taking some time to assess why you might or might not be comfortable pursuing an international adoption. As discussed in Chapter 2 on making key adoption decisions, whether to adopt domestically or internationally is one of the first adoption decisions you will need to make. Your decision should be based, first and foremost, on wanting to be a parent and provide a child with a loving home. You do not adopt a child because an episode of *20/20* or *60 Minutes* featured the conditions abroad and made you feel that you owe it to a child to do a good deed. You also do not choose to adopt internationally because it's "trendy," quicker, or because you've already adopted a child from a foreign country and want him to have someone to keep him company. You do that with cats, not children.

Explore the reasons that you are choosing to go abroad to adopt. Ultimately, your key reason for any adoption is that you want to bring a child into your life to love and raise. After that, your lack of restrictions (newborn only, Caucasian only, and so on) and your ability to bring that child something of his or her own cultural heritage will point you in the direction of international adoption. Yes, international adoption may be faster than domestic adoption, but if you cannot feel comfortable with a child of a different ethnic heritage or provide the child with some of his or her culture, you are doing yourself and the child a disservice. You owe it to yourself and your child to become familiar with that child's culture. Adoption agencies and support groups may assist you in finding other parents who have adopted from the country that you have chosen. Visiting such a group meeting or attending a social activity would be an ideal way to get a feeling for the culture of the child you are planning to adopt. Visit a library, check out the books available on amazon.com, look at web-sites, or attend lectures or seminars to learn more about the country. Once you adopt, you'll find culture camps for children born abroad sponsored by agencies such as Holt International and others.

Wendy Stanley, New York branch director of Children's Hope International, an international agency licensed in Missouri, New York, Illinois, Tennessee, and Washington, works with couples who are trying to decide about international adoption. "We run programs to several countries, and many people come in unsure of where they want to go. I tell them to shut their eyes and picture what they think their family should look like. They need to think about ethnicity and even their own prejudices. They need to feel comfortable about the country they choose."

According to her, some people want to hear about all of the programs offered while others are interested in a country from which a friend adopted, or they are interested because of a family background of heritage. "Everyone's family is different," she adds.

Once you have adopted, you will have to introduce your son or daughter to life in a new environment, outside of an orphanage or a foster home. You may have to deal with latent development and dietary concerns. It may take some time and patience to get a child who is used to a certain diet to start eating healthier foods. *In reality, it's a struggle to get most children to eat healthier food.* Children who have spent time in institutionalized settings may also exhibit more fearful behaviors than other children. Some children will be very clingy; others won't want you to touch them. In short, you need to familiarize yourself with what it will be like to bring a child home from another country and raise that child in your home environment. Many people are so focused on the process of adoption that they forget that the child is the end result and is a huge responsibility. The older the child, the more time he or she has spent in the institutionalized or foster-care setting and the more behavioral problems you might face while the child makes the transition.

Note: Generally, there are fewer developmental and attachment issues when a child has been in foster care than in an orphanage.

The International Process

International adoption requires submitting a substantial amount of paperwork to the Immigration and Naturalization Service (INS), having a home study completed by a licensed social worker, and working with an adoption agency licensed in your state of residency. One of your initial steps in any type of adoption is always to gather your own personal documents and get several copies of each. To meet the requirements of the

The Actual Adoption

The actual adoption of a child born overseas is a legal matter usually handled by the courts, or similar government body in the country in which the child was born. Neither the United States government or the Immigration and Naturalization Service can intervene with the proceedings in such an international adoption. Adoption laws and regulations will be guided by the individual country of origin. See Chapter 10, which looks more closely at some of the sending countries.

agency, home study, and country, get official copies of your marriage license and any divorce decree(s) if applicable, birth certificate, health and financial documentation, and letters of recommendation from three or four people who know you well. Other documents may also be required by the agency to complete the home study and meet requirements of the country.

The first and most important form that you will need to file with the INS is the Orphan Petition Form, known as either the I-600 or I-600A. The difference between the two is that you will fill out the I-600 if you have identified a specific child to adopt. The I-600A form will be used when you begin working with an agency and have not yet identified a child. Once either form is carefully filled out, it is then filed with the local INS office. The INS then reviews the form and, in most cases, it is approved. If the child has been identified, the INS notifies the U.S. embassy or consulate where visas are processed for residents of the child's country. A copy of the petition is sent with accompanying documentation to the National Visa Center, where the petition is assigned a computer tracking code.

However, in most cases, the child has not yet been identified, so you will submit the I-600A form. It will be sent to the U.S. mission in the country from which you are planning to adopt. Although you will then have to wait for a referral before filling out the I-600 petition with the identified child, you can expedite the process by using the I-600A. In fact, you can fill out and

The INA and Visas

The United States Immigration and Nationality Act (INA) will also factor into the process. The issuance of how U.S. visas for nationals of other countries, which include the child to be adopted, is detailed in this federal act. Section 101(b) of the INA grants immigrant classification to orphans who have been adopted or will be adopted by U.S. citizens. Under this section of the law, both the child and the adoptive parents must satisfy a number of requirements established by the INA. Once both parents qualify under U.S. regulations, the child can be issued a travel visa.

submit an I-600A without naming a country, so that you will get your INS approval. The INS will then hold it until you specify the country and travel information. You can even submit the home study at a later date. When submitting the I-600A form, you will need to include any preadopt certification that is required in your state plus your marriage certificate, any divorce decree(s), your birth certificates, and fingerprints as filled out on the INS forms.

As of 2002, fingerprint cards cost $50 per person and every member of the prospective adoptive family age eighteen or over needs to provide a fingerprint card for clearance by the FBI. Once you receive either the I-600 or I-600A form, the INS will provide appointment letters with the date and location for all adult members of the household to get fingerprinted. Take the appointment letters with you when you go to be fingerprinted.

Costs

As of February 2002, the cost of an I-600 or I-600A form, according to the INS was $460. Verify the current cost by contacting the nearest INS office or going to the INS website at www.ins.usdoj.gov.

The fingerprints will then be sent to INS for you.

The INS can take two to four months before getting back to you with approval, which is why you want to get a jump on the process by submitting the I-600A.

Russia or Ukraine and the I-600

If you are adopting a child from Russia or Ukraine, the child is not identified until you get to the country. Therefore you will need to complete the I-600 form when you are overseas. You can complete the paperwork at the U.S. Consulate abroad. Make sure you know the cost and have the correct amount of cash on you (in American dollars).

In the past, an affidavit of support was often requested. This is most often not asked for by the INS since your adoption agency will have screened to see that you can support a child and your paperwork will include financial statements.

To contact the INS for information you can call 1-800-375-5283 or go to their Web site, www.ins.usdoj.gov. The INS provides a booklet (M-249Y) which explains much of this information regarding bringing a child into the United States.

Same Name

"Women need to remember to be consistent with the name they use on their passport and documentation." notes Heidi. "I couldn't figure out why the paperwork was being delayed, and then I contacted the INS and found out that the paperwork was not going through because there were different names on my passport and my adoption papers. I had used my maiden name on one and married name on the other."

The Process Overseas

The process differs, depending on the country from which you are adopting. In some countries, such as Russia, you make two trips; one to identify the child and the second to adopt. The overseas process also differs greatly. In China you visit the U.S. consulate, in Russia you go into a Russian court, and in Guatemala nearly everything is done by proxy so you do not have to appear in court or the U.S. consulate. Your agency will tell you what the official adoption process is in the country you have selected. Since the process is subject to change, make sure your agency provides you with the current information. Generally, there is an appearance or hearing required in front of the courts or the department of the government responsible for overseeing adoptions. Your paperwork will need to be in order and you will be asked some questions which you should be briefed about in advance by your agency. In addition, your child will often receive a basic medical exam. The interview or hearing and medical exam are fairly routine in each country, and your adoption generally is not in jeopardy. Any good agency should walk you through the process.

Once the adoption process is completed, you will need to apply for an immigrant visa for your child. The U.S. consular office will handle the visa interview with you as the adopting parents. Contact the consular office in advance for a list of what documents are required for the specific country.

About the Agencies

The vast majority of international adoptions are handled by adoption agencies, which have programs in the various countries. Agencies will show you plenty of pictures of children from the country and lots of children's toys and items to attract your attention. Behind the photos and three color brochures are a wide range of agencies, some of which are placing children from all over the globe with families on a regular and routine basis, while others are still building their reputations as they look to establish strong ties with other nations. You want an agency with a track record of successful placements. You want an agency that has, for lack of a better phrase, "satisfied its clientele."

It is very important that you talk with other people who have used the services of the agency, preferably in the same program (for the same country). You want to hear their stories. You are looking for a situation in which the agency was there to help the couple every step of the way. Susan Soon-Keum Cox, of Holt International Adoption Agency, and charter member of the advocacy committee on intercountry adoption, points out that if you are paying $20,000 in fees, you expect that an agency should be able to handle the adoption from start to finish. One couple, using an East Coast agency, complained vehemently about the agency's not helping them when they were in the other country and not knowing the answers to many of their questions. The agency replied, "Why are you complaining? You got a baby, didn't you?" It shouldn't be that way. You should be able to rely on the agency to be the driving force in your successful adoption, not to simply go through the motions while you have to find things out for yourself.

Susan Cox also likens the process to having surgery or buying a new home. "You need to ask a lot of questions and be very well-informed before you start working with an agency. You wouldn't have open-heart surgery without knowing the doctor's credentials. You should know the agency's background and the credentials of the key people. They should be able to explain the process from start to finish. If they cannot or do not want to answer your questions, you should go elsewhere." She also adds that there are more options then ever before (meaning countries) and points to the Hague Convention as a way of monitoring the agencies working with these many different countries. "The Hague will benefit adoption. Agencies will be screened more carefully, and that will put adoptive families at ease."

The International Version of Twenty Questions

Questions to ask international adoption agencies include:

1. Is the agency licensed to place children in your state?
2. What is their fee structure and what is included? This should be clearly outlined.
3. How long have they been in business?
4. What kind of professional services do they offer?
5. What is involved in the home-study process (including how many visits)? Do they have someone in your state who handles home studies? Remember, you *do not* have to work with an adoption agency located in your state, only one that is licensed to do adoptions in your state. Most agencies will have referrals to home-study agencies or social workers in the states in which they are licensed.
6. What programs do they offer? Agencies have programs established with various countries. Assuming that you have decided on the country (or countries) from which you might want to adopt, you should ask about these countries and whether or not the agency has such a program.
7. How long have they worked with the specific country and how many adoptions have they done from that country? Most agencies will have a list broken down by country and by the number of adoptions they have done in each country. Look for an agency that has an established program in the country you want.
8. Roughly what is the average length of time it takes for adoption in that program?
9. Whom do they work with in the other country? Is it an orphanage? Are the babies in foster care?
10. How do the babies come into the program? Are the birth mothers involved in the process? Are these children abandoned? Are they already freed for adoption?
11. Whom does the agency have working overseas? Do they have someone on staff in the country? Do they work with facilitators? Is this person working exclusively for the

agency? It is very important that you know exactly how the agency is affiliated with the orphanage or foster-care program in the other country. This can help determine the better agencies from those that are "winging it" or do not have a solid program set up. An agency should have people working overseas, or at least have a very strong relationship with the director of the orphanage. Everything should be in place (in both countries) before you travel.

12. Will you have someone with you as an escort? You should have someone there to guide/assist you while you are in a foreign country. In fact, it has even been recommended that you inquire as to whether one of the principals of the agency speaks the language of the country. This way the agency's director or someone of similar status, can get on the phone directly and get involved in a problematic situation should one arise.

13. What kind of access does the agency's overseas staff have to seeing the children? Sometimes the government will not grant the agency workers much access. If this is the case, the agency should be forthright. This is not always a negative if you can get accurate assessments of the child's health through the orphanage.

14. What health assessment or medical records are available? This will vary from country to country. (Medical assessments are covered, below.)

15. How often, if at all, will you get medical updates prior to my traveling overseas? This will also depend on the country. For example, you will not get any advance information when adopting from Russia or Ukraine.

16. Does the orphanage also work with other adoption agencies? If so, how do you know that they won't place the child elsewhere? Couples have flown overseas only to learn that the child they thought would be there was placed with another

family from another agency or given to a facilitator. You need to find out how the agency handles securing that the child you are going to bring home is indeed there for you.

17. What if the child has too great a health risk for you to handle, and you therefore decide refuse this potential adoption. Will you get another assignment?

18. Do they work with, or recommend a travel agency? You can make travel arrangements on your own, but it doesn't hurt to ask. They may have a good relationship with a specific travel agency.

19. Will there be someone at the agency whom you can contact from overseas at all times? The difference in time zones will make it imperative that the agency be reachable at off hours (U.S. time).

20. What kind of postplacement services do they provide? Workshops? Cultural camps? Parenting groups? Family activities?

Along with asking questions, you need to review the contract carefully. It won't hurt to have an attorney look it over as well and highlight anything that looks questionable.

There are many sites in which to locate adoption agencies including www.adoptiondirectory.com. See Chapters 20 and 24, "Adoption and the Internet" and "Adoption Resources" for more information.

Heidi and Jerry from Connecticut had already adopted domestically when they headed to Russia for their second child.

"Our concerns with international adoption were the amount of travel and having to leave our daughter home or try to bring her with us. My dentist husband was also concerned about leaving his practice for long periods of time and we knew that travel in an international adoption might mean being away for several weeks. We considered Russia when we saw that you only needed to make one trip (at that time) and would stay no longer

than two weeks. In addition, my last name is Russian, so I felt some sense of connection.

"We hooked up with an agency in Pittsburgh. They were wonderful, the director is Russian, and she even goes to Russia herself and selects children for families . . . you see her in the videos. It was very comforting to have someone at the agency who was familiar with the cities and the customs . . . they also provided a personal touch. We flew to Pittsburgh for an interview with the agency and brought our three-year-old daughter with us. They made us feel at home.

"Eventually they sent a couple of videos for us to choose between. It was interesting because they tried to match a child with a sense of what you look like . . . a child who fits in with your family.

"We made copies of the tapes and sent them to a doctor who specializes in evaluating children from overseas who will be adopted. She responded quickly, which is very good because you want to have a quick turnaround time. We were supposed to make a decision within a week. (As of early 2002, agencies were no longer sending tapes of children from Russia.) Each of the videos was taken at two different times so she could evaluate the developmental growth of the children. One had a scary medical history which included hepatitis B; the other had some developmental delays. We contacted a second doctor whose opinions were similar in some ways but different in others. Doctors specialize in different areas. One will be able to detect an illness such as hepatitis B more easily, while another will focus more clearly on developmental delays. The second doctor was better versed in developmental delays and gave us a better idea of what to expect with the child who had such issues. We ended up choosing the child with hepatitis B and had him examined while in Russia. It was set up by the agency. Now we have him monitored.

"Then it was time for our court date. We were prepped by our agency in how to answer the questions. The Russian laws *at the time stipulated that there were ten days in which the child still had to remain in Russia, as a last-ditch effort for him to be adopted by a Russian family. We found out that we could get that waived and the agency helped prepare us in how to do so. We explained, when asked why we wanted the ten days waived, that we were away from our other child, our three-year-old daughter who was staying with relatives back home. We missed her and know she must be missing us. We knew they would not be as concerned about my husband's dental practice, but it was an additional reason we mentioned. The truth was that we were anxious to be a family all together at home. The ten days were waived and soon we were on our way, but not before a tea party was given for us at the orphanage. We handed out fourteen gift bags including cosmetics, scarves, and stockings to the people working there. It was a very positive experience and I think a lot of that had to do with our agency being on top of everything."*

Getting Medical Assessments

The leading concern of people adopting from overseas is not a fear of traveling, but a fear of adopting a child with potentially serious health problems. However, technology and the proliferation of doctors trained in Western schools who are now working all over the world makes it easier than ever to evaluate the health of a child.

Dr. Mark Magnusson, Clinical Associate Professor of Pediatrics at Children's Hospital of Philadelphia, explains that adoptive parents traveling overseas need to expect that children may be undernourished and that their development is not normal. "The question is whether this is a lack of loving care and physical contact or an underlying disease," says Dr. Magnusson, who is one among a growing number of doctors in the United States who routinely look at videotapes and photographs of children in orphanages overseas who have been assigned for placement in American families. "I tend to take a laissez-faire approach, whereby in most cases I think it's important to get the child into a loving nurturing environment for a period of time and see if any development and growth accelerates. In an infant, you will usually see progress in two months, while a toddler may take four to six months to demonstrate some change. A child may not make great strides, but you want to see that he or she is catching up."

Initial videotapes can demonstrate reason for concern. A child may not be moving all of his or her body, may possibly be walking on tip toe, or may not exhibit certain behaviors such as smiling during social interactions. However, Dr. Magnusson reminds prospective parents that just because they do not see something on the tape does not mean the child cannot exhibit other behaviors that were simply not caught on the tape. Ideally, you would like to have two tapes of the child; one when he or she is assigned to you and another a couple of months later. This will allow the pediatrician to determine whether or not there is some problem in developmental growth.

While serious developmental issues can often be evident on a tape, sometimes there will be other concerns when meeting the child. A good agency for international adoption should have a representative in the country that can help you find a Western-trained doctor who can examine the child if you so choose.

Keep in mind that many of the illnesses you may discover sound worse than they are. Intestinal parasites, skin rashes, and other such common illnesses, including the aggravating, but treatable head lice, can be dealt with easily. There are, however, some more significant concerns such as hepatitis B, more commonly found among Asian-born children, and fetal alcohol syndrome that need to be detected.

Once you return from overseas with your child, you should have an intensive evaluation done. Physicians screen routinely for HIV, tuberculosis, rickets, intestinal pathogens, metabolic disorders, syphilis, and anemia. Physical, motor, social, and cognitive evaluations can be done and should be followed up to make sure progress is being made in all areas. Your pediatrician's early intervention programs can do a world of good, as can school-based programs. The best you, as a parent, can do is be diligent about following the growth and development of your child, adopted or otherwise, and be proactive if some type of program or intervention is necessary. Do not shrug off physicians' recommendations for such programs because you've already been through a lot or assume that love and attention will solve everything. In short, try not to wear blinders. On the other hand, don't look for things to be wrong that aren't there because you've heard stories about children adopted from a particular country or because your child isn't as active as your neighbor's kid. Don't look for labels that are not there. Take a step back and try to take a realistic look. It will be the best you can do for your child in the long run.

As Dr. Magnusson mentions, it's also worth pointing out that "the growth curves in the United States are based on our population. Therefore, what is considered average height and weight for an American-born child of a certain age may not be the same for an Asian-born child of the same age." As long as the child is following the curve and making steady progress, you may have no reason for concern.

Whether your child is adopted from another country or domestically, much of the job of the pediatrician will be to create a more detailed medical history for an adopted child. Often, past medical history comes from answers on medical forms, which are not always detailed or inclusive. Immunization screening will generally be done for children adopted from overseas. Tests for the effects of drugs or alcohol, for example, may also be done if there is reason to believe that the birth mother used alcohol or drugs, or if there is no evidence pointing either way.

When adopting from Russia or Ukraine, you will not have referrals before going overseas. Therefore, you will not have videotapes or photographs of a child before you travel. You will need to have a system set up whereby you can get medical information, and possibly even digital photos (which you take yourself) to a medical adoption expert who will respond quickly.

Steve and Mary, mentioned in Chapter 2, planned in advance to have medical information assessed by specialists who were experienced in evaluating children adopted from overseas: *"We made arrangements to send digital photographs of the child in the Ukraine by e-mail to a doctor here in the United States. Once we were there, we rented a digital camera and, in the orphanage, took photos of the little boy we were shown. Then we used a nearby Internet café to e-mail the photos back home to both the doctor and to our agency. If you stay at a major hotel or a chain such as a Marriott, they will often have a business center that you can use to do this. It was clear that the child we were first looking at was a special-needs child . . . and since this was not something that we were comfortable with, we told the orphanage we were unable to take him. That was very hard to do. The next baby we met is our son today. We went through the same process, but we knew he was ours."*

Attachment Disorder

From the first visits, a medical professional should assess behavior and the potential risk of attachment disorder. Then, as the child adjusts to your home, periodic developmental and behavioral assessments should be made periodically. Your pediatrician should be apprised of the progress being made so that he or she can provide proper ongoing care.

The medical professionals listed below handle either preadoption medical evaluations, post adoption developmental evaluations and, or, in some cases provide ongoing care. *Not all provide the same services, as some specialize in more significant developmental or neurological issues.* Below are some questions for such medical professionals:

In what area(s) do you specialize?

Do you review medical records prior to travel?

Do you look at videotapes?

Do you review medical-related travel needs for the parents?

Can you be contacted while I am overseas? This is very important. Some medical facilities offer support via telephone and or e-mail.

What is your turnaround time? You will often need quick replies, especially if you are e-mailing digital photos from overseas.

What are your fees for each of these preadoption services?

Do you do postadoption medical evaluations?

Do you provide ongoing care for medical problems? (This will be in line with their specialties.)

Do you provide ongoing pediatric care?

What are your fees for post adoption services?

If you are not reachable, who is covering for you, and can they contact you if necessary?

Below we include several of the adoption medical experts in major cities throughout the United States. While you will want to have a pediatrician close to home, if you are planning to return from overseas to a major city before traveling four or five more hours home, you might try to schedule an appointment with one of these or another adoption specialist upon returning.

In the East

In the New York area, one of the most prominent physicians in the field is DR. JANE ARONSON, a leading doctor of osteopathic medicine. Besides handling a very busy pediatric practice, she holds on-line chats at http:/www.adopting.org/DrJane and conducts parenting seminars. (Dr. Aronson's office is at 151 East 62nd Street, Suite 1A, New York, New York 10021, 212-207-6666. E-mail: orphan-doctor@aol.com; Web-site: http://www.orphandoctor.com/.) Also in New York, you can contact DR. ANDREW ADESMAN, at the Adoption Evaluation Center at Schneider Children's Hospital (269-01 76th Avenue, Suite 139, New Hyde Park, NY 11040, 718-470-4000). In Connecticut you can contact the Yale University School of Medicine, where MARGARET K. HOSTETTER, M.D. and CAROL WEITZMAN, M.D. see children who have been adopted domestically or from overseas. (464 Congress Avenue, New Haven, CT 06519, 203-737-1623.)

If you are in or around Syracuse, you might contact STEVE BLATT, M.D. at the Adoptive Health Care Services Pediatric and Adolescent Center at University Healthcare Center (90 Presidential Plaza, Syracuse, NY 13202, 315-464-5831).

In Philadelphia, the Children's Hospital of Philadelphia has opened the Clinical Center for Adopted Children (34th Street and Civic Center Boulevard, Philadelphia PA, 19104, 215-590-7525). GAIL FARBER, is the director, and among the doctors is MARK MAGNUSSON, mentioned earlier in this chapter (E-mail: farber@email.chop.edu). In Pittsburgh, SCOTT FABER, M.D. and SARAH SPRINGER, M.D. head the Mercy Center for International Adoption Medicine. (Mercy Hospital of Pittsburgh, 1515 Locust Street—Room 315, Pittsburgh, PA 15219, 412-575-5805.)

In New England, LAURIE MILLER, M.D. is located at the International Adoption Clinic Floating Hospital for Children, which is part of the New England Medical Center (750 Washington Street,

Boston, MA 02111, 617-636-8121; Web-site: wwwnemc.org.ado ption). Also in Boston are Lisa Albers, M.D., and Kay Seligsohn, Ph.D. at the Children's Hospital and Harvard Medical School Adoption Program (300 Longwood Avenue, Boston, MA 02115, 617-355-5209; E-mail: albers_l@hub.tch.harvard.edu).

If you are in Washington, D.C., you might visit the International Adoption Health Resource Center and Dr. Nina Scribanu (3307 M Street, N.W. Washington, DC 20007, 202-687-8635). In Maryland, the renowned John S. Hopkins Medical Center features the International Adoption Clinic of Kennedy Krieger Institute (700 North Broadway, Baltimore, M.D. 21205, 410-502-8988; Web-site: http://adoptiondoc.org). And, if you're in or near Georgia, Amy L. Pakula, M.D. is at the Marcus International Adoption Center for Health and Development at Emory University Department of Pediatrics (1605 Chantilly Drive, Suite 100, Atlanta, GA., 30324, 404-727-9450).

In the Midwest

The International Adoption Center at Children's Hospital Medical Center (3333 Burnet Avenue, Cincinnati, OH 45229, 513-636-2877) handles telephone conversations with parents while you are in the foreign country and offers a range of services (E-mail: danq7g@chmcc.org; Web-site: www.cincin-natichildrens.org). In Cleveland, Anna Mandalaka and Karen Olness, M.D. are both well-versed in evaluating and diagnosing children adopted internationally. They can be found at the Rainbow Center for International Child Health, Adoption Health Service (11100 Euclid Ave. MS 6038, Cleveland, OH 44106-6038, 216-844-3224). The Rainbow facility has been treating children for more than a century, as a leading pediatrics hospital with funding from the National Institutes of Health. (E-mail: RCIC@po.cwru.edu; Web-site: www.uhrainbow.com/internationalhealth.htm). Also in

Cleveland, occupational therapist WENDY SCHMIDT, O.T.R./L., M.A. provides consultations regarding growth and development, prepares families for foreign travel, and works in assisting the family on transitional matters including attachment issues (2219 Devonshire Drive Cleveland, OH 44106, 216-231-1981; E-mail: wxs19@po.cwru.edu).

In Chicago, TODD J. OCHS, M.D. heads the Adoption Pediatrics group of the Ravenswood Medical Professional Group (1945 West Wilson, 4th Floor, Chicago, IL 60640, 773-769-4600; E-mail: t-ochs@nwu.edu). You can also contact TINA TAN, M.D. who does postadoption evaluations at Children's Memorial Hospital. (2300 Children's Plaza, Chicago, IL 60614, 773-880-4187). In St. Louis, MARY KAY BOWEN, M.D. at the Unity Medical Group (4305 Butler Hill Road, Suite 2, St. Louis, MO 63128-3717, 314-845-1780) provides assistance with your adoption medical needs (E-mail: bowenM.D.99@yahoo.com; Website: www.beansprout.net).

In the St. Louis area, you might call JENNIFER S. LADAGE, M.D. at F.A.C.E.S. (Foreign Adoption Clinic and Educational Services) at the St. Louis University School of Medicine, Cardinal Glennon Children's Hospital (1465 South Grand Avenue, St. Louis, MO 63104, 314-577-5643).

DR. JERRI ANN JENISTA at St. Joseph Mercy Hospital in Ann Arbor, (551 Second Street, Ann Arbor, MI 48103, 734-668-0419), is well known for her work in the international adoption community doing preadoption evaluations and postadoption work on complex medical problems. She specializes in infectious diseases and works with children with HIV, hepatitis B, and special needs. DANA E. JOHNSON, M.D., PH.D. also works with adoption and can be reached at The International Adoption Clinic at the University of Minnesota (420 Delaware Street SE, Minneapolis, MN 55455, 612-626-2928; 612-624-1164, E-mail: iac@umn.edu; Web-site: www.peds.umn.edu/IAC).

In the Southwest

In Texas, GALE L. HARADON Ph.D., O.T.R. is at the University of Texas Health Science Center at San Antonio (7703 Floyd Curl Drive, San Antonio, Texas 78229-3900, 210-567-8889; E-mail: Haradon@uthscsa.edu). In Houston try the Texas Children's Health Center for International Adoption, HEIDI SCHWARZWALD, M.D., DIRECTOR (6621 Fannin Street, A350, Houston, TX 77030, 877-824-5437; E-mail: internationaladoptions@texaschildren-shospital.org; Website: http://www.texaschildrenshospital.org). The health center provides preadoption review of records, posta-doption medical and developmental evaluations plus regular pediatric care.

In the West

In the San Francisco area, DR. TINA GABBY, specializes in devel-opmental behavioral pediatrics (2 Fifer Avenue, Suite 200, Corte Madera, CA 94925, 415-381-3255), while in southern Cali-fornia, DEBORAH LEHMAN, M.D., at Cedars-Sinai Medical Center (8700 Beverly Boulevard, Los Angeles, CA 90048, 310-423-4471) offers preadoption review of materials and postadoption medical evaluations. In Denver, you can try contacting SARA CARPENTER, M.D. and MATTHEW F. DALEY, M.D. at the Interna-tional Adoption Clinic, (1056 East 19th Avenue, B032 Denver, CO 80218; questions: 303-837-2830; appointments: 303-837-2740). In Washington, DR. JULIA M. BLEDSOE, at the University of Washington Center for Adoption Medicine (4245 Roosevelt Way NE, Seattle, WA 98104, 206-598-3006) handles a wide range of adoption services.

In Canada

In Montreal, you might contact JEAN-FRANCOIS CHICOINE, M.D. At Clinique de Sante Internationale, Hospital Sainté-Justine (3175 Cote Sainte-Catherine, Montreal, Quebec H3T-

1C5 514-345-4675) or DR. ANGELO SIMONE in Ontario at The
Canadian Clinic for Adopted Children in Mississauga,
Ontario. (2338 Huronterio St., Suite 200, 905-848-5227); E-mail:
asimone@attcanada.net; Web-site: http://CdnClinicAdopted-
Children.homestead.com/CdnMedClinic.html.

Chapter 10
INTERNATIONAL ADOPTION:
THE COUNTRIES

Over the past quarter of a century, international adoption has become a more viable means of forming a family. This is due in part to our society's having embraced adoption and increased social acceptance of many types of family structures, including those of various ethnic origins. It is also due to the ever-present condition of poverty in many nations throughout the world and a need for the children in these countries to have what they so richly deserve; a loving, secure, and permanent home.

Today, more and more couples, and singles, looking to adopt, immediately consider their international options. They approach adoption agencies with a greater knowledge and understanding of the adoption process and greater familiarity about the nations from which they may adopt. The process, as discussed in the previous chapter, may appear daunting at first, but international adoption works. Families are formed with children from all over the globe.

Yet, while the concept remains the same—that of taking children out of orphanages in hopes of providing a better life—the players are changing constantly. Economic conditions notwithstanding, policies change. Countries that were open to international adoption five years ago have closed their borders today. Conversely, nations that were closed to international adoption as recently as a year ago may now have several thousand children placed with American families in a year. Viable countries such as Chile and the Dominican Republic, which once saw many children adopted into American families, are no longer open for intercountry adoption. Even a country like Romania, which once made the headlines with a flood of people looking to adopt in the early to mid-1990s have also closed their doors to international adoption. Meanwhile, programs continue to emerge and grow in nations that are now open to, or may soon be opening to, international adoption. Some of the countries that were part of the former Soviet Union, for example, now have put programs in place for adoption in recent years.

The Joint Council on International Children's Services (www.JCICS.org) provides the latest updates from countries regarding adoption. Also, web-sites like Adoption Travel.com (www.adoptiontravel.com) serve as a portal, offering a great number of links to informative web-sites on the various countries from which you can adopt. You can look at web-sites with information about Russia, China, Korea, or any leading "sending" country for numerous links.

Note: Most of the international links are updated, but some are not. Look at the dates as you read. If the information appears to be more than a year old, go to a different site. Adoption Travel.com offers plenty of alternatives.

Countries change their requirements and restrictions, and in some cases simply put adoption on hold for a period of time. Nonetheless, we've included some of the basic information as of 2002 for the five countries from which the most international adoptions have taken place in the United States, over the past two years. You can use these as a general guide and seek out similar information regarding other countries, such as Colombia or Mexico. These listings will also provide an example of what to look for when profiling a country that you may be considering. Remember to always double-check to see what has changed before you start pursuing the country (including the five listed below) and keep up with news and information while you are in the process of filing your paperwork. Many prospective adoptive parents have had to change their country of choice because of policy changes issued by the country while they were doing their paperwork, so it's always advisable to have a second choice ready. In most cases, such as the closing of Cambodia to international adoption in 2002, the nation will complete the adoptions that are already far along in the process (paperwork having been completed and assignment of a child issued).

South Korea

A very steady program has been in place for many years. There are four government-run, licensed Korean welfare agencies; Eastern Social Welfare Society, Holt Children Services, Social Welfare Society and Korea Social Services that handle all Korean adoptions. They keep all records of the child on file, which can be very beneficial should medical information be needed about a birth parent.

Marital status: Married couples are accepted, singles are not. Only one divorce per each partner is acceptable.

Age limits: Both individuals must be no older than forty-five.

Travel: There is no travel required—children are usually escorted to the United States.

The children: Under one year of age.

Other requirements: A minimum of $25,000 in family income. What may be considered an odd requirement is a "weight limit" requirement listed by a couple of the Korean agencies. The requirement states that you must be no more than 30 percent heavier than the normal body weight for an individual of a specific height. These two agencies use a weight/height chart to make their assessments.

Note: The time frame is about one year from applying to adopt from Korea until the baby is escorted to the United States. You can adopt healthy infants who receive good medical treatment and are living in foster homes with families (not in orphanages) until placement. Unlike most other countries, you will have to complete the adoption process in the United States, since you are not physically adopting in Korea. Until you complete the adoption, you are awarded a guardianship of that child.

Russia

There are more than 250,000 children in orphanages in Russia and the surrounding former Soviet Republic. Therefore, there are plenty of children available for adoption. To keep the adoption process running smoothly, the Russian government has begun accreditation, and reaccreditation of adoption agencies. (Check to see that the agency you are working with has been accredited.)

Marital status: Married couples and singles are accepted.

Age limits: At least twenty-five years of age and no more than forty-five years older then the child.

Travel: Two trips are required and a stay of anywhere from one to three weeks is typical. One trip is to identify your child and the other is to adopt your child.

The children: You can adopt babies as young as three months old.

Note: A Russian adoption can be completed in less than one year. The names of the children awaiting adoption are placed on a national adoption registry, where they must remain for several months before the child is freed for international placement. This is to allow for domestic adoption by Russians. However, there are very few adoptions by Russian families taking place. Once a child is in an orphanage, it is unlikely that he or she will be placed unless it is by international adoption. Care in orphanages varies with some facilities having a 10-to-1 ratio of caretakers per child. Russia, which used to send videotapes to United States-based agencies (which would then make referrals to U.S. couples and singles), no longer sends such tapes or photographs. Essentially, you are given an assignment when you travel, but can choose to decline an assignment once you arrive in Russia and can bring home a different baby.

Note: The Russian Adoption Handbook by John H. Maclean is an excellent source for Russian adoption information.

China

Since 1983, China has emerged as one of the leading nations from which children are adopted into the United States. Nearly 30,000 children have joined American families through adoption from the People's Republic of China. They are nearly all girls. The one-child rule in China means that families can be penalized for having more than one child. Often, if a family has a girl they will place her for adoption in hopes of having a boy.

If they are already raising a girl, and then have a boy as a second child, families will raise the child and face the penalties, whereas they will more likely place a girl with one of the orphanages for adoption.

Marital status: Married couples, divorce okay. Singles can adopt, but the process is far more difficult.

Age limits: Between thirty and fifty years of age.

Travel: One trip of about two weeks, which includes picking up the child, completing paperwork at the local and provincial levels as well as going to the U.S. Consulate in Guangzhou for processing the INS documents, which will allow the child to legally enter the United States.

The children: Girls from six months to two years of age.

Other requirements: The "dossier" or paperwork for China requires you to include two bareheaded photos of each applicant and half a dozen photos of "family life." China also requires four visits by the social workers who are conducting your home study. Singles must provide a signed statement to show that they are not homosexuals.

Note: The popularity of adopting from China has slowed the process down in recent years and has increased the waiting time (more than one year for the entire process). There is a great deal of paperwork for all international adoptions, and China is certainly no exception. Certified documents go to the China Center of Adoption Affairs (CCAA) in Beijing in several dossiers and also to the INS. The government also receives information from orphanages throughout China on each child. They then essentially make the "match" of child and family, and the referral goes through the agency with which you are working. You are then provided with a photo and medical records. Until they are adopted, the children are living in orphanages, in which conditions vary greatly.

Ukraine

Since 1996, when a moratorium on adoption was lifted, Ukraine has become one of the most viable sources for adoptive families. Unlike most international adoption, however, there is no preselection of children for placement. You are offered a child when you arrive at the orphanage. U.S.-based agencies that have successfully established Ukrainian adoption programs can walk you through the rather complicated process. Make sure to check and see that the agency has established such a program and talk to others who have worked with them. It is suggested that you contact the U.S. consulate in Ukraine to make sure all procedures have been followed before attempting to complete the adoption process. The government office responsible for adoptions in Ukraine is called the Cabinet of Ministries.

Marital status: Married couples, divorced okay, or singles.

Age limits: Minimum twenty-five years of age.

Travel: One trip that may easily last three weeks.

The children: Under one year of age.

Other requirements: American prospective parents looking to adopt must register with the Adoption Center in Ukraine. The Ministry of Education heads the Adoption Center, which houses all data on available children for adoption. A petition must also be submitted to the Adoption Center requesting registration as prospective adoptive parents. This will grant you permission to visit orphanages in order to meet and select a Ukrainian orphan.

Note: Adoption from Ukraine can be completed in less than one year. Ukrainian children eligible for adoption are living in orphanages. The orphanages are responsible for providing complete information on children available for adoption to the Adoption Center in Kiev within one week after they arrive at the orphanage. A file for each child is then available at the office of the Ministry of Education. The ministry tries for one month to place the child with a local Ukrainian family. The same procedure of first seeking a Ukrainian family is followed for a second month at a district ministry office. There are, however, few adoptions by Ukrainian families.

Also, because you are not receiving a referral in advance and are essentially selecting a child once you are in the Ukraine, you will be given medical records and the child's medical history once you are at the orphanage. You may wish to have an examination of the child done at this point to get more information on any significant medical conditions. This will be up to the discretion of the orphanage. You can contact the American Medical Center or the Clinic of Oil Industry, both located in Kiev for such examinations. Medical examinations cost under $100. Unless you have an English-speaking physician, it is crucial that you have a competent translator with you. Also, you should ask for the immunization history of the child from the orphanage. If there is no such history, discuss this with the physician. (This applies to any adoption taking place from an orphanage in any country.) You can get a waiver stating that all necessary vaccinations will be given within thirty days of your return to the United States.

Going to Warsaw

To get an immigrant visa for an adopted child from the Ukraine, you will need to visit the American embassy in Warsaw, Poland. It requires three-business days for an interview appointment. Plan to go to Warsaw after you leave Ukraine.

Guatemala

Adoptions from Guatemala have become more commonplace in recent years, with the number of immigrant visas issued rising from under 100 in 1996 to over 1,000 by 2001. Several government authorities are responsible for adoption, including the Department of Social Services, the Procuraduria General de la Nación, and the courts. Adoptions are completed either through agencies recognized in Guatemala or through independent attorneys. An attorney can work with both the birth and adoptive parents. A court-appointed social worker will also be involved and will file a report and review the home study of the adopting family. All information and documentation will be reviewed by the Procuraduria General de la Nación, which is the equivalent of the Solicitor General's office.

Marital status: Married couples, divorced okay, or single women.

Age limits: All prospective parents must be over 25 and under 55 years of age.

Travel: One trip that is generally around one week in length.

The children: Under one year of age.

Other requirements: Couples adopting from Guatemala must be married for at least two years. DNA tests are conducted on the child and birth mother before the INS will approve the orphan status of the child.

Note: The time frame from signing up with an agency or, hiring an adoption attorney to the completion of the adoption process will generally take ten months to one year. Before you travel, you will receive material from your agency or attorney's office including the child's Guatemalan passport. You will obviously need to bring this with you. A child from Guatemala must be declared abandoned by a Guatemala court for U.S. immigration purposes. This is true even if the birth mother or birth parents have signed an irrevocable consent to relinquish parental rights. Also, certified Spanish documents must be sent with all English-language documents.

The U.S. embassy in Guatemala City is available to help assist you overseas (502) 331-1541.

Remember; the regulations and parameters for adopting a child from overseas may change by the time you finish reading this book. Check to make sure that other restrictions have not been instituted. Look for the criteria provided in the examples above, such as minimum or maximum age for adoptive parents, marital status, and travel required, for any country from which you are looking to adopt.

Citizenship

Under INS regulations, if you have identified a child, or children, overseas and completed the adoption process in the child's country of birth, then you are considered to have a full and final adoption upon returning to the United States. The child is considered a United States citizen. If, however, the child or children, were not seen by the parent or parents, then adoption is necessary in the state where you will be residing. According to the INS, children who were not identified overseas by their

Visas

According to the INS, children who were seen by all relevant parents will have been issued IR-3 visas and will be eligible for automatic citizenship. Children who were not seen by all relevant parents prior to the overseas adoption (including all Korean adoptions) will be issued an IR-4 visas, and are required by the INS to be adopted in the United States before they can become citizens.

adoptive parent or parents are not considered to be United States citizens until they are adopted in the United States. Since most children adopted from Korea are escorted to the United States, the child is *not* automatically a citizen upon arriving here in conjunction with the Child Citizenship Law of 2000.

Readoption

If your child is adopted abroad and enters this country with you from overseas, according to the Child Citizenship Law of 2000, you generally do not need to readopt. There are several reasons, however, why some families choose to do a readoption.

Original documents from overseas could be lost or destroyed. Paul, an adoptive father from New York City, points out that his son's documents from their international adoption were stored safely in their bank vault. Unfortunately, their bank was located in the shopping mall below World Trade Center Tower One.

Readoption provides documents that are easier to read in American schools, courts, or wherever necessary. In addition, attorneys often recommend readoption to protect inheritance rights. Also, readoption can sometimes make it easier to obtain a birth certificate for your child.

Readoption laws, like all domestic adoption laws, are governed by the individual states. Some states have specific requirements and necessary paperwork for readoption, which may include post-placement visits. It's recommended that you check with the state court for the appropriate information in your state.

If you would like an attorney to assist you with a readoption, you might contact the American Academy of Adoption Attorneys.

A Passport for Your Child

Along with allowing your child to travel with you outside of the

United States, a United States passport is an important document for proof of citizenship. The Child Citizenship Act of 2000, which automatically recognizes your child adopted overseas as a United States citizen (under most circumstances) also allows you to obtain a U.S. passport for your child immediately. If, however, a child was not seen by all relevant parents prior to an overseas adoption, or was brought to the U.S. for adoption here, and traveled on an IR-4 visa, the child does not fall under the guidelines of the Child Citizenship Act of 2000 and must be adopted/readopted in the U.S. before automatic citizenship applies and before he or she can be issued a U.S. passport.

To get the passport, you will need to have the child's adoption decree, foreign passport with visa stamp, or a green card. You will also need to provide your own identification and proof of U.S. citizenship such as your own passport or birth certificate. You will then need to find a location to apply for a passport locally and bring your paperwork with you including adoption papers. Make copies in advance, since these will be sent to the U.S. Passport Office. Also, keep in mind that if your child's American name is not on the paperwork, or you have not gone through a readoption, then your child's passport will be issued in the name the child was given in his or her country of origin.

For online information on passports go to:

http://travel.state.gov/passport_services.html.

Chapter 11
TRAVELING

Unless you're adopting from Korea, where your child will be escorted to the United States, it is most likely that you will be traveling as part of the adoption process. Most adoptive parents agree that traveling to bring home a child is a trip unlike any other. It's one with a very different itinerary and far greater perks than postcards, souvenirs, or even piling up those frequent-flier miles. Adoption travel is both exciting and nerve-racking. And no matter how well organized you may think you are, when you are ready to leave the house, you will likely feel that you are not fully prepared. That's a very common feeling, especially if you're traveling overseas. Make a checklist in advance and post it in a highly visible place in your home. Include all the paperwork you will need on your list.

If you are heading overseas, you will need to obtain a passport, or double-check to see that the one you have is still valid. If you need to get a passport, do it early on in the process. Go to the post office or a local government passport office and get this chore out of the way. A passport usually takes about three or four weeks to process. It's recommended that you make a photocopy of the cover of your passport and of the photo picture page. This way you can put your passport in a safe place at your hotel and not have to carry it around with you. Also, should you lose the passport and need to have one reissued by the local embassy, you will have proof of your original, which will make the process much easier.

Prior to traveling overseas you also need to consult your doctor to make sure you have any necessary immunizations. In fact, it's recommended that you also consult with your doctor to discuss the country you're going to be visiting. It's in your best interests to know which—if any—illnesses you may likely be exposed to and have an antibiotic with you.

Most overseas adoption travel will commence when the adoption agency you are working with informs you that a child awaits your arrival overseas. The agency will usually send you overseas with other adoptive families and should provide some type of escort or guide for you while you are in the country. Some agencies will have someone meet you when you arrive. Whether an agency has escorts or provides some type overseas assistance is a very important question to ask when first starting the international adoption process. A good agency should not leave you on your own in a distant land. In fact, some agencies arrange for housing with host families.

Making Travel Plans

Some adoption agencies work regularly with travel agents who help book flight and hotel arrangements. In other cases, you will need to make your own travel arrangements. Northwest Airlines and KLM Royal Dutch Airlines offer what they call "Special Delivery" discount fares for adoptive families. The fares provide a significant discount (as much as 65 percent savings) plus the much-needed flexibility, since adoption travel plans will often need to be changed. The program includes destinations in Asia, Africa, Europe, and elsewhere and allows for cancellations or changes without penalties plus open returns and stopovers. This is particularly important since you may not know exactly when you will be returning. In addition, discounted fares are offered for the return trip for the newest family member.

Your other alternatives are to either find an adoption-friendly travel agency or call customer-service of a major airline and see what (if anything) they can do for your particular situation. Sometimes, should you reach an actual human being at the airlines customer service department, you can get positive results when explaining your adoption situation. It all depends on making a connection with someone who understands and has some authority to do something other than quote fares off a computer screen.

Here are a few adoption-friendly travel agencies that are able to secure low fares and provide you with the flexibility you need with your travel arrangements. A good travel agency for this purpose needs to be there for you before and *during* your travels. They should be reachable when you're overseas, should your plans go awry.

Adoption-Friendly Travel Agencies

All Ways International Travel (specializing in travel to Russia)
225 West 34th Street, Suite 2001
New York, NY 10122
212-947-0505
Web-site: www.awintl.com

Federal Travel & Cruises: Adoption Travel Services
3320 North Federal Highway; Suite 1
Lighthouse Point, FL, 33064
1-800-551-8666 or 954-942-8666

Web site: www.federaltravel.com
E-mail: adoptravel@federaltravel.com

Four Corners of the World
1200 Pearl Street, Suite 50
Boulder, CO 80302
1-888-930-3777
E-mail: tgallinek@aol.com

Music World Travel (specializing in China, Vietnam, Thailand, and Bulgaria)
319 South Peabody
Port Angeles, WA 98362
1-800-500-8431 or 360-452-8431
E-mail: mwtravel@olypen.com

While making travel arrangements, read up on the country you will be visiting. Travel guides or travel web-sites can prove helpful. If you are going to be living in another country for two or more weeks, you will want to be acquainted with some of the local customs. It's also important to familiarize yourself with the currency and the seasonal weather conditions. In addition, check out some sights to visit while you're there, since you may have plenty of time on your hands.

Do not let the stress associated with the adoption process get the better of you. Remember that while you are in another country, you are playing by their rules and adhering to

Visas

Ask your adoption agency and your travel agent about visa requirements, which vary from country to country. In most cases, you will need to get a visa for your child. It's also important to check with your travel agent to see if you have a stopover in another country on the return trip. You and your child will need a visa for that country as well.

their customs and laws. You are adopting a child from *their* country, and United States laws do not influence their policies on adoption. Therefore, you need to understand their concern about documentation and proper procedures. It's been proven time and time again that an ounce of kindness and being polite will work in your favor. It's also very much in your favor to have an adoption agency that has established ties with the other nation and provides full escort services, which means translators and personalized attention.

Steve and Mary, last mentioned in chapter nine, had no idea of how much special attention they would get while they were in Ukraine:

"Our agency did a wonderful job. We traveled with another couple from the agency and had an "entourage," of sorts, traveling with us. We were not allowed to go anywhere without our escorts, which was fine because they took great care of us. We had a translator, a driver, someone who handled the bureaucratic process; there was even someone who cooked for us in the house that the agency had us staying in. It was all part of the agency's overall fee. They took care of the paperwork and helped us shop when we needed to buy things for the baby. The main thing is that they were there for us, which was so important when you're far from home . . . and nervous. We'd been trying to adopt for some time and had not been successful with our domestic efforts, so for us it was very reassuring to be with an agency that was very supportive.

"We eased our way into being parents slowly. Until our court date in Kiev, we were allowed to visit our son in the orphanage only for a few hours a day. When we finally had the court date, Steve went to get the baby's birth records, so I was alone with our son in the house where we were staying. I was very nervous. I started feeding him formula, which we had brought from home. The orphanage had given us a list of what he ate.

He had never had formula before, but he took it. I recommend to anyone traveling to bring powdered formula. We were fortunate that the stores near the house where we were staying had diapers and plenty of other supplies, but you want to be prepared in case you can't get what you need. As it turned out, the clothes we brought were all the wrong size, but the couple who was with us gave us some of theirs and we bought some new ones in a local store. You need to be flexible and ready to buy whatever you need when making this kind of a trip.

"All in all, I'd have to say we had a very smooth trip, mostly because the agency was with us at all times."

When preparing to travel, talk to other families who have returned recently from the same country. Through your adoption agency or a local support group, you should be able to find another family who has adopted from the country you have selected. Also, you can go to Rainbow Kids (www.rainbowkids.com), a web-site with e-mail lists where you can find plenty of information by connecting with others who have adopted from the country where you are headed. Yahoo.com (included in Rainbow Kids) also has adoptive parent groups on-line which can provide some of the most up-to-date suggestions plus the nitty-gritty details of life abroad for an extended time. They may also have suggestions on how to get the most out of your stay.

Laurie Kroll, an adoption professional who adopted what she calls "virtual twin boys" from Vietnam (same birthday, but born in different provinces) suggests that you inquire about a Western-trained pediatrician in the country. *"Through Rainbowkids.com or in a support group, you should try to get the name of a pediatrician that you can visit abroad. We took our boys to a pediatrician in Vietnam who had been trained in Western medicine."*

Such a pediatrician can usually be found if you are traveling to, or will be near a major city. A Western-trained doctor will be able to assess any illnesses common to the region, but will also be able to tell you how to best treat the child once you return home. Thus, he or she can provide you with medical information that helps you in making the transition.

It is also worth mentioning that when Laurie and her husband traveled to pick up their virtual twins, they brought their seven-year-old twin daughters on the journey. Laurie called it the trip of a lifetime, despite the cost. *"We felt that since the family had been the four of us for many years, it would be a major adjustment for them to absorb two little attention getters at once! I felt it was critical that they be part of the process, and that included making the journey with us, staying in the hotel room, seeing the sights and sharing the culture."* Laurie, and others who have taken older children along on adoption travel, have found that with the right planning it can be a very rewarding experience for your older child.

What to Bring

Important Documents

First, buy an inexpensive valise or briefcase in which to carry documents when you travel. It's best to have one specific place to keep your essential adoption and travel papers so that you do not find yourself rummaging through your suitcase in search of the papers you need. Laurie Kroll recommends that everyone make up an extra dossier to take with them. *"If the country requirements are for two dossiers, get three and if they require three, get four. It's much easier to have an extra one with you than to try to get paperwork sent to you from overseas."*

Double-check what you need with your agency/attorney and triple-check that you have it before leaving the house. Also, make sure you have copies safely at home so that mom, dad, a neighbor, or friend can FedEx anything you have forgotten. In addition, make sure someone has access to your home when you're away so they can locate papers you may have left behind or just to help you prepare for the arrival of your son, daughter, or both.

Money!

Take some cash, but mostly traveler's checks which you can cash overseas as you need them. Credit cards can be useful in large cities, but you can't depend on them since some places won't take them, especially outside of major cities. Also, carry money or traveler's checks in a safe place and convert your money little by little as you feel you need it.

A Camera

A camera is important for three reasons: First, you will want to document your journey for friends and family, to show your child(ren) photos of their homeland that are not strictly out of a book and—most important—to take photos of your child and have them sent to doctors elsewhere to review and evaluate health issues. For this you should buy, rent, or borrow a digital camera.

Don't forget:

Backpacks

Waist packs— good for smaller items so you can keep your hands free.

A bag that can be used as a diaper bag if you're adopting a baby.

Duct tape for when your suitcase breaks as it's tossed onto a baggage carousel or for covering those electrical outlets in the hotel room where your toddler will be scrambling about.

Easy-to-prepare foods. Boxes of cereal, snack packs, crackers, chips, and other comfort foods which are good to have on hand. If you bring instant foods that require you to add water, bring bottled water.

Pepto-Bismol. You (and your stomach) may not be ready for a steady diet of food prepared in another country. Imodium is also a good idea.

A calling card from Sprint, AT&T, or another major phone company.

Travel outfits for the baby, including several daytime outfits, pullovers, sleepers, bibs, outerwear and so on. Have disposable diapers on hand for a baby or toddler.

For an older child, try to find out his or her size and bring loose-fitting or slightly larger clothing—better being wrong with something that's a little big than something that's too small.

Powdered formula—enough for the duration of your stay—and bottled water.

Important phone numbers and e-mail addresses. Be ready to contact your adoption agency, travel agency, attorney, family, and pediatrician or a doctor who specializes in children adopted from other countries. Bring the numbers of the U.S. embassy and consulate.

Medication including an antihistamine, Lotrimin cream for athlete's foot, and Tylenol.

Baby shampoo and a thermometer.

Age-appropriate toys for older children.

Keep in mind that in most countries, you can find major hotels chains like Marriott, Hilton and Sheratons in the larger cities. You can purchase some of what you need for your stay at the hotel shops. The more cosmopolitan the city, the less you will need to bring. In addition, most of the major hotel chains have business centers. This will provide you with all the familiar communication tools including e-mail and fax capabilities, thus making it unnecessary to carry around an expensive laptop.

Todd Gallinek of Four Corners of the World Travel, an adoption-travel specialist helping families from all over the nation, recommends that you plan carefully so you have what you need but do not take too much, if at all possible.

"You don't want to take too much with you because you'll want to have your hands free with a child. Also, there are maximums for luggage which are now forty pounds per person." Gallinek, who is on twenty-four-hour notice, points out that good travel agents for adopting families should be reachable whenever you need them. "Families need to have a contact number wherever they are. For this reason I tell people traveling for adoption that they should not buy discount tickets over the internet. There is no support desk, and you will likely need to make changes with your plans." In addition, Gallinek adds that if you need to make connecting flights within a country, you can save money by purchasing tickets for those flights within the countries themselves. For some travelers, however, the security factor of having those connecting tickets in advance is worth the extra money, as long as there is flexibility with those tickets.

Travel hints: Do not wear your finest jewelry or your Rolex. You do not want to call attention to yourself.

Your cell phone won't work overseas. You can however, usually rent one in many foreign countries for the two or three weeks you'll be staying there. It's much less expensive than using the hotel phones.

Gifts

"We also brought gifts," adds Laurie Kroll. *"In a monthlong stay in a foreign country, you connect with a lot of people. We brought small items such as picture frames, calendars, and inexpensive watches to give to people. We gave necklaces to the caregivers of our sons. When we traveled, Beanie Babies were very popular, so we did a local fund raising drive to collect money and took one hundred Beanie Babies for the other children we met in the town, many of whom were living in*

conditions that were just as poor as the children in the orphanages."

Says Mary: "We were told by our agency to bring handbags and make up."

"These were for the orphanage director and the care takers. Being a nurse, I also was able to get children's Tylenol and Motrin at cost and took them to the orphanage. I knew these were probably things they would need. The director had never seen Motrin before and I explained to use it when a child had a very high fever. She appreciated this gift more than the handbag."

Agencies will generally suggest what you should bring. Families who have returned from abroad can also fill you in on what gifts were well received and what is needed in these orphanages.

Coming Home

You will need to be proactive concerning your return trip. This means confirming your return flight plans as soon as your adoption documentation is completed and everything is in order for you to leave. Remember: You will need a ticket for your new family member. There are usually significantly discounted fares for children and especially for infants who do not get an assigned seat. While you are making your return-trip plans (or your travel agent is making them), if you have an older child, take a moment to request a kid's meal. Most airlines have them, but unless you request them in advance, you cannot get them. Also, after making your return trip plans, but before departing, remember to gather up all of your paperwork. You may need to have all of your papers on hand for customs, so double-check that everything is signed, sealed, and easily accessible.

Confirm your seats at least seventy-two hours in advance and when traveling with a young child or toddler, try to get the bulkhead seats—they are roomier. Often, once you've confirmed that you are indeed on the flight, you can get the bulk-head seats simply by arriving at the gate early.

Aboard the plane, you'll immediately realize that with a child, "traveling light" is a thing of the past. You'll need a change of clothes for your little one, a backpack in which to carry things (you'll want to keep your hands as free as possible), food or formula, wipes and diapers for a baby, some activities or toys and gum for older children (for blocked ears, including your own). While abroad, make a list of all that you think you will need for a long flight home.

You will then need to pass through customs at the airport. Have passports and visas handy. Don't bring fruits, plants, or anything else that could possibly slow you down at customs. Explain that you were traveling to adopt and have your adop-tion paperwork handy. Waiting at customs can be exasperating, but remain calm and focus your attention on your child.

At some point during the flight, your child or even children will fall asleep. If you're still awake, this will give you a little time to unwind, relax, and realize that you have indeed "done it!" It's a good feeling when you finally have those few moments to take a deep breath and appreciate that all your efforts to adopt have finally paid off.

Customs: Two Lines

When returning from overseas, there are generally two lines at U.S. customs; one for citizens and one for non-citizens. Remember; your baby is a citizen if you've completed your adoption overseas. Get on the citizen line. It's likely that you will need to go into another room, anyway, to present the baby's paperwork.

Getting to Know You

Your child has a history—even a brief one—so learn as much as you can about that history. Talk with the caregiver(s) in the orphanage or foster home and get a good understanding of what life was like for your child in the orphanage. Find out what he liked to eat, whether he liked to be held, and how he reacted to meeting new people. Also, find out as much as you can about your child's health history. All children are very different in their characteristics and personalities. Get to know something about their early years. For this reason, you will want to have someone with you who will translate so that you can communicate with the caregivers more easily. Whatever you learn can help you and your child in the transitional stage that will follow.

Most likely, you will visit with the child for several days before taking your child from the orphanage or foster home. During these times, talk with caregivers or foster parents and observe their interaction with your son or daughter as well as begin your own bonding process. Remember; you are still "an unfamiliar person" to your baby who has not anticipated your arrival in the same manner you have anticipated this important meeting. You've been planning for months and dreaming about holding a baby. He or she has been growing, completely unaware that anyone is coming to change his or her life.

Sheila, mentioned in Chapter 2, flew to China with her mom to begin life as a single parent through adoption. She talks about her first few days overseas with her new daughter LuAnn:

"There was a group of us working with the same agency who flew over together. We had been in China for a few days before we actually got to see our daughters. There was paperwork to sign and a weekend to contend with before a day of travel from Beijing to Dianbai, the town the orphanage was in. When the bus arrived in Dianbai the orphanage director got on the bus and said we should go to our hotel in Maoming and the girls would be brought to us. At that point there was a rush of emotions—fear something was wrong and disappointment as more waiting was imminent.

"Later that evening, we were in our room after dinner, when I

heard a baby crying. We opened the door and almost all the expectant parents in our group were already in the hall; the babies had arrived and were in the room with our guide and representatives from the orphanage. One by one each baby's name was called and placed in the arms of her new parent(s). As my daughter was given to me, all I could think of was 'here I am in a strange place in the middle of China with this baby in my arms who doesn't know I am her mommy yet. What do I do?'

"The guide told us to take the babies into our rooms and undress them to make sure there were no marks or anything else on the child that concerned us. The orphanage representatives stayed for a very short while to talk to us . . . not nearly enough time to ask them all I wanted to. My head was swimming with ideas of what to do next with this strange child I was now holding. Luckily, my mom was there with a clear mind and we went into the room, fed her, changed her into PJs, and put her to sleep. Despite the strangeness of the place and all that was happening, my daughter slept very well that night, which is more than I can say for myself. I spent the night staring at her sleeping.

"The next few days were very difficult. My daughter did not cry. When I held her she clung to me as if for dear life. The other children seemed to be starting to bond, but not my daughter. Also, she was not responding to any sounds. We made all sorts of loud noises around her, and she never turned her head to see where the noise came from. We were beginning to think she was deaf. The orphanage director insisted that was not the case, and he brought her main caregiver to call her name to show that my daughter would respond. She didn't respond to the voice at all. The woman seemed genuinely concerned for my daughter, which was good to see; I had been told she was a good baby and favored at the orphanage, but it was nice to see her caregiver show concern for her. She finally responded to the sound of metallic paper crackling. At least it was a start. And after an entire day of not letting her out *of my arms, she seemed to start bonding. Yeah! Although the time spent in China was hard, I had been fortunate to contact a pediatrician prior to the adoption. I called her and she called me each day while my baby's health was uncertain. This helped keep me sane."*

Today LuAnn is six. She has overcome initial developmental delays and is doing well in school. Together with Sheila, they make a great mother-daughter team.

Not only will you be new parents, but you'll be new parents thousands of miles from home. This will mean that you'll be bonding, while completing your adoption and trying to communicate in another language. The more assistance provided by your adoption agency during your stay (which can often be two weeks or more), the less stressful your journey will be. If you're a single parent like Sheila, it's to your advantage to have support, which may be your mom or a friend who could manage to get off work or plan her vacation with you in mind.

> **Childproofing**
>
> *If you're adopting a toddler, he or she can get around the hotel room in a hurry. Therefore, you'll need to childproof. Block off all electrical sockets, sharp corners, and anything else that appears potentially hazardous, then sit on the floor and look around. You'll discover more from the child's-eye view than you imagined.*

While the adoption process can be stressful, you will not want to exhibit stress in front of the child. It's important that you provide a nurturing, consistent environment. Some adopted children will reject being held. Others will respond favorably. Either way, don't panic. You will both adjust.

Domestic Travel

There are no advertised adoption fares for domestic travel. That doesn't mean that a good travel agent won't be able to help you, or that customer service won't be accommodating. Fewer people

Todd's Ten Travel Tips

Todd Gallinek has helped over one hundred families traveling internationally over the past three years. Here he provides ten key travel tips.

1. *Always check the visa regulations for each country, then make a copy of the visa with the country's stamp on it, as well as the stamps in your stopover countries if there are any.*

2. *Use the hotel business center rather than bringing your own laptop. If you do bring a laptop, remember to get a converter, and don't leave the laptop in the hotel room.*

3. *Be careful with hotel-room safes. Often that are not bolted down, and the entire safe can be stolen.*

4. *Rent a cell phone and just pay for the minutes you use it.*

5. *Bring sunscreen if you are going to a warm climate.*

6. *International carriers can provide a bassinet for infants up to 20 pounds or under 18 inches.*

7. *Get travel insurance for lost luggage, etc. You can spend $200 for a good policy to cover a family going overseas.*

8. *Take one credit card. American Express is not as widely accepted as Visa or Master Card.*

9. *You'll get a better rate cashing traveler's checks at a bank.*

10. *Be aware of what's going on around you. Pickpockets look for travelers both in this country and abroad.*

are flying, so the airlines can provide better customer service—which doesn't mean they will. A travel agent familiar with adoption, such as those listed above, are often your best bet, since dealing with customer service is a hit-or-miss proposition.

Domestic travel is obviously less stressful than overseas travel for obvious reasons. Shorter flights, no language barriers, no customs to pass through and no visas or passports are necessary.

In addition, when you travel within the United States, you need not take quite as much along. You'll want to have some baby items with you, such as powdered formula for a newborn or infant or some toys to occupy an older child, but you won't need to stock up on items for your journey since you'll likely be able to locate a 7-Eleven or Wal-Mart to pick up what you need. You can also use your credit cards almost everywhere or find an ATM machine if you need cash.

If you're bringing home an infant, you will not need to pay an additional fare. Children under the age of two fly for free. Children from age two up through ten will generally receive a good discount (often 50 percent) off the full one-way fare. Again, you will want to get to the gate early in hopes of getting the bulkhead seats for more room.

Tim Swanson, the adoptive father of two, runs Federal Travel and Cruises, in Lighthouse Point, Florida. It has been specializing in adoptive travel for several years and now works with anywhere from 500 to 1,000 families annually, traveling domestically or internationally. Swanson suggests getting paper tickets:

If you have paper tickets, you can get changes made more easily. Electronic tickets only show up in their computers, and it makes it more difficult for you to make changes. In adoption-related travel, you will often have to make changes since you won't know when the birth mother is going to deliver or how long you might be staying until the interstate compact is signed. Also, many people go on-line and get a good price on a ticket, and then have to make changes, but there's no one to contact because the service is not there. It's important to have good service when making adoption-travel plans.

Unlike international travel, where adoption agencies often have recommended hotels or host families providing housing (plus guides who will serve as drivers), you are usually on your own regarding domestic travel plans. Often a travel agency can get a better deal on a hotel and rental car. If you are looking for a hotel yourself, try to find one that is convenient to both the hospital and some shopping for essentials. Look for hotels chains. This is not the time for a bed-and-breakfast with occasional running water.

Ask about cribs and other child-friendly accommodations. (Also, make sure to have your cell phone, since you can significantly increase your adoption expenses by using hotel phones!) Likewise, look for Hertz, Budget, or another major rental-car company that is consumer friendly. Remember, some rental-car companies are far more corporate friendly than consumer friendly.

As for traveling with an infant, "Each airline regulation is different but for the most part they do not inquire about the age of the child," says Swanson. "Families can get a letter from a doctor if they need to, but generally it doesn't come up."

Doctors will tell you that infants can travel by plane without any problem.

There is still no law, providing on-board baby seats for infants. The airlines lobbied against such a law, feeling that it was too costly. Therefore, you will most often have your son or daughter on your lap for most of the journey in whatever type of baby carrier you have brought. Swanson will often arrange the ticketing so parents have an empty seat between them, which they use as a seat for the baby.

Amid the busy adoption process and all of the paperwork and planning, travel plans can sometimes get lost. Therefore, it's worth taking a couple of hours well in advance and listing what you will need to take along. It's recommended to have an umbrella stroller (which can be checked at the gate), a diaper bag, some formula, and diapers. Otherwise try to travel light. You can take up to two bags of 70 pounds each domestically, but try not to reach this limit—remember, the most important cargo will also be returning with you.

Chapter 12
ADOPTION AND THE MEDIA

Adoptive families today take pride in how they came to be a family. The days of secrecy and shame are a thing of the past regarding adoption. Nonetheless, in the media, stereotypes, myths, and inaccuracies still linger. The media, in their haste to find "entertaining stories" and compelling drama, often overlook the realities of adoption in favor of fantasies and erroneous portrayals.

Of course, we all know that television programs are not a slice of real life—not even the so-called reality programs. Nonetheless, television *does* contribute to the shaping of views and attitudes, most significantly those of younger viewers.

Moving Backward?

Oddly enough, as adoption has become more widely accepted in society, it has taken a turn toward misrepresentation in the world of episodic television. The sensitivity of television programs dealing with adoption has taken a bold step backward. In the late 1970s, the character Jerry (the dentist) on the old *Bob Newhart Show* was an adult adoptee. The subject, when broached, was done so with sensitivity. Other shows followed suit. Murray, and Ted Baxter, leading characters on the old *Mary Tyler Moore Show*, both adopted children without great fanfare or an unrealistic or sensational portrayal of adoption. The two boys in the comedy *Different Strokes* depicted minority children adopted by a white family. Transracial adoption was displayed with pride at a time when it was still just emerging from the closet in America.

As adoption moved into clearer focus in America, it moved farther *out* of focus on television. *L.A. Law,* a rather well-researched quality program of the early 1990s had the classic scene of a birth mother arriving out of the blue and taking her child back in a heart-wrenching, child's-best-interest hearing involving two of the show's stars, thus illustrating a less than 1 percent probability as typical of the adoption process. The episode sent an extremely inaccurate message about adoption to millions of would-be adoptive parents: that independent adoption is fraught with great risk. The 1990s comedy/drama *Sisters* also painted a negative picture of adoption when one of four featured sisters on this long-running program adopted a child, then decided to overturn the adoption herself after she kept bumping into the birth mother everywhere she went. This, too, was far from realistic.

While adoption grew in the public awareness as a viable alternative for couples and singles wanting a child, it became one of the stumbling blocks for television couples looking to start a family. *"Why couldn't one of the five kids on the hit* Cosby Show *of the late 1980s have simply been adopted?"* asked an adoptive parent. *"It would have normalized the situation if they had simply been part of the household of such a popular series."*

Despite a highly praised episode of the sitcom *Coach,* which handled the subject of adoption in a very positive manner, many television shows have missed the mark, sending poor messages to an audience that generally knows little about adoption. Even Disney programs and films have routinely included comments or subplots that are insensitive. For example, programs have referred to adoption as a threat, with comments by kids such as "Mom, could you put him [little brother] up for adoption?" This tells children that if you misbehave, you'll be placed for adoption. It tells adopted children that they must have been bad, and that's why they were adopted. Other programs and films have featured an odd character and questioned whether he or she was adopted as an explanation of being different or exhibiting strange behavior.

Unfortunately, episodic television has routinely been insensitive to the adopted child sitting in front of the set and has not used the same political correctness or sensitivity that has been afforded to other minorities. Unlike most minorities in this country, adoptive families do not have many high profile speakers on their behalf. Jamie Lee Curtis, author of a children's book on adoption, went on the talk-show circuit and sang the praises of adoption. The late Dave Thomas, founder of Wendy's, was an adult adoptee, adoptive father, and strong, vocal advocate of adoption. Thomas not only started the Dave Thomas Foundation, which has been responsible for placing thousands of foster care children into permanent homes, but he also started an annual uplifting holiday television special called *Home for the Holidays*, which promotes adoption.

Pushed Too Far

While it's impossible to fight every battle with the broadcast media, there have been some issues that could not be overlooked. The overwhelming message that adoption was anything but permanent in the animated film *Stuart Little* generated numerous calls and letters of complaints to the studio and producers of the film. In another example, advance promotion of a new television program generated attention within the adoption community. In early 2001, a WB TV program called *Maybe I'm Adopted* was in development. It was essentially about a girl who felt that she didn't fit in with her offbeat family. While the concept was well intentioned, the adoptive community did not want a television show telling young teens (the target audience) that adoption means you are different. Letters poured in from adoption groups across the country. The show premiered in the fall of 2001 with the new title, *Maybe It's Me*. The adoptive community had responded, and the producers had heard their message.

Naïveté is usually the culprit for insensitivity toward adoptive families and particularly toward children. For example, a recurring sound byte popped up during one network's teen TV programming asked the musical question "Why are some families giving back adopted children?" It was followed by "Details on the news at six." The story was about some parents who had adopted special-needs children from Russia and were considering disrupting the adoptions. To the adoptive children watching television, however, it appeared that they could be "given away." When I called to discuss this sound bite, an associate producer explained, "Well, these shows are really for teens and younger kids shouldn't be watching." True, but younger children do watch teen television programs and even a teen does not want to hear that he or she could be given back, even if not in the literal sense. Adoption means a permanent family and to exploit the idea that it means anything else to draw attention to a news story is misleading to the general public as well as offensive to adoptive families.

It is therefore important that adoption support groups and everyone else touched by adoption educate those around them. The Kudos section of the Celebrate Adoption web-site: (www.celebrateadoption.org) provides a place to complain about negative adoption portrayals on television or in the media. It also lists names and addresses where people can write to the networks responsible.

As you become a member of the adoption community, which means being touched by adoption in any manner, you will become more aware of how adoption is presented. The more you learn, the more discerning you will become when confronted by episodic television and films that present adoption. It is then up to you to speak up when you feel that the message is being presented inaccurately.

In the News

The proliferation of prime-time television news-magazine programs has created a need for more so-called human-interest stories. Thus, we see more adoption stories emerging on television, on programs like *48 Hours and 20/20.*

Depending on the network and the tone, the stories have varied from poorly researched and produced to extremely effective. When thirteen couples were stranded in Cambodia, unable to leave the country with their children because of an ongoing investigation of the practices of an adoption agency, it was a television news-magazine story that directed great attention to the case. The attention helped facilitate a resolution of the problem, which was favorable for the families involved.

Adoption has showed up in news reports on numerous occasions. The tearful Baby Jessica story tugged at the hearts of millions as she was taken from the only home she had ever known and returned to her birth parents after a long legal battle. Stories from the Olympics in Seoul (as mentioned earlier), embarrassed Korea by claiming that babies were the nation's biggest export (hence shutting the nation down to adoption for a short time). A national story surfaced in 2001 about a twenty-two-year-old in New Mexico who learned that his adoptive parents had allegedly kidnapped him to keep his birth mother from taking him back. The adoptive parents later pleaded guilty to kidnapping charges. A story of child abuse by newly adoptive parents while en route home from Russia also gained national attention as other passengers turned them in.

The reality is that some stories can serve as a call to action and help, while other stories are simply exploiting the oddities that occur in a very nonscientific process. The stories selected for the broadcast or print media are most often not the stories that most accurately represent adoption. "Family successfully adopts a child, story at eleven!" does not make for the heart-wrenching, or hard-hitting news that producers are looking for when they use adoption to bolster their viewing audience. Again, the best you can do as a viewer is to respond with calls or letters to news producers when you see stories that are greatly exploiting the negatives without much foundation in fact.

Note: Media watchers note that negative adoption stories outnumber positive adoption stories two to one.

Sincere Misconceptions

While much of the media is naïve about the adoption process and, because of time constraints and tight deadlines, may take shortcuts in the areas of research and accuracy, there are writers and psychologists who take to the airwaves (or printed page) with a great understanding of adoption from personal experience. Many such adoption books are enlightening and provide touching personal accounts. Others, however lack a sense of much-needed objectivity because the author is using the book (often unconsciously) as a means of either venting or preaching.

A few years ago, there was a song called "Blame Canada." In a humorous verse, this Oscar-nominated little ditty essentially made Canada the cause of whatever went wrong. Unfortunately there is a small camp of writers and speakers who will preach the notion that adoption and the trauma of separation takes a lifetime of work to overcome. They blame adoption for all that goes wrong for adult adoptees. Authors, convinced that their pain is universal, and that adoption, like alcoholism, requires a twelve-step program, higher powers of healing and other lifelong healing mechanisms, will prey upon the emotions of other adoptees. The reality, as evidenced by the writings and interviews with numerous adult adoptees, clearly indicates that the adult adoptee has a broad range of emotions. Many adoptees do not feel—and never did feel—that their lives would be complete only through finding their birth parents or working their way through programs and ritualized healing processes for the trauma of separation. There would be no successful international adoptions if this was the prevailing theory and if everyone followed a single boilerplate emotional response to having been adopted. Clearly, as no two adoptions are alike, neither are the circumstances, situations, or emotional responses of the people involved. When it comes to adoption, the notion that *"everyone feels this way"* or *"everyone experiences such-and-such"* must always be looked at with a grain of salt, because such an argument—and this holds true for nearly any subject—can rarely ever carry much weight.

"No, I didn't spend most of my youth bemoaning the fact that I was adopted and looking for a twelve-step program to make me function and come to terms with this reality. I appreciated and loved my adoptive parents and enjoyed what my life was all about. Sure, I had questions and issues about adoption,

but it was a part of my life, like issues about dating, sex, self-esteem, and plenty of other concerns," responds Miriam, a twenty-nine-year-old adoptee, when asked if she needed to join a group or follow a program to work through her feelings about having been adopted. *"I dealt with the issues as they came up in my life but did not feel that having been adopted was an over-riding theme. I met my birth mother when I was twenty-two. Until that time I didn't think I was ready emotionally and didn't really feel a need to meet her."* Chapter 23 has more information on adult adoptees.

The Effects

When adoption is depicted in a negative manner, it can affect children adversely—not only those who were adopted, but all children. For this reason it is important to teach children (and adults) what adoption is all about.

A marvelous quote can be found on a very adoption-friendly web-site, that is appropriately called Celebrate Adoption. The quote comes from a ten-year-old boy who said, "It is not adoption that is a problem, but what everyone thinks about it."

Perceptions of adoption are learned, very often from the media. Television influences how we look at all facets of life. The increase in adolescent eating disorders, for example, has often been tied to the unrelenting desire to have the perfect "TV" (and magazine-cover) image and appearance. This is what is promoted by network television and the advertisers who sponsor it. Therefore, it is no surprise that inaccurate depictions of adoption can evoke the same negative perceptions.

"Studies"

There are studies, and then there are "studies." Adoption includes a wide range of possible scenarios, many of which can be interpreted in many ways (depending on which member of the triad is doing the interpreting). Because of this potentially limitless number of variables, the more scientific the study, the less likely it's validity. One study, for example, said that adopted children were more likely to steal things than other children. When pressed for more details, the clinician behind the study elaborated. It became clear that her study was based on her study group, consisting of children who came to her for behavioral problems. Most of these children had been adopted, primarily at an older age. Therefore, the many adopted children, who did *not* come to see her (or the overall population of adopted children) was not represented—only a subgroup that already had been considered to have behavioral problems. As it turned out, many of these children specifically came to her *because* they were stealing.

The point of all of this is that there are organizations and even foundations that are funded by grants to conduct Ph.D.-level research studies in areas that cannot usually turn up valid answers. In addition, such researchers are being funded to *find something*—not to find typical results. Therefore, you should take such clinical adoption studies you may read with a grain of salt. Also remember that many clinical researchers may not spend much time with real families formed by adoption, which is what adoption is all about.

Overly Sensitive?

There is also a case for oversensitivity.

A woman called me one day, frantic about a film that she had seen with her young daughter. In the film, a man found out he was adopted and was very upset about it. He was, as she put it, "very negative about adoption." The woman on the phone was aghast and rushed her young daughter out to the refreshment stand for a while during this "awful movie." Of course, her young daughter did not pick up on this minor subplot in a movie that was otherwise geared for kids. But the mother's reaction told the child that something was very wrong.

Often a child will not pick up on subtleties that adults will grasp. They may be quite unaware of what you hear and take objection to. In addition, in the case of this particular example, the reaction of an adult being upset to find out that he was adopted was a natural reaction to being kept in secrecy about such an important aspect of his life. If nothing else it points out the importance of telling even a very young child that he or she was adopted. This way, the child can grow up comfortably with the notion of adoption and what it is all about. By the way, this movie had a positive ending about adoption, and I received no other phone calls from outraged parents.

Weigh the facts and evaluate the overall theme and meaning before jumping the gun. You also need to evaluate the situation from the vantage point of your child and not overreact. Adoptive families will be less effective in educating the world about adoption if they appear to be supersensitive and ready to fly off the handle at the mere mention of the word "adoption."

Chapter 13
ADOPTION FRAUD

No matter how emotional and personal adoption is, there is still a business aspect involved. You are working with agencies, attorneys, and other professionals. And, where there is business—especially one tugging at your emotions—there is, unfortunately, room for dishonesty and fraud.

Fortunately, the unscrupulous players lurking around the business side of adoption are still the vast minority, and most adoptions are completed with reputable professionals and without the scenarios or difficulties discussed in this chapter. Nevertheless, it is worthwhile for you to know what can take place, so that you can exercise caution.

When you are adopting a child from thousands of miles away, through the good word of people *you* do not know very well, who are working with people *they* may not know very well, there may be some improprieties along the way. What can you do about it? Several things. First, be informed. Do your homework, learn as much as you can, and be proactive in your approach. Ask questions and expect answers. Know exactly how your child will come into your life and as much as you can about his or her background. Get references from others who have worked with the agencies, attorneys, or social workers whom you are planning to hire. One of the things we stress more than anything else at meetings of the Adoptive Parents Committee (an adoption support group) is networking with other people and gathering information.

What Constitutes Adoption Fraud?

First, let me clarify that adoption fraud is *not* when a birth mother changes her mind. Adoption fraud is also *not* when you are working in good faith with an agency or international attorney, and the country you are working with closes its doors to adoption. These are heartbreaking circumstances, but do not constitute adoption fraud.

Adoption fraud most often occurs either when you are not provided with full disclosure of information, or when money is paid for specific services or expenses and is used for other purposes.

The most commonly heard cases of adoption fraud center around information being withheld about a child's physical and/or mental health. Agencies may not only withhold information but in some instances may simply misrepresent the child's emotional and physical history. Lack of such information is a significant concern for adoptive families and can be grounds for fraud if it is proved that the agency knew about the medical or psychological problems and did not disclose the information.

Adoption fraud also occurs when an agency charges fees to be paid to the orphanage as a donation and does not send that money to the orphanage. Agencies, attorneys, or facilitators who accept money for a specific purpose, such as birth-mother expenses, and do not use the money for such expenses are also misrepresenting themselves.

Preventive Measures

If you are looking to adopt from China and are using Agency

A, then find someone else through a support group, on-line chat, or through networking who has adopted from China using Agency A. Find out about the agency costs, services, manner of handling problems and, very importantly, how the agency worked overseas. What orphanage did this person visit? With whom did they work in China? Ask people questions about the entire process from signing up through receiving medical information to picking up your child overseas. Ask families if there were significant medical conditions that they were not informed about.

In addition to checking with references, you can contact the Better Business Bureau in the city or town where the agency is located and in other locations where they are licensed to do adoptions. Spend one entire day contacting every source you can, including the local chamber of commerce, district attorney's office, state licensing bureau (which may be affiliated with the Department of Health and Human Services) or the attorney general's office. Any office where someone could file a business complaint against the agency or attorney is worth checking out. If you are looking at an international adoption, you might check with the consulate or embassy.

While seeking information on an agency or attorney, you should also visit pay a visit to the Adoption Guide at www.theadoptionguide.com, which provides stories and warnings about agencies, facilitators, and any other individuals involved in adoption that are considered questionable.

Smarts
What to look for and what you should know!

If you find a pattern of complaints against an agency, you might be happier setting your sights elsewhere. One agency was found to have some sixty complaints in the New York, New Jersey, and Connecticut, and had received nearly

Get everything in writing

Have an attorney look over the contract very carefully before you sign. Contracts can be amended (within reason), so you should not have to accept the "nonnegotiable, sign it or leave it" approach. Also, do not let them slip you a waiver to sign while they're busy showing you the adorable children they have placed. A waiver may say basically that no matter what happens, you can't sue them.

$300,000 from two dozen families who walked away empty-handed, after being promised a child. Needless to say, legal action followed bringing the attorney general of one of the three states into the picture.

Note: If an agency tells you that once you are in the other country you should pay someone "x" amount of money in cash or suggests any shady or potentially illegal action, say "goodbye." Find out from other people who worked with the agency if they were asked to pay such fees.

Full Disclosure

The agency should provide full disclosure not only about the child's background, but also about the people whom they are working with overseas. Stories of couples not being allowed to get out of the country without paying their country guide a certain amount of money have been documented. Stories of guides freelancing for several agencies and pulling scams on their own have occurred. One couple told a story about having their passports suddenly disappear and reappear after they tipped their guide more money to help them locate the "lost" passports. Instances of shady facilitators taking bribes and other such stories have also been reported. These are the exceptions, but you want as much information as you can get. Look for an agency that has staff overseas and is not relying on freelancers or facilitators whom they have little control over. Get as much data as possible about exactly whom the agency works with overseas.

You should also get copies of the original medical records from the orphanage. Have the medical records translated yourself and then looked at by a pediatrician whom you find on your own. One agency provided its own medical records to a client and neglected to include that the eighteen-month-old child had spent the first twelve months of his life in a hospital with serious illnesses. It is more likely— although not guaranteed— that the original medical records from the orphanage will include this information.

The bottom line is "full disclosure" by the agency. Lack thereof has resulted in several significant legal cases. The 1988 case of *Michael J.* vs. *L.A. City Department of Adoptions* stated that in an adoption "there must be a goodfaith full disclosure of material facts concerning existing or past conditions of the child's health."

In addition, adoption fraud claims, and those of misrepresentation on the part of agencies, have been filed in situations where agencies withheld information about the birth parents. One family sued the adoption agency with which they had worked to adopt their son after discovering that their son was mentally retarded and that his birth mother had also been diagnosed with mental retardation. The agency had not disclosed this information to the adopting family.

You should also try to get specific details following any claims an agency makes. For example, if the agency representative tells you that they have a very successful Ukrainian program, get the details of that program. One woman told of signing up and paying a fee to an agency that specifically claimed to have a successful program with the Republic of Georgia. After waiting several months, she inquired further only to find out that the so-called "success" was placing one child. The agency admitted that the program was new and tried hard to sway her to adopt from Ukraine instead, where they had a more active program.

Ultimately she went with the Ukrainian program and did adopt. However, she kept a very close watch on the agency and asked for backup information on the claims they made.

Catherine, now the mom of a daughter adopted from Russia, recalls sitting down at dinner one night with her husband and each commenting that they had spoken to someone at the agency that same day.

"The woman I spoke with told me she expected to have a referral of a girl for us in about two weeks and would get us a videotape. The man my husband spoke to told him that the situation had slowed down in adoptions from Russia [the country from which we were looking to adopt] and that it would probably be about another month before he would have any news for us. We were a bit concerned at this lack of a consistent story and called the agency together the following day. This time we asked to speak with the director, who told us she'd get on the matter at once and get back to us with the correct information immediately. Three days later she did, giving us a story that the first woman thought we were another couple and that she was very sorry. She promised us that in a month we would hear from her and she would let us know how soon we would likely have a referral. It was two months before we heard from her, and from that point on we taped our phone conversations with the agency. We did end up adopting through the agency, but it took considerably longer, and many bogus apologies on their part until it happened. We had to stay on them every step of the way for information. I tell people to watch the agency closely, and if you see signs of inconsistency early on, don't get started with them. There are plenty of good agencies out there. Plenty of people we know used agencies that they swear by. Next time we'll use one of those."

When working with an agency you will often be speaking to several different people. It is very important that the information you receive is consistent and that you do not get different answers depending on whom you are speaking to. If you are getting conflicting responses, insist upon speaking to the head of the agency. Also, get as much as possible in writing to verify what you are being told.

Short of taping your phone conversations, you should at least keep a log of when you spoke to the agency and what you were told from the initial meeting onward. As you feel more comfortable and gain more confidence in the agency personnel, this may become less formal, but it is still worth keeping just for the record, should you ever need it. If nothing else, and all goes well, you can put it into your adoption scrapbook!

Where's the Money Going?

Get an itemized breakdown and get receipts. If the agency says it is paying the birth mother's rent, get a copy of the receipt. If the agency tells you that you need to pay $2,000 as a donation to the orphanage, get a receipt. It's your money that they are taking for valid reasons—have them justify their expenses. The same holds true with attorneys who bill you for expenses.

Some agencies have been reported to take an amount, such as $2,000 for the donation to the orphanage, but then send only a $1,000 donation. Where's the rest of the money going? You're entitled to know.

Recourse

Short of court battles, in the event that you may have finally adopted but dealt with issues and practices through the agency or with an attorney that were not completely kosher, you may want to file complaints with any of the following, as suggested by Mary Mooney, who runs the Adoption Guide web-site. The attorney general's office, the local Better Business Bureau, Joint Council on International Children's Services (www.jcics.org, 202-429-0410) or the adoption licensing department in your state are all places to turn for recourse. However, as Mooney points out, "The licensing bureau will only file a complaint if it is in regard to a licensing violation." Elected officials, the attorney general's office, consumer advocate groups and of course adoption support groups are also places to inform about improper treatment by an agency or attorney, including surprise hidden fees, incorrect information, unusually lengthy waits for a referral or the old "switch the child" routine, whereby you are not given the child you are told had been referred to you. Also, if you should experience what you believe were improper activities on the part of an agency or attorney, let Mooney know at www.theadoptionguide.com.

Another very effective means of recourse is letting the agency know you are not pleased and are taking your information public. Be sure your information is valid and that you are not just upset over the long and tenuous adoption process. Agencies and attorneys operate largely on their reputations and if your story is truly one of documented impropriety, it can damage the agency or attorney's reputation if you speak up. Be sure you are correct before making any statements or claims against an agency or you can also become liable.

For more significant situations of fraud and deception, you may need to take legal action. Your best recourse is to find an adoption attorney who handles such cases or, if the case is not overly complicated (in terms of adoption law), a family-law attorney. You can do investigative work yourself and track down other families who have worked with the agency or attorney in question. If you can find others who, for example, are also out thousands of dollars with no child after several months of waiting (as in the case mentioned earlier in the chapter involving three states), then you may have a class action suit.

Fortunately, most adoptive situations do not end up this way. You'll hear some complaints, but the vast majority of adoptions proceed with only a few bumps along the journey. Be smart,

> ### *Passing Along Scam Information*
>
> *An example of how adoption support group members can help one and other comes from the following e-mail. "I was speaking to a member who says he is talking to the federal government about investigating a birth-mother scam artist. (He and his wife were victimized by her). She answers prospective-parent ads in western Pennsylvania newspapers and uses the names Laurie or Debbie and last names Jones or Collins. She has contacted several couples and gets them to meet her, claiming she is three months pregnant and really wants to work with them. She asks them to forward "small" amounts of cash (usually around $300, nothing that would cause alarm). Folks advertising in the Pennsylvania area should be aware of her."*
>
> *Signed, Connie*

learn as much as you can, and don't look for shortcuts or fall for people who claim to have an "easy way to adopt." There is no legitimate shortcut and no "easy adoption method." Be diligent and ask plenty of questions!

Facilitators

One final note. Facilitators are not mentioned in this chapter, because outside of California, where they are licensed (as mentioned earlier in this book), you should be *extremely* leery of using a facilitator. Agencies and attorneys are licensed and governed to some degree by their respective states. Facilitators generally are not. This makes it very hard to track their activities.

Chapter 14
OPEN ADOPTION; IS IT FOR YOU?

Open adoption . . . it's entirely up to the adoptive parents and the birth parents. Therefore, you should not be fooled by the propaganda for or against open adoption as there is no proven right or wrong method. Many well-adjusted, happy, wonderfully gifted and talented children have grown up in closed adoptions, and many are growing up today in open adoptions, a concept that has arisen over the past twenty years with much success in the right situations. Either way you choose, as adoptive parents, you need to handle adoption issues in a positive and honest manner for your child. Denying, hiding, distorting the truth, or downright lying are reasons why either method will fail, not the methods of open or closed adoption themselves. In addition, you need to go into an open or closed adoption anticipating the future and how you will deal with the situation not for yourselves, but for your child. In fact, therapists suggest that you try to anticipate your child as an adolescent and determine how the situation will affect his or her life at that time. To do so, you need to be aware of the pros and cons of open and closed adoptions and how they can affect your family dynamics and the emotional well-being of your child(ren).

"We have a good line of communication with our son's birth mother," says Dawn, whose son Teddy is now turning five.

"We send her photographs a couple of times a year and on

some occasions, such as holidays or Teddy's birthday, we talk on the phone. She's nearly 2,000 miles away so it's not likely that we can get together very often. However, we know where she is if we need her and she knows we're here if she wants to communicate with Teddy at some point in time. Basically, openness for us is simply a matter of having peace of mind . . . knowing each other is there and keeping the lines of communication open. We are also comfortable knowing our roles in this, which I think is very important."

Is this an open adoption? By definition, if a birth mother (or birth parents) and the adoptive parent (or parents) know each other by full names and have contact information, it is considered an open-adoption. For many adoptive and birth families, this is the extent of an open-adoption situation. It provides a level of communication that is comfortable for both parties and inclusion of the birth mother, while not clouding the respective roles of the adoptive and birth parents in the child's life. It preserves a "peace of mind" for both sides, knowing that each other is there and that a bond has been established.

Do you need to have this scenario to proceed successfully in raising a child whom you have adopted? No. Nearly 20,000 children are adopted annually from countries all over the globe. In 99 percent of those adoptions, there is no communication between birth and adoptive parents. Can children adopted from other countries grow up in a healthy manner without any contact with their birth parents? Obviously they can, whether or not they ever chose to search for their birth parents when they get older.

Therefore, open adoption is primarily limited to domestic adoptions. And there is a broad range of variations that fall under the heading of "open."

Defining "Open"

When an adoption agency talks about open adoption from the

perspective of a birth mother, it means that the birth mother can select the adoptive family from various portfolios. This is a different definition than the more standard meaning of open adoption, which signifies ongoing contact (or the potential for such contact by identifying information between the parties involved). Identifying information is usually not provided to a birth mother who is selecting adoptive parents (unless mandated by the state). California is currently the only state that mandates open adoption with full identifying information for all parties involved.

Note: Neither agencies nor attorneys should decide the issue of openness in a postadoption situation. This is not their responsibility. They should not be telling you how you will proceed with your life once you have finalized your adoption.

Fallacies

Before discussing the levels and pros and cons of open adoption, it is worth noting that you do not have to choose open adoption for the wrong reasons. For example, the argument that you cannot get medical information in a closed adoption is incorrect. An adoption attorney or adoption agency will almost always maintain records of all of your adoption information in their files. They should be able to contact the birth mother for you if you need medical information. Through court orders, if necessary, or letters from doctors, records can be—and have been—opened for information if such information was necessary for the child's well-being.

Note: The argument for open and closed adoption records for access by adoptees is a separate argument, which is not discussed here.

If you need medical information in an open or closed adoption, it is important to remember that locating a birth mother does not always mean she will know all of her family's medical history. Most of us have no idea what illnesses our grandparents may or may not have had.

Your emotions may also play into your decision-making process when contemplating the degree of openness you are seeking in an adoption. Much of open adoption centers around the degree of comfort on the part of two sides of the adoption triad; the birth mother and adoptive parents. Well intentioned as this may sound for the child, the truth is that the emotions of the adoptive parents may cloud the real issue; the child's well-being as he or she grows up. Often adoptive parents are either scared, intimidated, or threatened at the idea of having birth parents in the picture as they raise the child.

"I just felt that now we are her parents and I just don't want someone else being in the picture," says Arthur, the adoptive father of two children. *"It would seem kind of weird to have to deal with her [the birth mother] after the adoption ... telling us how we should handle things or making decisions for us."*

Conversely, adoptive parents may want to maintain a relationship with the birth mother because of guilt feelings.

"She gave us a child. How could we not keep her involved in our life after that?" asked the adoptive mother of a five-year-old girl.

The Birth Mother's Wishes

Regardless of your gut feelings, the birth mother will often take the lead in the situation based on her needs at the time. If you cannot be accommodating, you should not make an adoption plan with that particular birth mother. Therefore, this issue needs to be discussed ahead of time. However, keep in mind that you need not set anything in stone since life will change for both of you. In fact, you cannot set up a binding legal agreement for this type of situation—again, because circumstances change.

"We would have liked to have a photo or two from our birth

mother for our daughter," says Carol F., mentioned last in chapter three. *"I think if she wanted to maintain some contact through letters or photos once a year, we would have been okay with that too—but she didn't want to. In fact, she even asked us to wait to show up at the hospital until she had left. We had to follow her wishes."*

The decision to place a child for adoption is a painstakingly difficult one for a birth mother. She may not want to continue with a relationship because it is too painful for her. A clean break may be the best way for her to move on with her life, knowing the child is in a good home and will be well cared for. Should you try to persuade her otherwise because you've been told that open adoption is the best way to adopt? No. You cannot know how she feels and cannot understand her need to do this in her own way. Therefore, you need to show her respect and have a closed adoption if this is what she so chooses. Will this be detrimental to your child's growth? As evidenced by thousands of adopted children, no, it will not be, unless you try to hide or deny that she was indeed your child's birth mother or keep adoption a closed subject between you and your child.

Problems in both open and closed adoptions occur when the adoptive family does not embrace their situation and move forward. As stated at the beginning of this chapter and discussed later in Chapters 22 and 23, how *you* raise your child(ren) will be the biggest factor in their development.

On the Positive Side
An open adoption can certainly help in answering some of the hard questions, such as "Why was I given up for adoption?" or "Did my birth mother love me?" It can help the child through the sense of loss that comes with adoption and also provide a much clearer picture of what he or she will look like and (to some degree) act like when he or she grows up. A child can

embrace his or her full two-family background and learn about his or her cultural background.

On the Negative Side

An open adoption, where the child is in contact with the birth parents, can present a confusing situation in which the authority of the adoptive parents is diluted or even undermined. A child can be confused by differing views on life, love and anything else from adoptive and birth parents who may be coming from very different places. The adoptive parents may feel as if they are caretakers, and the child may not embrace the same sense of security that being with one permanent family can bring. It can also provide the child with a clearer picture of what he or she will look like and (to some degree) act like when he or she grows up.

Note: The last sentence of the above pros and cons is repeated because it's important to remember that birth parents (like adoptive parents) come in all shapes, sizes and temperaments . . . some for better *and* some for worse.

Wide Open

Since the concept of wide open or completely open adoptions, in which a birth mother plays a major role in the upbringing of the child, is still new and relatively uncommon, the jury is still out on the effects of such situations on adoptees as they mature into adults. While it may take a village to raise a child, the commonly held belief is that one set of parents, or a single parent, at the center of that village is the most important and influential factor in a child's well-being. Therefore, the roles of the adoptive and birth parents must be defined clearly. The birth mother is not the "real" mother, and the adoptive family is not the child's "only family." The birth mother needs to be defined in such a matter that the child understands the connection.

Note: In the vast majority of domestic adoptions, birth mothers today do want to meet the adoptive parents (around 60 percent) but do not want to be involved in parenting decisions.

Older Children

Most of this chapter talks about adopting newborns or babies. However, domestic adoption also includes the adoption of older children, generally through the foster-care system. Since these children have spent time with their birth parents as well as in foster care, you will likely have a lot more background information about them. These children may still have contact with their birth parents. You will have to discuss with the social worker assigned to the case how to best handle the situation. Sometimes there will be visits with birth parents that include you and other times they will include only the social worker. Situations are very different, and you will be guided by the social worker and the agency involved. In some cases, it may be in the best interest of the child to not only maintain contact with birth parents, but with grandparents, foster parents, and *especially* siblings.

So What's the Answer?

In a domestic adoption, if there is a degree of openness that you and the birth mother, or birth parents, find acceptable, go with it. You can always alter it over time if it's uncomfortable for any of the *three* members of the adoption triad. Ambiguity in regard to structuring the "openness" of the adoptive relationship is the root of most problems that arise between birth and adoptive parents.

Also remember, that as the child grows up, it is he or she who needs to participate in the further development of this relationship.

Adoptive parents are often maligned for "not wanting to let their child have communication with the birth parents" as the child gets older. Three possibilities come into play here:

First, as parents, you are responsible for the well-being of a child, emotionally as well as physically. Just as a young child is not ready to light a match, that same child can get burned emotionally if he or she encounters a situation that before he or she is mature enough to handle it. Adolescents and teenagers often believe they are fully ready to face the world as adults. Most often they are not. Depending on the child and the birth parents, this is a judgment that adoptive parents have to maintain control over.

Second, the adoptive parents may know that the child is in for a disappointment if he or she meets the birth parents, and they are therefore choosing to protect the child from birth parents who may, in fact, not want to meet the child at all.

Third, the adoptive parents may be insecure about the reaction that their child may have in meeting the birth parents. In many instances, a birth family has come a long way from the time it was struggling and unable to raise a child and are now in a far better life situation. They may pose a threat to the adoptive parents. This reason is why many adoptive parents receive negative press about not promoting contact with birth parents for their child(ren). However, it is only one of the possibilities.

More often than not, the adoptive parents are considering the maturity of the child, adolescent, or teen in question. In situations where there is openness from early on, the adoptive parents must work with the birth parents to manage this interaction for the best interest of the child.

P.S.: Do not rely on adoption agencies, attorneys, grandparents, friends, neighbors, books, social workers, or even Judge Judy to make the open-adoption decision for you. Make the decision that is right for all members of the triad in your own individual situation. Remember, as mentioned several times throughout this book, adoption does not follow a boilerplate, and there is no one-size-fits-all approach.

Chapter 15
ADOPTED AND BIOLOGICAL CHILDREN

Families with adopted and biological children are sometimes referred to as "blended families." Since my own family falls into this category, I am quite familiar with the term and take it with a grain of salt. Such a family can blend very nicely and smoothly. However, there can also be moments of frustration and aggravation, especially when a biological child uses the adoption of a sibling as ammunition in never-ending sibling rivalry. "Well, you're not *really* part of the family" is a sharpened arrow that stings both the child through adoption and the parent(s) who hear this.

However, the vast majority of the time, your children will clearly be your children, regardless of where they come from, or who they look like. When one of them calls you into his or her bedroom because of a tummy ache, or a bad dream, the adopted or biological part of becoming a parent is the farthest thing from your mind.

When you tell people that you adopted your first child and had your second one biologically, they'll inevitably respond, "It always happens that way. You adopt a baby and then you get pregnant." If that was the case, fertility clinics would first send couples to adoption agencies or adoption attorneys. The reality is that less than 10 percent of families who adopt a child ever have a biological sibling.

There are also instances where couples have a biological child but are experiencing "secondary infertility," the inability to get pregnant again. Such couples may turn to adoption. In some cases, the couples are simply getting older and the chance of a pregnancy becomes slim. In other situations, second marriages present an excellent opportunity to bring an older child into the family.

No matter which sibling is older, the closer the children are in age, the more you can expect typical battles to ensue. This is normal of any family. The above-mentioned ammunition, however, needs to be dealt with on a "zero-tolerance" level. The biological child must always be fully aware that his or her sibling is just as much a part of the family as he or she is and that such talk will not be tolerated. It falls into the category of hurtful behavior and should be disciplined accordingly in the same manner as you would handle any other teasing or name-calling.

More difficult to handle than the sibling battles are the honest questions from both sides and from their friends. It can be stressful trying to explain to a child why he or she was placed for adoption and what adoption means. It's also very difficult to explain to the other sibling what adoption means and that you have no intention of placing him or her for adoption, which is the question a younger biological child might ask. It is, however, an area that you will need to address as a parent. The harmony of the family is in jeopardy if the biological child does not understand and accept the adoption of the other child.

You'll have to explain to your children that some other children (in reality, it's actually *most* other children) don't know very much about adoption, so you have to help them learn what it's about. The toughest situation is dealing with a child who is nasty or has a negative attitude about adoption learned from his or her parents. Children can be cruel to one and other under general circumstances, and since they don't understand adoption, it gives them one more thing to use when teasing. You'll need to provide comfort and reassurance when your son or daughter comes home with hurt feelings no matter what the cause. It's advantageous when their siblings are helpful, rather than jumping on the bandwagon and teasing as well. You'll have to promote the family idea of sticking up for one and other and offer age-appropriate examples of how family members support each other through books or perhaps in television shows.

Differences and Similarities

Children who were adopted will notice the differences between themselves and their parents. When they have a sibling who may also have a similar look to their parents, it can make matters more difficult. "Why am I the only one in the family with blond hair?" asks the adopted child. He or she will often follow with "Why am I the only one adopted?" You need to explain that you *all* have differences from one and other.

"Why am I the only one who's gone bald?" I responded to my daughter, who laughed.

"No, dad, seriously, why was I adopted and he [her brother] wasn't?" she insisted.

You will then need to explain that families are formed in many different ways, and some family members come into the family by adoption. Point out other types of families that you know. There are single-parent families, stepparents, situations where grandparents are taking care of a child, and so on. You should also focus on the many things you share as a family, and what brings you together. As the family grows and adoption becomes one of the many aspects of family life, it is no longer the distinguishing feature, but part of what makes up your background. Joining a support group may also afford your child the opportunity to be with other children who were adopted.

Every family has their share of similarities and differences. You can be sure that children, based on their competitive nature, will point out who is better at a particular activity. However, you have to look at and acknowledge differences for better and for worse. One child may be the athlete, another may be the scholar, another the artist. (If you do not try to prejudge your adopted child and put him or her into one of these categories you will be better off.) You cannot push square pegs into round holes. Your image of what your child could or should be and who he or she really is, may be different. Likewise, you cannot compare your children or expect one to follow in the footsteps of the other—not that this is advisable with two biological children either.

Communicating Adoption

Today, an adopted child grows up knowing about adoption and is both proud and curious about his or her heritage. Therefore, you need to learn about your child's background, whether he or she was born in another country or another state. Children usually take great pride in where they come from. Our daughter was adopted from Phoenix, Arizona, and our son was born to us in New York. She's proud of being from Arizona and tells everyone that she was born there. Our son is a baseball fan. He tells her how the Arizona Diamondbacks are doing if he's watching a game in which they're playing because it's a way of being closer to her (although he won't admit it). Even though she doesn't really care much for baseball, she says she's rooting for the Diamondbacks when they're on TV because it brings her closer to baseball and, hence, to her brother (although she won't admit it, either). It's a small, unspoken bond because baseball is a big part of his life and Arizona is a big part of hers.

Despite their differences and their so-called "disdain" for one another, siblings usually find ways of bonding with one another without the help of their parents. Young children don't see prejudice or differences as we see them through the biases learned in society. Two culturally different children from two ethnic backgrounds can be brothers or sisters. If they are cared for and made to feel that they are part of a family, they will establish a bond. Only society can teach them otherwise. You'd also be surprised at how they will stick up for one another once that bond is formed early on. If anyone dares to bring up adoption in a negative way, the biological sibling will defend his or her sister or brother.

Essentially, there is no special trick to making a family work with adopted and biological children. The key is emphasizing love, fairness and family. Acknowledge all the similarities that make you a family and all of the differences that you have as individuals. Celebrate what makes *each* of you unique, not just the child who was adopted. Often appearance needs to be downplayed, especially when other people comment on your biological child having your eyes, your nose, and your spouse's hair. That is the time to refocus their attention *on both* children and their attributes.

If you take the proactive stance that your family is a unit, other people will follow your lead and eventually forget the adopted and biological history of your family. In fact, one day my daughter sneezed, and my mom thought she might have been allergic to the oregano in the sauce. "I'm allergic to it, and so is your sister. She might be also," she told me. I looked at her. There was a moment, and then she responded, "Oh, that's right . . . I forgot," she commented with a smile, suddenly remembering that her granddaughter was adopted. Families tend to blend together, hence bringing a positive aspect of the term "blended family."

Note: I always find it a bit disconcerting when "studies" are made by psychologists and clinicians who work in private practice and write about blended families. They will cite ideas such as the family having a difficult time with the birthday of their adopted child or having a stronger bond with the biological child. Anything can be found if you are speaking with the population that is coming to therapy for that specific problem. However, what these so-called "clinical studies" miss out on are the many families that are just that: families, without distinctions. Sure, you know which child was biological and which child was adopted into your family, but you love them both equally. I know.

Going Through the Adoption Process with Kids

If you have a child in your life while you are adopting his or her soon-to-be brother or sister, you will need to include this child in the process in some manner. Unless your child is an infant, he or she is going to be aware that something is going on. Children are very intuitive and can sense change is about to happen. Find an age-appropriate way of letting them help you to bring a baby brother or sister into your family.

The biggest fear of your child will be that the new family member will take away your time and love—not to mention some of his or her toys. Any child will feel threatened when a new baby is on the way, including a biological sibling. That is why your child(ren) need to feel involved. Since adoption is not an exact science, it's important to limit the information you share because a situation—whether it's a domestic or international—may not result in an adoption. For this reason, some parents choose to have their son or daughter spend a few days with grandma and grandpa while they travel to bring home your new family member.

Adoption counselor and consultant Leanne Jaffe adds that kids will ask a lot of questions: Be prepared. "If a situation does not work out, children will still know that something is wrong in the household. They will pick it up from how the parents act.

While you may not want to get into all of the details, you can let them know about the process and that sometimes it requires more waiting to have a sibling. I would rather that parents let children go through some of the grieving process because they are a part of it no matter what. They should be included in the process, not every detail but not protected."

There are many ways in which even very young children can be involved in the bringing of a sibling into the home. They can take on new responsibilities as the big brother or sister and be given jobs to do to that match their age and abilities. If the newly adopted, or even soon to be adopted, brother or sister is, in part, the responsibility of everyone in the family, then the child or children already in the family will feel a positive energy toward the new baby. Of course, this will disappear at those times when everyone visiting makes a big fuss over the newest family member. Therefore it is up to you to consciously keep a portion of the spotlight shining on the older children. And as Dr. Ruth Westheimer suggests, "Have a bag of toys stashed somewhere in the closet for when those forgetful visitors show up with just a gift for the newest family member."

Chapter 16
RELATIVE ADOPTION

By law, relative adoption is usually defined as the legal adoption of a brother, sister, grandchild, niece, or nephew. Depending on laws and circumstances, cousins or great-grandchildren may fall into this category as well. While this type of adoption is quite different, and generally much easier to complete than most of the adoptions discussed throughout this book, it is a subject that should be addressed. Relative adoptions make up a significant percentage of the overall number of adoptions that take place in the United States every year.

As in domestic adoption, state laws govern the process. Therefore, you will need to locate an adoption attorney to review the specific laws of your state. The America Academy of Adoption Attorneys (www.adoptionattorneys.com) and Adoption Directory.com are places to look for such an attorney.

In some states, a home study is not necessary as part of the process and in other states a more concise version of the home study can be used for a relative adoption. As in the case with other forms of adoption, termination of parental rights by the birth parents must be granted. A Judgment of Adoption will be filed in the courthouse in your county, and a date will be set on which you will go to court to complete the actual adoption.

The complexities of relative adoption are not usually found in the legal aspects of the process, but in the practical and emotional aspects. Depending on the circumstances and the relationship between family members, such a situation can range from very positive to difficult and even dysfunctional. In cases where the birth parent has died, the focus of attention is directed toward helping the child deal with loss and making a smooth transition. If the birth mother is living, but unable to care for a child because she is either too young or unable to support a child emotionally or financially (or both), the situation can become more complicated.

On the positive side, the child can have a close, open relationship with his or her birth mother, and she can be part of the child's life. The child can get his or her questions answered about adoption, and his or her health information is also readily available. The adoptive parents know much more about the birth mother's personal situation and can be supportive and maintain a special bond. A birth mother may also feel a greater sense of comfort knowing that someone close to her is raising the child.

On the other side of the coin, the awkwardness of the situation that can lead to many problems. These adoptions can strain a relationship between birth and adoptive parents who may be in close proximity and see each other at family gatherings. If the birth mother finds herself, in time, financially and emotionally able to raise a child, there may be a greater strain and resentment that she cannot suddenly be the mother again. Should she have another child, whom she raises, the adopted child will wonder why he or she was placed for adoption and this other child was not. In addition, the child will ask who is his or her "real" mom. The birth mother, who may be the sister of the adoptive mother, may also disagree with child-rearing methods and feel she has a right to be involved in such decisions. In short, there are many scenarios which can cause stress within the family.

It is therefore very important that all of this be discussed in detail in advance and in most situations, a reasonable amount of space between the families is essential for making this work. This way they will still see each other, but will not be involved in the day-to-day life of the child. All family members need to understand and respect each other's roles in this process.

Sometimes the family scenario can get very confusing, and new issues will arise as the family dynamics change.

"We each met separately with social workers a number of times," explains Lisa, who, with her husband, and their older daughter, adopted her niece's daughter at nine months of age.

"The social workers counseled us to make sure we covered all the bases. They wanted Gina, my niece, to know exactly what she was doing and both of us to understand what we were getting into. They talked about what this would mean within the family in the future as Annie [whom I adopted] grew up.

"Gina was nineteen years old, living at home with her mom, and the birth father had taken off and wanted nothing to do with the situation. She tried to make it work for several months but felt she couldn't do it. I really wanted another child, and since we were not having a second one biologically, I was already thinking about adoption."

The actual process of the adoption for Lisa went very smoothly. However, the concerns and potential issues are within the family structure. *"Right now she doesn't understand anything about adoption yet, but she's getting there. We want to be very open about it but don't want to confuse her. Gina [now twenty-two] still sees us often, and Annie calls her Gina and thinks of her as a best friend. She calls Gina's mom, who's my sister, "Grandma," which will get confusing because my other daughter calls her "Aunt." But I didn't want to take the grandma part of the relationship away from my sister."*

What confused matters more was that Gina had another daughter since Annie was born and that baby, Heidi, is now

Annie's cousin, but also her biological half-sister. Lisa wants Annie to know Heidi as her cousin, since she has a sister and would not understand it in any other manner until she gets older.

Lisa finds that she has to speak up from time to time to keep everyone in their respective roles:

"Most of the time everything goes pretty smoothly, but now and then I have to tell them to back off a little bit and remind them that this was the decision we all made. For example, one day Gina had a professional photographer at her house taking family photos. She had Annie over that day and had the photographer take a picture of her with Annie and Heidi. I didn't realize it until I saw it hanging in their house. I was not happy and told her she had to take it down. I don't think she meant anything by this, other than seeing a nice photo opportunity but I didn't think it was something that Annie should see.

"When Annie gets older and starts asking questions about the adoption, I'll have to talk with Gina so that we can both be on the same page in explaining why Annie was placed with us. I'm sure she is going to wonder why Heidi is living with Gina and why she was placed for adoption, and we'll have to explain carefully. Gina loves Annie and wouldn't do anything to sabotage the situation. My older daughter knows all about this, and when the adoption first happened, she had a thousand questions a day. But now she hardly ever talks about adoption, they just fight like typical sisters. Right now Annie is very happy and her world is very secure here, but I know there's a lot ahead of us."

Grandparent Adoption

Grandparent adoptions have increased in the past two decades. It is estimated that over four million children in the United States (under the age of eighteen) are living with their grandparents. The primary reasons are either because a teenage girl gave birth and could not handle the responsibilities of raising the baby, or the parents were ill and the grandparents stepped in and adopted the child. In the case of teen pregnancies, the grandparents are often in their forties which today, is a common age for parenting young children. However, the stress and stamina needed to parent young children may be more difficult for grandparents in their fifties or sixties. In either case the situation needs to be handled carefully so that the child understands everyone's role in the process.

A great deal of communication is needed between all members of the triad in any relative adoption whereby the birth mother or birth parents are living. The birth mother needs to understand that she will still have a role in the life of the child, but has, by placing the child for adoption, taken a secondary role once a relative has adopted legally and assumed the role of mom or dad. This is not a situation where the aunt or grandparents help out and raise the child until the birth mother is old enough and ready to resume the role as mother. In those situations, an official adoption is not necessary or appropriate. Adoption is a decision that indicates permanency. Therefore, the decision should always be made after careful consideration.

Family counseling is often advised for all parties involved in a relative adoption. A good family counselor should be able to help all members of the triad feel comfortable with their roles and help initiate open lines of communication. Get references and shop around for a good family counselor.

Stepparent Adoption

The issue in stepparent adoption is once again not the legality, but the emotional and practical elements. The process usually entails contacting an adoption attorney in your area who knows the state adoption laws and files all necessary paperwork with the court. The adoption will generally be held in family or surrogate court, and a court date will be set up, at which you will need to appear. Most states will have certain guidelines, such as stating that the couple needs to be married for at least one year. The court will inform you of what you need to know or provide an information package. Your attorney should also be able to fill you in on the process. Once the child is adopted, the stepparent will assume all legal and financial responsibilities regarding the child.

The vast majority of stepparent adoptions are by stepfathers. Among the reasons why a stepparent may wish to adopt is that it allows for the child to have a legal parent should the biological parent die and also allows the child to receive Social Security benefits should the stepparent die. It also allows for inheritance benefits. From an emotional standpoint, it can bring a family closer together and solidify the bond between the child and the stepparent.

On the other hand, a stepparent may choose not to adopt because he or she does not want to interfere with the strong bond between the child and his or her biological noncustodial parent. In fact, the noncustodial parent can even contest the adoption and cause a legal battle.

Each situation must be evaluated individually. If the noncustodial parent is in the picture and the child is old enough to understand the situation, a conversation would likely ensue between stepparent and child. The stepparent would explain that he or she wants to adopt the child, but only if it's okay with him, or her. A stepparent needs to add that he or she is not trying to replace the child's father or mother. All parties need to communicate, especially when dealing with a child who is over the age of five. Understanding the feelings and attachments of a child are very important. If the noncustodial parent is in the life of the child, maintaining openness between all parties can be very important.

In situations where the noncustodial parent is out of the picture, not taking any parental responsibility, or is unknown, and the child therefore does not feel an affinity for that parent, it may be more practical and easier to promote the idea

Amended Birth Certificates

Once the adoption has been finalized, apply for the amended birth certificate with the child's new last name.

of adoption as a means of bringing together a strong family unit. As mentioned above, each situation is different. The best interest of the child should always be the determining factor.

As a child grows and matures into adulthood, he or she is likely to understand why the stepparent legally chose to adopt . . . but as a young child, this may not be obvious. The stepparent should not promote adoption until he or she has a clear reading on how the child is likely to react. This may not always come from a conversation, since kids are sometimes reluctant to talk. Therefore, especially with a younger child, parents need to observe how that child is behaving.

Chapter 17
GAY AND LESBIAN ADOPTION

Twenty-five years ago, this chapter would not have existed. Today it is here because of the changing views of society. As of the writing of this book, by law, gays are allowed to adopt in every state except Florida, Mississippi, and Utah. While that may seem to indicate great strides forward, it should be noted that as of early 2000, the number was forty-nine states. Other states are currently considering laws to make adoption by gays illegal. In fact, several on-line surveys questioning whether or not gays should be allowed to adopt have rejected the idea by a significant margin. In addition, a half-hour television special on gay adoption, aired by Nickelodeon, received over 200,000 complaints. Therefore, even in our progressive society, the debate over gay and lesbian adoption continues.

Critics of gay adoption fear that gays will provide unfit role models and that they lead a lifestyle that is unsuitable for a child to see. They are also concerned that the child will have a very hard time fitting in with other children who will not be kind to the son or daughter of a gay or lesbian couple.

Supporters of gay adoption respond that gays and lesbians provide the same loving and nurturing environment as any other parents and have strong convictions, as they have often had to fight for their own rights and life choices, as well as their right to adopt. Therefore, they will make very strong advocates for the best interests of their children. They also point out that all children will be teased by other children who don't understand any different lifestyle (such as adoption in general). This should, therefore, not be a reason to prevent gay adoption, but rather to educate other families and inform them that gay adoption can and does work, providing children with loving, nurturing homes—which is what "family" is all about.

Despite the favorable laws in most states, there are numerous obstacles that make it quite difficult for gays to adopt as couples. First, many agencies will not accept a gay couple. Second, many birth parents will not select a gay couple. Third, some social workers may make it very difficult for a gay couple to get through the home study process.

Different Approaches

Often, agencies and others guiding gay and lesbian couples into the adoption process will recommend that to make the process easier, or faster, the couple should be open to adopting a "hard-to-place" child (which may mean an older child, child of color, or special-needs child). This may expedite the process, but does not make the adoption easier and may not be fair to the child. Julie, of Berkeley, California, who adopted two infants of color with her partner Amy, points out: *Being told to take a "hard-to-place-child" for the sake of adopting more quickly is a bad piece of advice. These adoptive situations present various other issues. For example, a transracial adoption adds a layer of complexity. You've adopted a whole other culture and need to address that and offer the child his or her culture. It worked for us because we are a biracial couple, but it won't work for everyone and it should not be advised to simply make an adoption happen more quickly."*

Another approach is for a gay or lesbian individual to adopt as a single parent and simply not disclose information about his or her sexuality. The "don't ask, don't tell" policy works well. Many social workers will simply avoid asking questions along those lines even if they suspect a gay or lesbian relationship. In many states, the second parent can then adopt a short time later. However, one concern is that if something happens to the adopting parent that there will be difficulty for the other parent to gain full custody, even if he or she has adopted as a second parent. The idea of one parent adopting and a second parent adopting at a later date brings up a debate about the lack of "full disclosure" to the social worker conducting a home study, and also raises a question of ethics. *"For us it felt like we were hiding the ball, or skirting the edge of ethics,"* says Julie. *"I wanted us to be open and encourage others to be open as well. This way you start a family with honesty."* Some adoptive couples feel strongly about being a couple in the process, while others are comfortable with one parent adopting and feel that sexual orientation should be a nonissue.

"We looked long and hard for an agency that would accept us as a couple," says Gloria, who along with her partner Linda, wanted to adopt together. *"It took a while, but we finally found an agency that accepted us. We did not want to have to deny who we are. We communicated with others in the [gay/lesbian] community and connected with other couples who had adopted. From there we found not only the agency, but plenty of support. In fact, we even started our own little support group."*

The decision whether to adopt as a couple or as a single is a personal one that needs to be discussed by each couple looking to adopt.

Networking is particularly important for gay couples because many of the advertised adoption agencies will turn them away. Support groups are valuable for all prospective adoptive couples and singles as well as families that have already adopted. Some resources listed below may help start the "networking" ball rolling. Gay and lesbian parenting resources are also a prime location for gaining information.

After making the decision that they wanted to be parents, Julie and Amy proceeded to talk to couples they knew who had adopted, and gathered information. They subsequently found a facilitator in their area (Berkeley) who worked with lesbian couples and placed children of color. Julie, being African-American, found this to be a perfect match and within a month they were in the process of adopting their first child. *"We were somewhat naïve when we started the process and didn't know anything about the potential pitfalls,"* says Julie. *"We learned a lot through PACT, an organization I'm now very involved with. They offered education workshops and we learned about adoption."*

For Julie and Amy, the adoption process went extremely smoothly, so much so that when they adopted for the second time, they were even less prepared. *"The second time it took over six months"* recalls Julie. *"We remember being very stressed and saying things like, we'll never have a second child. It felt a bit like going to your first prom and thinking . . . is someone ever going to pick me?"* Sure enough Amy and Julie were picked by a birth mother, and they now have two little boys running around their home. *"People still see us in the supermarket and try to figure out the family constellation, but that's okay. We're fortunate that we're in Berkeley, where this type of family structure is more common. It really helps for a gay family to be located in the right place, where they can fit in."*

As Julie points out, living in "the right" neighborhood can certainly make it easier for a gay or lesbian family to raise a child.

International Adoption

International adoption is almost impossible for gay couples. No countries allow gay couples to adopt. Therefore, the adoption would have to be completed as a single-parent adoption, and his or her partner would need to adopt the child in the United States in a state that allows second-parent adoption. The problem then arises with countries that do not allow for single parent adoptions (although there are fewer of these) and the scrutiny that is sometimes involved. Some countries, such as China, go out of their way to determine that an individual is not gay. Single applicants for adoption from China need to explain why they are not married.

In addition, there are slowdowns in the process, claim some gays, who have tried international adoptions as singles. One adoptive father from New York City noted, *"Even if you do find a country from which you can adopt, if it is suspected that you are gay, you'll find your I-600 form somehow gets lost somewhere in the process."*

Resources

Naturally, adoption becomes much easier if, like one former daytime talk-show host, you have a lot of money. However, for most gays and lesbians, adopting means to doing your homework and discovering the adoption-friendly resources available. It is also advisable to look at the laws of the various states when it comes to such same gender adoptions. There are situations where you may legally adopt in the state of the birth parents, but not in your state of residence. You will therefore need to finalize adoption in the home state of the birth mother.

Through networking, gays and lesbians seeking to adopt can locate gay-adoption-friendly agencies, attorneys, and support groups. If you do not want to address the issue openly, then you can start out by inquiring if they have single-parent adoptees.

A few resources for gay and lesbian adoption include:

> PACT, An Adoption Alliance, 3315 Sacramento St. Suite 239, San Francisco CA 94118 415 221-6957. This organization facilitates adoptions for children of color and placement in gay and lesbian adoptive families. www.pactadopt.org

COLAGE, Children of Lesbians and Gays Everywhere, is an international organization that supports young people who have gay, lesbian, bisexual, and transgender parents with various chapters and an informative website featuring pertinent resources and more. 3543 18th ST #1, San Francisco, CA 94110, 415-861-KIDS.

In Washington state, DSHS (Department of Social and Health Services) has been known to place special-needs children with lesbian and gay couples. More recently they have also started placing infants.

Who Chooses A Gay Couple?

The process is difficult. Gay couples often find themselves asking what often feels like a hopeless question. Why would a birth mother choose us over a heterosexual couple?

There are several reasons why a birth mother might select a gay couple. First, a birth mother may have been abused by a man and may be more comfortable placing her child with two women. Some birth mothers have brothers, sisters, or other relatives or close friends who are gay and can see beyond the labels. As mentioned earlier, gay couples have to show great strength in society. This strength to stand up and be who they are can be uplifting to a birth mother who is being strong in making such a difficult decision as to place a child for adoption.

> ### Second-Parent Adoption
>
> *Twenty states currently recognize second-parent adoption, with many other states granting them on a case-by-case situation. Second-parent adoptions occur when one person is the biological parent of a child or the adoptive parent (after a finalized adoption) and the second parent adopts.*

Chapter 18
SINGLE PARENT ADOPTION

It is clearly not as easy for a single person to adopt as a couple, but you probably knew that already. Today, however, single parenting is much more common than ever before. Over the past two decades, there has been a consistent rise in the number of adoptions by single parents. Nearly 25 percent of all special-needs adoption, and over 5 percent of all adoptions are by single parents.

For singles looking to adopt, the possibilities are limited. Some adoption agencies and several countries will not work with singles. In addition, a single trying to adopt through independent domestic adoption will not be selected as often as a couple by birth mothers. Nonetheless, there are still many singles who adopt. Sometimes it is just a matter of patience. A birth mother who was raised by a single mother or who feels men have mistreated her may feel more comfortable selecting a single mom. A birth mother who was raised in a one-parent family may also have a great respect for single parents and the difficult job they undertake.

The fact that people have not been married or have previously been divorced should not preclude them from the joys and responsibilities of being parents. In recent years, more easily available and affordable day-care facilities and jobs that allow for more flexibility (including telecommuting) have made single parenting more manageable. Therefore, single women and men who feel they can handle the time commitment involved in parenting now turn to adoption as a viable route to parenthood.

If you are considering adopting internationally as a single, you will need to carefully review the countries that are open to single-parent adoptions and what the process will be like. China, for example, is technically open to singles, but as of 2000 it became increasingly more difficult to complete an adoption. As of mid-2002, Russia and Guatemala were better choices.

It is suggested that a single adopting overseas arrange for a travel companion because it is a long and very emotional journey. The support will be needed and welcomed. Discuss this with a friend or relative in advance since he or she will have to take time off work.

Are You Prepared?

First prepare yourself carefully by calculating both the costs of the adoption and the cost of raising a child on a single income. Next, you will need to determine how you will balance your time between full-time parenting and a full-time job. You will then need to assess the strength of your support system. This can be tricky because some of the people you may be counting on the most will be ones to rain on your parade. Seek out those people whom you can count on.

Your family and friends may not understand why anyone would intentionally assume the responsibilities of parenting alone. They may try to talk you out of such a preposterous idea. If you believe you can and will succeed in adopting as a single, then stand your ground.

You will also need to network!

Look for adoption support groups and ask specifically if they deal with single-parent adoptions. Yes, some hand-holding is important, but you want to pick the brains of other singles to find out what agencies they used or from which countries they adopted. You also need to talk with adoption attorneys and ask them point-blank, "Have you worked successfully with singles?" Before beginning the application process, you should know whether or not an agency works with singles and its previous track record.

Next start getting your paperwork together; it is required for all types of adoption. Plan a schedule since you will be gathering the paperwork for the home study yourself, while still showing up for work.

Note: Single parents find that they can broaden their possibilities of adopting enormously if they are open to children of different ethnic or racial backgrounds or older children, as there is less competition from couples.

As a single, you will need to be tenacious and proactive. Single parenting is still breaking new ground in the eyes of much of the conservative portion of the population. Therefore, you must work that much harder. In the end it will pay off. Your tenacity will make you a more involved, proactive

> **Positive Parenting Results**
>
> *Children who grow up in single-parent families often mature more quickly and are forced to take on greater responsibility around the house earlier than children who grow up in two-parent households.*

parent—which will be necessary since it's all your responsibility. There is also a strong bond formed by single parents and their children that is unique. It represents a "you and me against the world" connection that is very special. It is also sometimes advantageous to be able to parent your own way without having to debate differences in parenting techniques with your partner.

Karen from Connecticut, a single mom mentioned in chapter four, who now has a two-year-old boy, had the usual apprehensions about becoming a single parent:

"Before I got serious about adopting, I was concerned about the impact on my personal life. I thought that if I didn't meet someone to marry that I should adopt a child. But I also realized that once I was with a child I might never meet someone. How many men want to hang around a woman with a two-year-old? I had to get my priorities in order. Once I decided that it was a child I really wanted, I felt confident. I thought it would have worried me more, but it didn't. The idea of not being able to get away more often and little concerns like needing to run to the store to get something and having to dress him to come with me or even going to take a bath make things a little more difficult than if there was someone else here, but you just adjust to those kind of issues. For the most part, people around me have been very helpful."

There are nearly 20 million children in single-parent homes today, many through divorce or teen pregnancy. Clearly, there are difficulties that these children may face and behavioral problems that may occur as a result of the child missing the father, or mother, figure. However, the conscious choice to adopt a child and start a single-parent family offers a parent the opportunity to work on remedying such problems by learning to address them early on.

Single Men

There are clearly more obstacles for single men trying to adopt. The long-held notion that a child needs a mother is still prevalent. In addition, men in general, are often not seen as nurturing or comfortable in a child-rearing situation. The potential of child molestation and the lifestyle of single men are also issues that are questioned by placement agencies and birth mothers.

Today, however, more fathers are becoming increasingly involved in the raising of their children. In fact, there are now over one million single dads in the United States. These numbers bode well for single men looking to adopt. However, it does not mean that it will be easy. Even a man with the best of intentions, who would make an excellent father, may still be turned down by an agency based on the staff's own preconceptions and fears of having a hard time making a match with a birth mother.

Adoption agencies have found that single fathers can make good parents for older boys (five and up) who need strong role models. Marshall, single dad of a teenage boy, wasn't even looking to adopt as a single parent:

"It was sort of by accident that I came to adopt, I met a woman who was a foster mom back in the late 1980s. There were a lot of African-American children to place for adoption who were in foster care homes, [and still are], and since she was African-American it was easy for them to find children to place with her.

"We were talking about marriage, and for me to be in the same home with a foster-care child, according to the state we were living in, I would need to be a licensed caretaker for foster children. I was out of medical school and in residency at the time. I took a few classes for the prelicensing and as I was taking the classes, my girlfriend and I broke up. So there I was, still in this program."

Marshall debated whether or not to proceed, and after some soul searching decided to pursue the process. Shortly thereafter he was introduced to Gregory, a five-year-old with a high IQ but from a very rough background. A crack baby, he was taken from his parents at a young age and had already been in several foster homes. The agency working with Marshall felt that he and Gregory would make a good match. Gregory was very verbal, an expressive and intelligent child. He was also explosive, with attention deficit disorder which required him to take strong medication. Marshall, a young physician, was intelligent and sensitive to the needs of such a child.

After several visits, Marshall did end up adopting Gregory, but at first he had his reservations:

"We formed a very strong bond. In fact, he tells me with great conviction that when he first saw me walking across the yard at the placement facility, he told the boy next to him, "That's going to be my father." But at the time I remember telling the social worker that he was a kid with a lot of energy and I thought he'd do better in a two-parent home. She spoke honestly and explained that at almost six years of age, he probably would never get selected since African-American couples have no trouble finding a newborn if they want to adopt, and as a child got older they became much harder to place. She wasn't trying to pressure me, but was simply being honest. I didn't do it out of a feeling of guilt, but because it was what would be best for him."

Marshall was the first single African-American father to adopt in his state. He worked out the logistics, and had a good support system of friends. Nonetheless, Gregory presented many challenges. At different times, he was in and out of special education classes, not for lack the ability to learn but for behavioral problems. Varying medications and much home schooling (in addition to regular schooling) were provided by Marshall. *"I taught him the multiplication tables, reading, even Shakespeare—in fact, one summer we read six Shakespearian plays together and when we visited New York City, I took him to see A Midsummer Night's Dream,"* Marshall recalls fondly.

Also, Marshall did not feel a stigma about being a "single parent."

"Being an adoptive parent made it a little bit different. I wasn't responsible for his life situation. Unlike a broken home or having had some affair, I had chosen to do this, so the moral

and ethical problems weren't there. People, in fact, were often amazed and impressed by my having made the choice to take on this difficult responsibility. The problems were mostly logistical by nature. Even the transition period, except for a major tantrum when we first started out, a battle I had to win as he tested me, went well . . . he always behaved like he belonged."

Nonetheless, Marshall still felt obstacles from being a single dad.

"We're in a culture today that is disparaging about traditional mores, but the ideal way to raise a child, I believe, is still in a committed home with two parents . . . so in many ways I can look back and see that I've been inadequate as a parent. There were times I couldn't do something for him and had no one to pick up the slack for me. I did Little League and as much as I could, but it was hard without another person there, even with a good support system of friends."

The concept of being a single dad in a maternal world also weighed heavily at times.

"As a single man I can't ring a married woman's door and say "let's sit down and talk about our kids." Women can more easily develop communities among the shared experience of mothering and child rearing, but as a single man, you don't have access to that kind of support . . . you don't have guy friends with which to share your child-rearing stories . . . there's no sense of community. I felt like he suffered because he didn't grow up in a home which had a greater tie to the community. At times I felt very single. Along with that, he has never had a mother, and one of the things I regret for him was not being able to deal with the loss of his mother, who died shortly after he moved in here. His mother is still a big issue subconsciously and sometimes consciously. He writes poetry . . . he once wrote a poem about his mother that started out, "Mothers mothers everywhere but where is mine?" He then proceeded to get *angry. I hurt a lot for him and feel a lot of pain to see how he struggles. I remember on the first Mother's Day after his mom had died, we went and planted a memorial tree for her. But the next year he did not want to go back and see it. He is still very angry and won't work it through . . . at least not yet."*

Role Models

One of the most important issues you will face as a single parent, through adoption or otherwise, is how you view the opposite sex and how you incorporate the opposite sex into your family life. No matter what your personal sexual preferences are, you will need to provide role models of the opposite sex. If a woman displays anger or resentment toward men, her daughter may grow up with a negative opinion of men. Similarly, a single male who belittles or treats women in an unflattering manner will paint an inaccurate picture of women for a young boy. There are many variations on this theme. Single moms often admit that their sons would have benefited from having a strong male role model around, whether it's a personal friend or even someone in a Big Brother program.

You will need to compensate for not having a dad or mom in the household by finding such positive role models. Marshall, quoted above, added that Gregory had a very good relationship with his grandmother, Marshall's mom. However, you can't replace loss the child may feel, and you should not expect to.

In addition, you will have to explain two-parent families to your child in a positive manner. One single mom refused to let her son play at a friend's house because the friend had a father and she did not want him around fathers. This did not paint a realistic picture of the variety of family situations that exist. Let your son or daughter know how wonderful having either one or two parents can be. You will need to highlight the positives of your own family situation, but not deny that other types of families exist.

How you answer the question, "When am I going to have a mother/father?" is significant. Keep in mind that no matter how well you explain the various family situations, a child may sometimes feel badly that he or she does not have one parent. Allow him or her to feel sad and to explore and express those feelings.

Some resources for single parents looking to adopt:

The National Adoption Center, 1500 Walnut Street, Philadelphia, PA 19102, (215) 735-9988 or 1-800-TO-ADOPT.

SPAN, or the Single Parent Adoption Network offers numerous links and books for single parents. *(http://members.aol.com/Onemomfor2/)*

The National Council for Single Adoptive Parents. (formerly The Committee for Single Adoptive Parents) can provide a listing of adoption agencies that will work with you to locate a foreign child or children. NCSAP are located at P.O. Box 44, Wharton, NJ 07885; e-mail: ncsap@hotmail.com; Web-site: http://www.adopting.org/ncsap.html Inquire about their book.

Also, check the Department of Public Welfare or Social Services in your state and the state listings of available children from the foster-care system.

Chapter 19
FINANCING YOUR ADOPTION

Whether you choose a domestic agency or work with an attorney, adoption will likely cost you between $15,000 and $25,000. International adoption will be comparable. Only when adopting through a public placement agency will you incur little to no expense. In fact, you may even receive a subsidy.

For many people, a major concern is that adoption will simply cost too much money. If you've priced new cars lately, it may put adoption costs into perspective. The fees that you will pay throughout the adoption process will vary and are not payable all at one time. You should not be paying the bulk of—or even half of—your $15,000 to $25,000 in expenses up front. If an agency, attorney or particularly a facilitator asks for the $20,000 up front, this is not for you.

So how do you plan financially?

Once you have decided on your method of adoption, you should consider the sequence of steps involved. For example, if you are planning to adopt domestically through private placement (working with an attorney) your initial steps will include paying an attorney's retainer, paying for any state precertification necessary and paying for a home study. You should then add on additional money for buying books on adoption, such as this one, paying dues to join a support group, obtaining certified copies of various documents (such as your birth and marriage certificates) and perhaps some money to pay to attend an adoption conference. Home studies will usually range between $750 and $1,750. Assuming that your attorney asks for an initial fee of $2,000, you might estimate $4,500 (including other factors mentioned) as your initial costs for starting out in the adoption process.

Next you will want to look at fixed and variable costs that will arise during the adoption process. Installing a 1-800 phone line for birth mothers to call you on will be a fixed cost. However, paying for the calls that come in on your 1-800 number will be a variable, as will advertising costs. Estimate how much you will need for monthly advertising and phone calls, plus any expenses incurred by your attorney for phone calls, copies, and so on. If you are looking at for $500 monthly advertising, then you might need a total of $700 monthly to also cover the calls.

Once you are working with a birth mother, you may be paying some of her expenses. Try to keep this at a reasonable amount in accordance with the courts and what are considered legitimate adoption expenses. Also, remember, this should not be a "pay x amount or don't adopt" scenario. In addition, you will need to pay the birth mother's attorney fees and some expenses. Finally, you will pay when your attorney completes the adoption process—including finalization. This is the rest of the attorney's fee beyond what is already in escrow. Then of course, there are the travel expenses for when you fly or drive to the state in which the birth mother is giving birth.

In addition to all of this, you will be paying for a pediatrician to look at the birth mother's medical expenses and for counseling for the birth mother, and possibly for yourself.

Once you fill in the numbers on a monthly basis, you'll get an idea of how much your adoption should cost. You can then plan accordingly. With agency adoption, the set fees should be spelled out for you when you sign up with an agency.

Financing: Loans

A home equity loan, or borrowing against your home, is one way to procure a loan that allows you to use the money as you choose. Interest rates are usually low. You could also borrow against the cash value of your insurance.

> **Liquidity**
>
> *When adopting, try to keep a small portion of your assets liquid at all times since you may suddenly find yourself at the next step of the process, meeting or picking up your child, sooner than you expected. You want to keep at least three to six months liquidity at any given time in the process.*

New York City-based financial planner Loretta Goldberg, of Planning Center for Professionals, Inc. also notes that you can borrow against your pension plan as long as you are in a position where you expect to remain for a while. "The loans are good only as long as you're with the company," says Goldberg.

Friends and family should lend you money with very low interest rates, or none at all, considering the reason for the loan. Anyone who charges you a high interest rate to adopt a child gets limited visiting privileges and no photos! You can also cut back on some of your own expenses and perhaps take a less exotic vacation or milk your current car for another 20,000 miles.

The National Adoption Foundation (NAF) offers low-interest secured and unsecured loans to adoptive families who have completed home studies. (100 Mill Plain Road, Danbury, CT 06811, 203-791-3811; web-site: www.nafadopt.org. Also, MBNA America offers loans for the purposes of adoption: 800-626-2760.

Insurance

You may wish to have life insurance in place prior to your home study. In some cases, you can get a low-cost group life policy through your company or from a union or professional group to which you belong. Loretta Goldberg recommends getting six to ten times your annual income and also having disability insurance. Goldberg and her associate, Connie Cohort, emphasized the importance of disability insurance in several articles they wrote. They pointed out that people list various assets such as homes and cars as most valuable, but rarely include their jobs. They site statistics that one out of every two thirty-five-year olds will experience at least one ninety-day disability. They also note that disability claims are on the rise, particularly for carpal tunnel syndrome, which leaped by over 500 percent in recent years.

When planning to adopt, it is in your best interest to review and consider insurance options that will benefit yourself and your family in the future.

Company Benefits and Employee Assistance

A growing number of companies offer employee assistance for adoptions. Some will help by providing direct cash assistance while others will offer low-interest loans, reimbursements of approved expenses or paid leave. Check with your company's human resources department. You might also look at the website, www.adoptionbenefits.com, which has a chart listing over 400 companies and their policies regarding employment assistance for adoption. Policies may have changed since the chart was last updated, but it can give you an idea of what your company has offered in the past.

Remember: You won't know what company policies are until you ask. In many cases, smaller companies have no formal adoption-assistance program, but may work something out because of your inquiry. You may, in fact, break new ground in establishing a policy at your company.

Tax Credits

The federal government will also help you out with a $10,000 tax credit per adopted child, based on family income for the year in which the adoption took place. This credit starts to phase out at a family income level of $150,000 and goes up to $190,000 before the credit fades out completely. Expenses include reasonable and necessary adoption fees, attorney or agency fees, court costs, some travel costs, and other expenses directly related to, and whose principal purpose is for, the legal adoption of an eligible child. To claim the adoption credit, file Form 8839 with either your 1040 or 1040A form. Keep a copy of your records to support any credit claimed. It's advisable to ask a tax professional for guidance when determining which expenses qualify.

Expenses related to stepparent adoptions are *not* included.

For more information on the adoption tax credit, get IRS Publication 968.

> ### Dependents and Exemptions
>
> *Families must provide more than half of their children's support to list them as exemptions. Some adopted children receive subsidies, which may provide more than half of their support. For example, if a child receives $3,000 per year in subsidies, the adoptive family must provide at least $3,001 per year to claim the child as an exemption.*

Chapter 20
ADOPTION AND THE INTERNET

Yes, the Internet can help you spread the word that you are looking to adopt, let you look at photo listings of waiting children, read about the adoption process, communicate with others through chat rooms and e-mails, and learn about agencies. But no, you cannot adopt through the Internet.

There are numerous web-sites devoted to adoption, spanning a wide range of sub-topics from adoption how-tos to the heated debate on open adoption records. Information can be very easy to find, yet a bit harder to substantiate. Furthermore, even the most well-intentioned web-master will have a difficult time keeping up with the constantly-changing information regarding adoption laws and policies.

As you are learning, adoption has plenty of room for controversy and differing opinions. And where there is a wide range of opinions, there are both understated and overstated manners of expressing those opinions. You will encounter web-sites with strongly worded opinions playing on your (potentially vulnerable) emotions. If a web-site is preaching one form of adoption over another, you can be sure another site has the opposite opinion. You will also encounter web-sites providing objective nonjudgmental resource materials on adoption methods, costs, travel information, and so on. The best sites provide a broad range of viewpoints but are based mostly on factual information.

Below you'll find an overview of some of the less-opinion-oriented, more-information-based web-sites. Some of these sites are affiliated with agencies; others are not. This list is based on the overall merits of the site to provide easily accessible, objective information and is not an endorsement of any particular agency or web-site.

Note: You can potentially connect with a birth mother, learn a lot of valuable information, get help choosing a baby name, find a pediatrician in your area, locate an adoption attorney, find numerous agencies, get information on countries worldwide or play solitaire while waiting to become an adoptive parent—but you *cannot* formally complete an adoption over the Internet.

Adoption Web-sites

National Adoption Information Clearinghouse

The clearinghouse provides a wealth of official information and extensive resources on all areas of adoption for professionals, policy makers, and the general public. The information is updated frequently and is impartial because the site is not sponsored by an agency or adoption professional. You'll find statistics, adoption laws, state child-welfare agencies and photo listings, frequently asked questions and a lot more. Hot topics and recent adoption news and legislation, such as the Hague Convention on International Adoption can be found in the "What's New" section. There's also a handy conference calendar with regional and national adoption events. "Publications" is a vast resource section featuring fact sheets, statistics, international resources, federal publications, and more. *www.calib.com/naic*

Faces of Adoption

The National Adoption Center, a nonprofit organization founded in 1972 to expand adoption opportunities for children with special needs and from minority cultures, sponsors this very innovative and significant web-site in hopes of placing as many of America's 100,000+ waiting children as possible into permanent loving homes. The power and promise of the Internet and its ability to make a difference in the world is no more evident than looking at the faces of these often abused or neglected children. Information can be sent with details on how to adopt one of these children through the NAC's National Adoption Exchange, which allows for interstate placement of children in state foster-care systems throughout the country, after parents have completed a home study and are approved in their own state to adopt. Read the questions-and-answers section to learn how to use the photo directory and get more information about the children in the photo listings. The "Adoption Quest" section provides informative articles on a range of topics. Also browse the bookstore. *www.adopt.org*

Adoption.com

Be patient—this extensive web-site may load slowly. From birthmother.com, where birth mothers can look at parent profiles (sponsored by an agency) to an extensive community of boards, chats, and newsletters, this is a very comprehensive web-site. Resources run the gamut from baby names to a glossary to adoption laws and an adoption registry for searches. A directory lets you search by state or country for professional services including agencies and attorneys (starting with paid listings, followed by full listings). Much of the data is culled (by permission) from the National Adoption Information Clearinghouse, but there is a lot of additional material to peruse on this well-organized web portal. *www.adoption.com*

Rainbow Kids

An international on-line adoption magazine, Rainbow Kids provides a world of information. Click on one of the countries listed for country-specific requirements or link to one of nearly fifty international agencies. The site includes articles by experts on various topics of interest and concern. A popular e-mail list features a community where people who are interested in a specific aspect of international adoption can exchange information and share their knowledge, worries, triumphs, tragedies, hopes and dreams. Perhaps the most unique and worthwhile aspect of the Rainbow Kids web-site is the long list of stories from families who have adopted internationally. Read them whenever you're getting that sinking feeling that adoption will never happen for you. *www.rainbowkids.com*

Adopting.com

Adoptive parent Julie Valentine is the woman behind this massive portal that has grown into a significant adoption source. Sponsored sites are included on the home page and links lead to extensive alphabetized listings of agencies, facilitators, and attorneys. The "Getting Started" section connects with several large sites featuring general information on the important first steps to adoption. Photo listings feature waiting children, and you can find links to international support by country. *www.adopting.com*

The Adoption Guide

It's unfortunate that this site needs to exist, but it's a good one to have in mind when you venture into the process. Before clicking on the adoption guide, remind yourself that adoption *does* work, (read some of the stories on Rainbow Kids.com), there are many very happy adoption stories, and the majority of agencies and attorneys are reputable. The

Adoption Guide serves as a consumer-protection site featuring listings of agencies that have earned bad reputations, facilitators being investigated by the FBI, and cases of adoption fraud or scams. You'll find a warning list worth checking to make sure your agency or attorney is not listed (we've already warned you about facilitators) and a consumer-protection list. Despite winning a Forbes award for excellence, the site is slow loading and clunky to navigate—in fact, you may lose it and have to get back to it. Contact the Adoption Guide site if you run into anyone operating in an unethical or illegal manner. *www.theadoptionguide.com*

Joint Council on International Children's Services (JCICS)
JCICS is the oldest and largest affiliation of licensed, nonprofit international adoption agencies in the world. Parent, support and advocacy groups are all members of JCICS. The web-site includes updates on adoption legislation including the Hague Convention on International Adoption, a list of member agencies, an excellent country-by-country update, and a listing of agencies accredited to work with Russia. Plenty of postadoption information can also be found. *www.jcics.org*

Adoption.org
It's a beautiful day in the adoption.org neighborhood, as evidenced by the bright and cheerful buildings and planes flying overhead on the colorful home page. Designed to meet all of your needs, you can get the latest adoption news, post your profile for birth mothers to read, or join adoption discussions in the café. From informative links on all facets of the adoption process to thousands of baby names, some games and even a children's' Lullaby Library, you'll find a wealth of information at your fingertips. Search for adoption professionals by state or country, find info on the adoption tax credits, link to adoption laws, or

look for your employer on a company-by-company listing of adoption benefits. *www.adoption.org*

Hannah and Her Mama

Susan Ward, who adopted her daughter Hannah from Russia when Hannah was six years old, has put together a site that focuses on adopting an older child and single parenting. The site includes listings of agencies with waiting children, books, single-parent information, and very real, honest articles from Susan. Discussion listings, a bookstore, information on reactive attachment disorder, and a concise, to-the-point FAQ section are also included. Hannah has her own section on the site for kids called "Adopted Like Me!" *www.hannahandhermama.com*

Celebrate Adoption

A clean and simple uplifting site, Celebrate Adoption provides fact-based reasons why you should understand adoption and how it works. Misconceptions presented by the media are discussed. The goal of the group behind the site (a coalition of adoptive professionals, adoptive parents, birth mothers, and others) is to generate increased attention to the positive aspects of adoption. The site also provides a place for Kudos and Complaints and a list of media contacts where you can send a letter, e-mail, or make a phone call to discuss inappropriate references, comments or stories in the media regarding adoption. *www.celebrateadoption.org*

Adoption Directory

Several other sites link to this extensive portal which helps in locating adoption professionals nationwide and worldwide. Search by state, category, country, or keyword for an agency, attorney or one of the other professional services listed. Most have links directly to web-sites. The directory is updated often, and the listings are alphabetical. *www.adoptiondirectory.com*

Other sites worth checking out are the Dave Thomas Foundation web-site, for information on adopting from photo listings (*www.davethomasfoundation.com*); the Adoption Council of Canada's web-site (*www.adoption.ca*) for Canadian adoption information; the Immigration and Naturalization Service web-site with details of the international paperwork (*www.ins.usdoj.gov*); and the American Association of Adoption Attorneys web-site, mentioned earlier (*www.adoptionattorneys.org*).

Assessing a Good Web-site

1. Is there a range of opinion, or is the site pushing one viewpoint? Is the site objective or does someone behind the site have his or her own agenda?
2. Is the material up to date, or are the facts and figures outdated?
3. Is the site adoption-savvy? Hint: Words like "real parents" instead of "birth parents" may indicate that the site is run by people who are not well versed in adoption.
4. Is the site easy to navigate, or are you constantly getting lost?
5. Is the site trying to sell you everything under the sun or asking you to pay for information that is free elsewhere?
6. Is the site loaded with adoption (or other) ads? This may weaken the site's credibility when it comes to listings.

These questions will help you evaluate adoption web-sites. Remember, anyone can put together a good-looking web-site. Also, keep in mind that nearly every agency has a web-site. It should be clear that it is the *agency's* site and not disguised as a site offering generic information just to draw you in.

Finally . . . remember that there's a great deal of emotion involved with adoption. Even the best web-site, cannot offer a shoulder to lean on, so combine a real-life adoption support group with your web endeavors. Use the Internet to access information, then verify it through direct communication with adoption professionals and get honest opinions and support from other people in the adoption community.

Chapter 21
POSITIVE ADOPTION LANGUAGE

Let's face it, adoptive families have feelings too. Since so many people misunderstand adoption, it is often misrepresented, leaving many people unsure how to handle the subject.

Adoptive families frequently encounter language that is adoption unfriendly or simply does not present a positive image. When adoption is portrayed in a negative manner, it continues the negative perception about adoption, as discussed earlier in the chapter on adoption and the media.

However, it's not the media alone that perpetuates the negative image of adoption. Very often well-meaning individuals use terminology that is insensitive. Words can be very powerful, and children, in particular, not only pick up on such wording, but often find a more literal connotation to what is being said. As adults, you may need to step in and correct the speaker politely. I've used the phrases "you mean birth mother" or "*we are her real parents*" many times to do this.

As adoptive parents, you are indeed real parents. Just as a couple is married by law and no one doubts that your spouse is your real husband or real wife, your child is just that; your *real* child. Therefore, being asked if you know his or her real parents is both troubling and insensitive. "Birth parents" more clearly defines the role of birth mothers and fathers. It's hard not to feel like "real" parents when you're washing a scraped knee and wiping away the accompanying tears, playing editorial assistant on a book report about Pocahontas, or praying that he or she will make contact as a pitch sails toward home plate. Parenting is very real, no matter how you get there.

The adoptee will also very often feel confused and troubled by a statement such as "Have you ever met your real parents?". Young children don't understand. Are they being told that their parents who love and take care of them are fake? As children who were adopted grow up, they learn to respond, "These are my real parents." Likewise, the term "natural parents" insinuates that adoptive parents are not natural.

It's important to correct individuals when they use phrases that clearly insinuate that you are not the parents, or that your child is less than your real child. You need to support the fact that you are very much a real family that came together through adoption. Your children's friends may wrestle with the concept because they do not understand adoption. Hopefully, their parents will understand what adoption is all about. Unfortunately, that is not always the case. Often well-meaning parents will say the wrong thing in trying to explain adoption, which is an odd concept for a young child to grasp, especially one who has not previously been exposed to it.

Phyllis, who adopted her daughter Rita as an infant, talks about how she helps Rita, now eight, deal with inquisitive friends:

> *"My daughter had several friends who asked me whether or not Rita was adopted. Rita liked to tell her friends that she was adopted, and that was always entirely up to her. Most of her friends took the news in stride. One friend, however, just kept saying that it seemed weird and asked if we knew her real parents. I*

explained that Rita's father and I were indeed her "real" parents, and that she did have birth parents. She didn't quite understand, but as she saw how Rita loved us as her mom and dad, it became more understandable to her that we were indeed Rita's real parents. In time we also met her mother who had a greater understanding of adoption, but still used terms like 'real parents,' which we corrected. It takes time to readjust people's attitudes about adoption. They generally don't understand that adoption is a very real and common way of forming a family."

Adoption has other questionable terms, such as "gave a child away" or "gave up a child for adoption," which makes a child feel that someone gave up on them or simply did not want them. This can lead to feelings of inferiority or low-self esteem. "Placing a child for adoption" or "making an adoption plan" are more positive ways of explaining this process. Such phrases also portray the birth mother in a more positive light, showing that she consciously placed the child or made a well-thought-out plan and did not just give up or reject the child.

Other phrases may also tend to rattle members of the adoption triad or give off the wrong message. For example, when someone introduces your son or daughter as your adopted child, it makes adoption sound like something unique that must be specifically singled out. Your children are your children, and they should not be labeled. No one introduces a child as your birth child. Likewise the phrase "is" adopted gives off the impression that the child deals with being adopted on a daily basis, as if he or she is taking medication for it. "Was" adopted indicates that the adoption happened, in past tense, as was the case, just as the birth happened and is now over.

Some adoptive parents are more sensitive than others. As is

the case with the media, it is a matter of picking and choosing your battles. You need to understand that because of your affinity for adoption and understanding of the process, you will be more sensitive to how adoption is discussed by those around you. You do not need to be on the defensive every time the subject comes up. Some adoptive parents are ready to argue any time the word "adoption" comes up. The reality is that adoption is a word used in other contexts, and sometimes misused, but nonetheless is not defined only as the adoption of a child. Supersensitivity also suggests discomfort about adoption, and that, too can reflect upon a child. If mom or dad always get upset when they hear anyone mention adoption, a child may get the wrong impression and think of it as a negative term. Therefore, while you are looking to improve how adoption is presented, you also do not want to present yourself to your children as someone fighting windmills.

Remember: The vast majority of people you meet are not against adoption, they simply do not know nearly as much about it as you will, once you have adopted a child.

Some Other Words / Phrases You Might Think About

Negative	Positive
Foreign adoption	International adoption
Natural parent	Biological parent
Unwanted child	Waiting child
To take a child	To adopt a child
Paying for a child	Paying fees toward adopting a child

Chapter 22
THE ADOPTIVE FAMILY: SHARING INFORMATION

Congratulations! Once you've adopted, you'll hear that word many times. The relief from the stress of being on the waiting side of the adoption process will be very much welcomed. You will have numerous opportunities to tell your adoption story, and each time it will have a happy ending. However, once the story of adopting a child concludes, life begins as a family, an adoptive family. I separate the two points because you will be both; a family and an adoptive family. There will be numerous issues common to all families and additional issues relating to the fact that your family was formed by adoption. You cannot deny this part of your family story any more than you can deny the other characteristics that make your family—and every family—unique. For too many years, adoption was closeted, concealed and tucked away as a deep, dark secret. People denied how their family was formed. However, adoption is not shameful, nor is it "unusual" as the media might insinuate. It is simply how your family came to be.

When reading about adoption, you will hear from one person that the adopted child is growing up with great pain, while someone else will tell you that the child experiences loss and then moves on through that loss without being caught in an emotional impasse. The truth is that there is no right answer. People write and speak from their own life experiences, which are a combination of their environmental and genetic history. Why is one person more sensitive than another? Why does one woman say, "I thought about my birth mom and considered doing a search, but it never really mattered to me." Why does another woman say, "I never felt like I was complete. I always knew I had a birth mother out there somewhere, and I wanted to meet her to find out who I really was."

The answer is that people experience life based on their physiological make-up and their temperament in conjunction with how they were raised, including their culture, and the place(s) where they grew up. The blank slate that is the child, may be more analogous in modern culture to the workings of computer programs. Some programs have more advanced features and can achieve finer results because of how they were created. Other, simple programs can achieve great results because of the skills of the person at the keyboard. You will create the final draft of the project you are working on. You will be able to shape, mold, and encourage positive traits and characteristics in your child. A child who is athletically inclined and is encouraged to play sports may gain great self-confidence because he or she excels at such an activity. This will happen only through positive reinforcement and encouragement. A child who is stifled when looking to pursue an area of interest will not feel the support necessary to excel in that area. Similarly, a child who is brought up in a household that encourages communication about adoption, and neither hides nor overdramatizes the adoption story, will feel more self-confident and more comfortable when the subject is addressed.

Environment will shape the child in so many ways, and *you* play the significant role in this portion of a child's life. By adopting a child, you are environmentally shaping the child's life in a major way from the moment he or she joins your family. When adopting an older child, you will find that there has already been writing on that blank slate and numerous environmental influences. The older the child, the harder it is to influence the child's behavior significantly. It will take greater effort and greater reinforcement.

In this chapter, I discuss one of two key issues regarding raising your child; the handling of information. In the next chapter, I'll discuss a child's understanding of adoption as they develop, how you talk with your child about adoption, adult adoptees, and what a search may or may not mean to your son or daughter—and to yourself.

The Handling of Information: Everyone Knows and No One Knows

If you are a Caucasian couple walking down the street with an Asian baby, it will be fairly obvious that you have adopted the child—either that or are you are taking care of a friend's baby. Most international adoption is clearly discernible to the naked eye. By contrast, most domestic adoptions afford you the opportunity to decide with whom you choose to share the information.

However, there is a lot more to it than who knows that you have adopted. "When a child is a baby you can't anticipate the problems that will be caused by sharing information with other people," says Anne Malave, New York City-based clinical psychologist, and adoptive parent. "How you handle sharing information with others is very important. It's hard to balance openness and secrecy. You need to think about what you tell other people . . . what to disclose and what to keep private."

The issue of privacy and openness about your adoption is a touchy one. On one hand, although you will enjoy sharing your adoption story, you do not want to ramble on about adoption and make it appear to be something out of the ordinary. Adoptive families want to be thought of as "typical families" like all others and do not wish to be singled out. However, if you remain too private about adoption, then you are perceived as cloaking adoption in secrecy.

To talk or not to talk: That is the question. Often you'll find that you're damned if you do and damned if you don't. You'll wish you had not broached the subject in some situations with people who are naïve about adoption and may judge you. You'll also wish you had been more forthright with other individuals who would embrace the situation.

When adopting an infant, it is tempting to share a wealth of information with other people, forgetting that when your child is seven, his aunt or uncle may share information about the birth parents or birth siblings that you are not ready to explain. Not that the information is classified, only that you want to explain it first and not have it blurted out accidentally or incorrectly. You may find it advantageous to share general information with others, but not divulge that which you feel should come from you as the parent(s). Draw a clear line between such general information and private matters just as you would with issues that take place in the privacy of your own home. For this reason, I reiterate my earlier comments about not telling everyone under the sun that you are looking to adopt. You don't need thoughtless remarks, later on, from someone who knows your child was adopted but is insensitive regarding adoption issues.

Naturally, the older the child, the more he or she will know about his or her background. You will need to steer conversations onto more adoption-friendly tracks when someone asks you, "Was her real mother a druggie?" in front of your daughter whom you adopted at the age of seven and fully understands the question. You'd be surprised at how insensitive people can be. Therefore, you need to balance private and public issues as you would with financial matters, your sex life, or any other topic that is not for the general public.

Positive Image

Adoption is a positive thing. It may take children from an institutionalized situation and place them into a loving family. It may also allow for a birth mother to give a child much more than she feels she can offer emotionally or financially.

Therefore, you need to reflect adoption as positive and normal.

Talking about adoption at home, in general terms, makes the subject more familiar. *"We talked about adoption, not necessarily our adoption, but about the subject,"* says Carol F. (mentioned earlier in the book), mother of two, one child that was adopted and one biological child. *"Our kids never thought of adoption as anything out of the ordinary. They grew up knowing that it is one way in which families are formed. By not whispering about it or avoiding the topic, we normalized it around our children, our families and our friends. If someone made a comment that was insensitive, we politely corrected them."*

"Get used to talking about adoption so that you're not nervous discussing it with other people" says Anne Malave. "If others see that you are calm in discussing adoption, they will follow your lead. Sometimes this takes time." Dr. Malave adds that adoption is full of meaning and can be disturbing to people who have not come in contact with it. "Adoption evokes strong feelings. Even though it is centuries old, it is something which goes against what the majority of people culturally understand. Family is most often defined by bloodline, and adoption is crossing those bloodlines. Even though it's acknowledged, it's still different or mystifying to others."

Today, nearly 60 percent of Americans are touched by adoption in some manner, many through a relative or a friend. Just as you had to adjust your thinking to proceed down the path to adoption, others are asked to adjust their thinking to understand your adoption.

This may take time. If you fly off the handle every time

someone says something you don't like, you present adoption as something that is a very touchy subject, hence not normal. If you shush the subject away or do not want to talk about it, you create secrecy. If you handle the subject in a manner that radiates confidence and a belief that adoption forms families, then you can spread that message and normalize adoption for others. Also remember that your children pick up on how you present things. Although you may not even respond verbally, a child can pick up on how you react.

Comments

When others ask about her "real parents," correct them and say, "You mean birth parents; we're her real parents now."

When others ask if you know anything about her background, tell them you have some information, but then share only the details you feel she will be comfortable talking about when she gets older.

When others ask how someone could give up such a beautiful child, tell them that the adoption plan was made before they ever knew how beautiful she would be and that there were reasons why her birth mother made the plan to place her for adoption. You need not go into the details. Correct the phrase "given up" with "placed" for adoption.

When someone asks how much you paid to get her, explain that you did not pay to get her, you adopted her and paid only for services rendered by an agency/attorney just as you pay for services rendered by a physician.

Note: *One nine-year-old boy adopted from Brazil was with his family in a supermarket when an adult asked the parents how much they paid for him. Before his parents could respond, the boy shot back, "How much did your parents pay for you?"*

When others ask whom he or she looks like, say "himself, or herself." If you want to raise eyebrows, say "the mailman."

Stay calm, be humorous if the situation fits, correct others if necessary, and don't volunteer more information than you feel anyone else needs to know. The less someone understands adoption, the more you should explain the basics. For example, if someone is pressing you for how much all of this costs, explain that you paid for x, y and z—the services rendered. You do not need to give them exact numbers unless you are talking to a couple, or single, who is actually looking to adopt and you feel comfortable disclosing such information.

Adoption and The Schools

To tell or not to tell? Again, a tough question.

This is an issue that may sometimes begin at the application process. If you are applying to a school, the question should not be on the form as to whether or not your child is adopted. However, sometimes it is. Look at forms in advance and determine how you wish to answer this intrusive question. You can always leave it blank, but that can also be an answer.

There is no reason why a school application should force you to disclose personal information and every reason to wonder how this will be used. You may find yourself in the precarious position of explaining to the school that while your child is adopted, there is no reason why this should be public information. However, this also puts you in the position whereby it appears that you are trying to hide adoption. Therefore, you are in an unfair position no matter how you look at it.

When discussing adoption, every school will most certainly reassure you that they are "very sensitive to adoption issues." Some may put their foot in their mouth while doing so. One principal told a mother, *"We never addressed the issue with the child or ever mentioned anything about his* real *parents."* Now, there's sensitivity!

Most often the choice is yours to discuss adoption with the school your child attends. One mother went to broach the subject to her daughter's first-grade teacher, who responded, "Oh I knew she was adopted. Cynthia's mother told me." This goes back to whether or not you spread the word in a big way.

The key to telling teachers and administrators about adoption is evaluating their response. How they react and what they say or do with the information is your primary concern. You may need to follow up by asking if they have had other adopted children in their classes? Are there lesson plans in which there could be a problem (such as the old "family tree")? How the teacher responds will give you a tremendous sense of security or panic. You will either breathe a sigh of relief knowing this teacher is sensitive and understands adoption, or you will curse yourself when you leave, knowing you may need to do some damage control after this teacher says something insensitive— or what I like to call *j.p.s.* (just plain stupid).

I recall our daughter coming home all excited when she found out her fourth-grade teacher was an adult adoptee. My daughter gladly told her that she was adopted, too. Suddenly this was her favorite teacher—she was "cool." They shared a bond that she had not shared with her other teachers.

The arguments against telling a teacher are centered around how the teacher or school will use (or misuse) the information. If a child misbehaves, do the teachers look at one another in the teachers' cafeteria and say, "Well, you know she's adopted, don't you?" Adoption can be used as a label or an easy excuse for why a child does poorly or misbehaves in school. The real reason may be simply that like millions of other children, the child is not paying attention or talks too much. You don't want old, stereotypical attitudes about adoption thrust upon your child, nor do you want your child discriminated against or even receiving preferential treatment.

If your child is adopted from another country, and your story is "public," you will still need to determine what lesson plan(s) may come up that might be potentially more difficult for your child. You may also want to see how his or her cultural background is addressed in the studies, if it should come up. You will have to assess the teacher's comfort level and, again, note how the teacher will or will not use this information.

Once the school is aware that your child was adopted, try to keep track of any issues that arise from it. Without asking, see if your child hints at, or tells you outright, about any comments or concerns about adoption that came up in school and need to be addressed, especially if they came up from a teacher or administrator. Bring up the subject of adoption periodically at home in a general manner and see how your son or daughter responds. Sometimes a child will tell you that so-and-so mentioned adoption in school. Other times your child will not want to talk about it. How he or she dismisses the topic will indicate whether or not it's just of no interest at the moment, or there is something that he or she does not want to address.

> **The Ol' Family Tree**
>
> *Most teachers should be able to find an alternative manner in which to do a family tree. Some children make what is called a grafted tree, which has a section for the biological parents, and their history, connecting to the section with the adoptive parents and their history.*

Like all parents today, you will need to be proactive and advocate for your child when necessary. If he or she needs special classes to catch up developmentally, should be in a Head Start or a gifted program, you will have to get involved in making this happen. You will also often have to ask for evaluations when necessary, sometimes outside of the school to avoid labels on permanent records.

Your Child's Own Story

Once your child has a clear understanding of how adoption works, which may be at six, seven, or eight years of age, your adoption story becomes his or her story. At that time, you need to start respecting his or her right to tell or not tell others. Follow your child's lead, but "float balloons" once in a while to see if the child wants to discuss the subject. Children may have more to say than they express verbally. Chapter 23 has more on talking with your children about adoption.

At some point, your child will begin telling other children that he or she was adopted. Keep in mind that when children start talking to others about adoption, they may be in for a rude awakening by the responses they receive. Many kids have discussed adoption at home and around their family, where the responses have been nothing but positive and uplifting. Other children do not understand adoption and may rain on their parade. Allow your child to feel hurt, and don't offer to run out and fight windmills for him. You need to explain that adoption is not something other people are as well versed in as your child. If you get bent out of shape your child will likely overreact, which can lead to more conflict because children who antagonize others feed on weakness in other children.

On the other hand, don't glorify adoption. It is ill advised to tell a child that he or she was "chosen," or to portray adoption

---

"Blame Adoption" School Syndrome

The perception that adoption is at the root of the problem may be valid, but often is not. Sometimes a problem in childhood, preadolescence, or the teen years is simply a problem that needs to be addressed. However, watch that teachers and other important people in your child's life understand that adoption is not to blame for everything. Make distinctions between adoption-related and non-adoption-related issues.

as something to be exalted. You want to normalize the process, not build it up so that the child is in for an obvious letdown. Think about future repercussions of your statements.

Laying The Groundwork

Family and close friends need the short course Adoption 101, and perhaps some required reading. Be proactive (not demanding) and make the effort to gently educate those around you.

The responses and reactions to adoption from the people in your neighborhood or community will vary by the nature of where you are living and raising your child(ren). Often parents who have adopted internationally, gay adoptive parents, or in some cases single adoptive parents, will be more conscious of selecting a town or city that they feel will better accept and understand not only adoption, but their choice of lifestyle. Children adopted internationally will particularly benefit more from a "mixed" ethnic diversity. *"I didn't want my daughter to be the only Asian child in an all-white school,"* explained one parent who chose not to move to the suburbs. *"In the city she is able to fit in more comfortably."* Comfort and normalcy are very important when assimilating into a culture that is not one's own.

Chapter 23
ADOPTEES: UNDERSTANDING ADOPTION

Once upon a time adoption was not discussed or even disclosed to children until they were in their teens or adulthood. This was a great disservice, as the news was shocking and upsetting to a mature individual who had no prior knowledge of such information. Suddenly all that this person knew about his or her life was turned around. Today, the overwhelming sentiment on the part of adoptive families is that children should grow up knowing that they were adopted. The subject should be part of the child's life.

Children under the age of five will generally not understand what adoption means but they will know it is something positive if it is presented as such. The subject can be discussed around the house and they can become familiar with the word "adopted." Often a three-year-old will mistake the phrase "I'm adopted" and tell people "I'm a doctor." As long as the term becomes familiar in the household, it doesn't matter.

Of course the idea of talking about adoption does not mean it should become the focal point of household conversations. You also do not want to label your child as your adopted son or daughter. Nor do you want to make a major issue about adoption and overemphasize the point with comments like "adoption means you were chosen" or "adoption makes you very special." Adoption is how a child came to be a part of the family. When you're looking at baby pictures with your four-year-old you might comment, "That was taken the day after we adopted you." Try to fit adoption in as a part of everyday life.

Young children enjoy stories, and there are many books that include adoption. In addition, *Sesame Street, Barney,* and other television programs geared for preschoolers have also presented episodes on the subject. As a child approaches school age, you can tell the story of how you became a family. Often a child will start asking questions about being a baby, or where he or she came from. The most common scenario for adoptive parents is to explain that mommy and daddy (or mommy for a single mom), wanted a baby but could not have one grow in her tummy. You can then explain that he or she grew in another woman's belly and after being born, was adopted, which meant becoming your son or daughter. That's how you became mommy and daddy. Keep it simple.

Naturally, children will ask plenty of questions. "Why didn't the other woman want me?" is among the toughest questions the child will ask. You need to explain carefully that it was not that she did not want you, but that she could not take care of any baby as a mommy and wanted to make sure her baby had a very good mommy and daddy. It's always important to tell a child consistently that he or she is not at fault for the birth mother placing them for adoption. By the way, they won't know the term "birth mother." You also need to emphasize that the birth mother did this out of love.

"At four-years-old, she started asking me whose belly she had been in," says Sheila, single adoptive mom of LuAnne, mentioned previously in chapter two. *"By the time she was five, she started saying she wanted to go to visit China. So far I have told her that we can go there when she is a teen, and she has*

been repeating this to people. As far as who her birth parents are, I tell her they couldn't take care of her, but brought her to a place where she could wait for me to come for her. I have told her that we probably will never know them."

While a young child will not grasp what all of this is about, he or she will have the basic story and eventually will come back with some questions. You can then provide information about adoption, in small doses as you see fit. If you squelch the discussion or tell a child that you do not want to discuss adoption, you will be sending the wrong message. If you feel the child is too young to process too much information, you may put off some of the details for a later time. Young children can grasp only so much information at one time and it's easy to steer a conversation onto something else after a few minutes. Buy time when you need to, but always be willing to talk about adoption and allow your children to ask questions and ponder possibilities. For example, your child might make up a scenario of what her birth mom is really like. Allow her to do so. If it sounds negative, try to paint a better portrait in kid-friendly terms.

One of the best ways to learn how your child feels and thinks about the concept of family, including adoption, is through play. When you play house, or watch them playing and creating different scenarios, you learn a lot about how they view the world. This is especially important with children who are not very vocal about expressing their feelings. Drawings by young (or even older) children can also be very enlightening. You can sometimes get a glimpse into their understanding of "family" through the pictures they draw.

As children process the information and as they hear stories of mommies, daddies, and babies, whether it's sheep, cows or people, they will make connections and begin to understand the family unit. In some instances, they will think that every baby will be adopted, while in other cases they will ask again if they grew in your belly. This is a hint that he or she is catching on to the differences in adopted children and biological children. "I grew in my mommy's tummy," one little girl told a friend who responded, "I grew in another lady's tummy." The other little girl didn't believe her friend and told her she was wrong—she had to grow in her mommy's tummy. You will need to reassure her, lovingly, that her story is indeed correct, that families are formed in all different ways . . . and that's perfectly okay. Your child will educate other children about adoption slowly with help from that child's parents, who will inevitably be fielding questions as well.

If you have a young child first grasping the concept of adoption, you will need to discuss adoption with your family as well. Mike, father of an adopted ten-year-old girl, explains, "*My sister told her seven-year-old daughter that we brought our daughter home from the hospital. While that was true, she never told her that our daughter was adopted, and* then *brought home from the hospital . . . a major difference. Apparently my sister could not figure out how to tell her own daughter that her cousin had been adopted. Nearly a year after we adopted our daughter, our niece was surprised to find out that she had an adopted cousin. It troubled her at first, but not for long. It's fortunate, however, that my wife and I discuss adoption frequently so the subject came up. Otherwise our niece might not have found out their cousin was adopted for several years. She would have been much more upset at that time. She would have felt her parents had lied to her, and in a way they did, or simply didn't tell her what she should know.*"

By the time a child reaches seven, he or she may begin seeking out more answers about his or her birth parents, state or country of origin, and cultural background. Children experience curiosity and begin to experience sadness and loss, realizing that they are not connected to their biological family in the same manner as most of their friends are connected to their families. It is very important to understand that you should not deny them these feelings. The sense of loss is very real and very normal, as they are now more fully beginning to feel a sense of separation from the birth family. Adoptive parents need to understand that this is not a reflection on them. This is not an either-or situation in which your child suddenly wants his or her birth family over you. If anything, the child may be searching for you to reaffirm your love and build his or her sense of security. It is a time when a child is trying to understand where he or she fits into the world. Don't be surprised if your child tests you.

At times, a child may feel sad or angry about adoption. While you will have the parental urge to try to make everything all better, do not deny your child these feelings, or try to convince him that adoption should always be thought of as "happy" and "wonderful." Like everything else, there are highs and lows. Too many adoptive parents panic when their child has negative thoughts about adoption. That isn't fair to the child. Most adult adoptees agree that open and honest communication is the cornerstone.

Early Understanding

"Children start understanding what adoption means at about the age of six or seven," explains Ronny Diamond. C.S.W., and Director of Post Adoption Services at Spence-Chapin, a century-old New York City-based adoption agency. "Kids will get different responses from friends than the message they have been getting at home, and they will react. They may suddenly think, this isn't as great as my family thinks it is. Their best friends may react with statements like 'you don't look adopted,'" explains Diamond. "Children begin to understand the bittersweet element, and that not everyone understands adoption."

Children may try to piece together a lot of issues in their own ways. An active imagination can fuel a lot of interesting scenarios regarding adoption. Sometimes such scenarios will cause a child to act out because he or she is angry about adoption. No matter how you handle discipline issues or other behavioral problems, you must always make your sure your son or daughter feels the security and permanency of being part of a family. A punishment for bad behavior has nothing to do with adoption and being loved.

How much your child tests you, questions adoption, wrestles with his or her personal history, or handles the issues of adoption throughout his or her life will be very much a part of his or her own temperament. "If you are intense and struggle with things, you will struggle with adoption issues," says Ronny Diamond. "However, if you are more carefree, easygoing, and laid back, then adoption will become another part of who you are and will not be an ongoing struggle. Temperament is inborn and constant. Some people will continue to grieve, and others will move on."

Diamond and other postadoption experts do not deny that there will be some hurt associated with adoption. "Just as adoptive parents may always feel some hurt that they were not able to give birth," adds Diamond. "It is not directed at anyone, nor does it affect their ability to give love. It is just something that will remain inside."

The Middle Years

The middle years (ages seven through eleven or twelve) are difficult for kids in so many ways. Their bodies are changing, and they are moving into a phase in which their peers are their cornerstones in life. With any luck, you have joined a support group and can offer them at least a few peers who were also adopted. You cannot create friendships, but you can let them know that so-and-so was also adopted. Knowing other children who joined their families through adoption is valuable because it lessens the feeling of being unique or the only one.

By the time a child reaches puberty, he or she should know as much as you can give them about their background and history. If you are in an open relationship with the birth mother or birth parents, this might be the time where they can write a letter or establish their own line of communication. There are several schools of thought as to whether this is really in the child's best interest. A lot will depend on who the birth mother is and how she will react to such contact. Some staunch believers of "very" open adoption feel that because the birth mother can provide all the "correct" answers, this is in the child's best interest. However, if the birth mother is not tuned in to the child's sensitivity, she may make the child feel worse. Instances of being disappointed by a birth mother at this young age have proven very difficult on a child emotionally, whereas an older individual may have developed the emotional resources to handle the situation better. Some birth mothers do not want to be found, and others do not want to remain in contact. In fact, several families report that the birth mother was in the picture when the child was younger but has had less and less contact, having moved on with her current family situation. This can also be more hurtful to the child, who is now experiencing loss yet again. Remember, "openness" is a double-edged sword and while it can be a problem solving solution to closed adoption, it can also present a new set of problems.

When contemplating a child's contact with his or her birth mother at a young age, it's also worth mentioning that a child develops abilities, self-confidence, and self-esteem through play and by using his or her imagination. Children dream of being major-league baseball players, world-famous dancers or actors or actresses . . . they don't see the practicalities of every issue and do not usually understand things like financial implications. A child is going to fantasize. When children are young, they believe in the tooth fairy. As they get older, they place enormous credence in what their peers say and do, even if that includes hair dyeing and body piercing. Therefore, taking the framework in which children grow and develop into account, you need to evaluate whether or not contact with the birth mother will fit into that framework. Remember; the child is not coming from the same perspective of openness in adoption that you are envisioning as an adult. If everything is taken into account early on and the relationship with the birth mother remains strong, open adoption can work very well, but it needs to be established so that both sets of parents are united on maintaining the best interests of the child.

In a closed adoption, you can try to get information through your agency or your attorney's office. In the case of an international adoption or one in which the birth mother specifically wanted to move on with her life, not allowing for any communication, you will need to do your best to help your child speculate about his or her birth mother. When your child is older, he or she might be able to search, but for now you can go with his or her perceptions of the birth mother and what you infer based on the child's looks and abilities. "I think your birth mother or father must have had beautiful blond hair because you do," says a mother to her daughter as they try and figure out more about her birth mother. Remember, it's okay to allow children to use their imaginations; that's what kids do. The best you can do is help shape their perceptions.

International Adoptees

In the case of a child adopted from another country or of a different ethnic background, it is very important to provide aspects of his or her culture. You may read books about the child's country of origin, learn recipes, play music, and eventually take a trip overseas. Be prepared to help them embrace some of their culture. You need to address the positives and even the negatives, such as stereotypes, that he or she may come in contact with. As is the case with adoption, people who are not familiar with a specific culture may have misconceptions and may not always respond politely. You cannot gloss over this when it happens to your child, who will inevitably hear some ethnic slurs while growing up. Try to help put everything into perspective and accentuate the positives.

Heritage camps and tours are ways to allow your child to experience his or her own ethnic background. Holt International and other agencies sponsor such heritage camps, where children can learn about their cultural history. In addition, there are groups, like Families with Children from China (FCC) (www.fcc.org), who meet to share their children's culture. FCC now has over eighty chapters nationwide. You can also find heritage tours, which provide a journey into a nation's culture and history. The idea of experiencing culture and traditions allows adoptees to build an awareness of their roots and origins. Tours are designed for all family members, so they can learn and share these experiences together.

Keep in mind that heritage tours, culture camps, and other means of acquainting your child with his or her culture may not be for every child. As children get older and find their own interests, they may not want to focus on issues of heritage. In fact, they may not want to discuss adoption issues, either. Understand that children will be very caught up in pop culture, school, peers, playing, and "being cool." This is quite typical and age appropriate. Just as a biological child of any background may not want to spend the day at a museum dedicated to his or her heritage, you can't push a child who was adopted to learn about his or her culture. And, you can't push the subject of adoption. Some children simply are not interested. This does not mean he or she is harboring any great turmoil inside. From the perspective of different temperaments, you will find some children who simply will grow to adulthood without focusing on adoption issues very much at all. Try to understand what your child is feeling about adoption issues. Look for nonverbal cues and be ready if and when your child wants to discuss adoption and or his or her culture.

"I think that being around other Asian children would have meant a lot to me," says Marilyn, who was, adopted at the age of six from Korea by an Irish family in suburban Long Island.

"Adoption was never talked about in my house, nor was my culture. Until I was in the fourth grade, I thought I was Irish. I didn't know other Asian children or anything about my culture. Someone called me a "chink" and I knew it was a bad word. It was a rude awakening and the first time I realized I was Asian. My family was very conservative and just assumed that I would fit right in . . . they did not acknowledge the cultural differences. I felt part of the nuclelus of the family, but didn't feel the same attachment that I feel now for my own son. When

When Will Adoption Come Up?

You never know when your child will suddenly throw an adoption question your way. Often it is when you're trying to parallel-park an SUV or racing around the backyard to turn an outdoor barbecue into an indoor party as the first rain drops hit. Nonetheless, you need to stay calm, poised, and be ready to either talk in brief about the subject or set aside a time later to talk. There are, however, certain times in life that adoption is more likely come up in the household. Below are some common times when your child(ren) may bring up the subject of their adoption.

1. Birthdays;

2. Mother's Day, Father's Day, plus some other major family holidays;

3. Major transitions like starting at a new school or moving to a new house;

4. Changes in the family, including birth, marriage, divorce, or death of a relative;

5. School lessons on family, biology, or reproduction;

6. Getting a family pet.

adoption issues were brought up, my family joked about them. I was brought up to joke about adoption and shrug it off. If it wasn't for the cultural differences, I might not have ever even known that I was adopted. Instead, I had very low self-esteem and felt ashamed of being Asian."

Marilyn agrees that if the subjects of adoption and cultural distinctions had been addressed at home, she would have felt better about herself. Instead she kept journals and wrote about her feelings of loss. She wrote about feelings that she could not discuss with her parents.

Birth Parents and Adoptive Parents

Yes, both adoptive and birth parents will feel threatened at different times. It's important to respect and acknowledge each other and understand your differing roles, whether or not there is contact between the parties. Like it or not, your child has two sets of parents. Neither set of parents should belittle the other's role or who they are as individuals. If there is an open line of communication, it can work very well if everyone understands who they are in relationship to the child and are comfortable with themselves. When either side starts to lie, belittle, or destroy the image of the other party, the child suffers.

Adopting Older Children

When you bring an older child into your family, obviously he or she has a much clearer picture of his or her life up to that time. The child knows very well where he or she has been, whether it's a group home or foster-care homes. There is more work on everyone's part when adopting older children. There is a much greater level of distrust. After all, the child may wonder why you should keep him since he has already been moved from home to home before. "Therefore, it's up to you to provide unconditional love," says Ronny Diamond. "A child needs to feel secure in a family, and then he or she needs to be able to grieve and feel angry and know that it's okay to have these feelings."

Children need to understand that there are different parts to their story. Whether it was various foster homes or an abusive birth parent, they need to be able to explore and understand what each part of their story was all about and know that they are not at fault for the lack of a secure home environment until now. You can provide the child with mementos and items from his or her past and discuss where they have been. However, some children may not want to deal with their past and you cannot force them to confront these issues. Your job is not to solve all of the child's issues instantly—this can be said for any child who was adopted. Yours is to help them recognize where they have been and that they are here now and are loved. Trying to keep a child who comes from such a background in the present is helpful as you can create a less stressful environment in the present.

Teens

Adolescence and the teen years are tumultuous, in general. Personal appearance, dating, peer pressure, school, and a host of other issues are all vying for attention. Depending on the individual child, adoption is somewhere in the mix. Teens, by nature, do not share a lot of information or discuss their opinions or feelings with their parents. The are very protective of their thoughts and are guarded in general, especially around their parents. How many teens really want to spend much time around mom and dad, anyway?

Teens will test you when they can. They'll see how you react to threats that they are going off to be with their "real family." Whether adoption is used as a trump card or not, you cannot let them manipulate or intimidate you. You will need to hold your ground on the many issues you will have with teens.

Teens also want information and, in some cases, to find their birth parents. You can be supportive, help point them in the right direction, but let them know that a search can sometimes lead to disappointment. Often a teen's desire to search is more a desire to see how you will react. They want to see if you will "freak out." Keep in mind also that teens seek easy short-term solutions to problems and may believe that a search, or contact with their birth mother, will solve everything. Of course, this is generally not the case.

You may find that discussing adoption issues on more general terms may be an easier, less intrusive way to communicate with an emotionally guarded teen.

Teen adoptees run the gamut from those who want to know their birth mother or birth parents to those who would just assume wait awhile to deal with the subject. It is all a matter of what is going on in life at any given moment, and for teens that can change radically from day to day.

Rite of Passage

"My real mom would let me" is a common statement from a child who was adopted. It's considered almost a rite of passage. It's a time when you are being tested—how will you react to this statement? Your child has played the trump card—throwing the emotional issue of adoption at you.

Hopefully, you will not fall for this tactic, and will have a simple, calm response: "Well she's not here right now, so I guess it's my call." Children test their parents, and a child who was adopted simply has some extra ammunition.

It might be added that in an open adoption where the birth mother is in the picture, this is not the time to call her and find out what she would or would not do. By doing so you are undermining your own ability and authority as the parent. The birth mother's role must be defined, and it does not include having parental authority. Otherwise, the child can play one side against the other and ultimately will be left feeling let down by both when he or she is older.

Adult Adoptees

"My family now has everything on the table," says Leanne an adult adoptee whose family did not talk frequently or openly about adoption when she was growing up. *"There was much resistance to discussing adoption when I grew up and now there is much more openness. I felt an enormous sense of loss. I felt a need inside of me to know more and I knew it wasn't good to shut off to it in order to survive psychologically."* Leanne had an inner quest to discover who she was, and then a quest for more information. As she grew up, she investigated on her own to find answers to her own adoption quest. Leanne searched for her birth parents and as an adult, she established a relationship with them.

> *It's always better to know then not to know. It doesn't fill all your holes, but you want to know about your own story, not to look at it as a panacea that life is going to be great, just to fill in some of the pieces."* The longer you grow up with information, the easier it is to integrate it into your life. Then, should you seek a reunion, it will be much easier because your expectations will be more realistic."*

Camellia, a forty year-old adult adoptee, was one of three children including a biological older sister who were adopted by her parents. Today she and her husband are raising two young children, whom they have also adopted. She recalls that while growing up, life did not focus heavily on adoption issues, although the subject was always discussed around the home.

> *"It came up at different times in life. When the subject came up I would think about it and certainly there were times I had questions, but for the most part it was not a part of everyday life for me or my brother or*

sister. It was always in the back of my mind that someday I could search or find out more if I wanted to, but I really was not very interested.

Camellia's father gave her all of the paperwork and information that he had when she grew up. *I think it was important that we were open about adoption in the household. My dad used to tell me about how when he brought me home, everybody in our Brooklyn neighborhood was waiting outside for us. It was always a very positive thing. I'm trying to do that with my own children, telling them about their adoption stories and talking about it openly. They know that I was adopted, and so was one of their aunts and one of their uncles."*

Searching

The Internet has been a great help for adoptees looking to search for birth parents. Web-sites like *www.Reunite.com, www.adoptionretriever.com,* and *www.adoptionregistry.com* all provide ways to begin the adoption search process. By law, adoption searches can be done once the adoptee reaches eighteen years of age unless there are medical or psychological concerns that need to be addressed. In such cases, adoptive parents can request— generally with the support of a doctor and or attorney—that birth parent files be opened.

Of course, adoptees searched well before there was a World Wide Web. "Searching starts with gathering information," says Susan Cox of Holt International Children's Services. "Go to whoever originated the adoption. In some states where records are open, you can get the information from the agency. In other states, where there are not open records, you need to get more creative. There are organizations like the American Adoption Congress (*www.americanadoptioncongress.org*) that can be of help. In my case, since I was born in Korea, I placed ads in newspapers in the area where I was born. In time it started me on the path to finding my birth mother."

Placing ads, finding search-specific books in the library or bookstore, and utilizing as much information as your state allows you access to are the ways to proceed on a search. Also, by joining on-line chat and information-sharing groups, adoptees can learn the methods others used in their searches.

In addition to the how-tos of searching are the emotional factors. Adoptees need to be mature enough to handle the situation. When is someone considered emotionally mature? That's debatable. Many adult adoptees and adoption experts agree that you need to be emotionally prepared. "If someone is looking to search, they should know what it is they are searching for and why they want to search. It's more than just locating another person, and that's what makes searching tricky," adds Cox.

Some international adoptees are in search of learning more about their culture and their roots before even desiring to search for their birth parents. However, domestic-born adoptees by and large, want to meet their birth mothers. For many it is curiosity, while for others there are unanswered questions and unresolved issues they are hoping to solve. An individual's temperament, level of emotional security, and self-esteem will all factor into how one approaches a potential meeting with a birth mother or birth parents.

There are numerous individual factors involved in this complex emotional issue. There are ongoing debates over the availability of information and what records should and should not be opened, by whom, and at what age.

Search factors that come into play include:

- The emotional maturity of the adoptee;
- The reasons why he or she is searching: Curiosity? To learn more about his or her identity? A desire to connect? Medical information? Anger at the adoptive parents? Anger at the birth mother or birth parents?
- The image the adoptee has of the birth parents. Does he or she have unrealistic expectations?
- The reality of who the birth parents are and whether or not they want to be located;
- The circumstances surrounding the adoption;
- The degree or quality of information provided by the adoptive parents;
- The openness about adoption in the household;
- State laws, agency policies, and other extenuating factors;
- The post-search reaction. This is very important. Often the meeting is the crescendo. What then? This should be thought about in advance.

All of these factors will determine the success or failure of the search.

The last point is worth further discussion because it is one reason why adoptive parents may persuade the adoptee to wait until he or she is older before searching. In general, parents protect their children as best they can. Adoptive parents are often very concerned that a young adoptee—especially a teen—will want to search in hopes of finding "the all-fulfilling answer" and will be disappointed.

As noted earlier, teens look for short-term cures. For that matter, so do many adults. Most often when a teen (or anyone) is seeking a solution, meeting birth parents is a letdown. They are simply people—good people—but there is no wizard in Oz who will make everything better. Many adult adoptees who have searched on their own accord admit that afterward they felt some letdown. This is not meant to deny in any way the many wonderful meetings that have forged new relationships between birth parents and adoptees. With the right emotional attitude and perspective, the adoptee can discover a whole new family. This serves only as a warning that adoptee-birth parent relationships are not always what you see on television and need to be approached with realistic expectations.

Interestingly enough, many children are aware that they are too young to meet the birth parents. They commonly say, without much concern, "I think I might like to meet her when I'm older." Often children, teens, and even adults do not want to give up the fantasies of their birth family. They also worry about not being able to connect automatically with their birth parents beyond that of physical resemblance. Says Camellia: *"I think for most people, like 90 percent, it's curiosity that leads to a search. I was in my thirties and I figured what the heck, I'm going to try to contact my birth mother and see who she is. My dad had given me the paperwork, so it wasn't all that hard. My biological sister and I found her number and called, but she just told us it was a wrong number. We double-checked and were sure it was her, but when we tried again, she didn't want to talk with us. I was surprised that she didn't want to meet us, but I guess she had put it behind her and did not want to have to deal with that part of her life. She certainly could not have put it out of her head to the point where she wouldn't remember. I sent about ten letters but did not receive anything back. A short time later I called once more, just to say thank you for giving us the good life we had, but the number had been disconnected. I was disappointed, but figured this is what she needed to do. I never looked at it as a mother-daughter kind of thing, but I was just curious to meet her."*

Sometimes searches also lead to siblings, explains Camellia: *"I had also been curious about whether I had any other siblings and did locate her son, my half-brother who knew nothing about my sister or me. He did meet with us, and we had a lot in common. He agreed that it was his mother's choice and she had to deal with that in any way she could. We had a nice meeting and that was about it. We later found out that around the holidays he told her that he had met us and she didn't really know what to say. She has my number, address, last name, so if she contacts us, great, and if not, I'll understand."*

Unlike Camellia, Marilyn, mentioned above, is more fearful of starting her search. *"I've started filling out the papers to search many times,"* she says. *"I never go through with it. I think I'm afraid I won't find anything. I do have a feeling of loss, but also a sense of curiosity about what my birth mother looks like, what her character is and what she's like. I share blood type with someone and don't know her . . . I don't even know if she's wondering what ever happened to me. I hope she is."*

For Marilyn, discussing adoption is cathartic. She didn't have many opportunities to discuss it as she grew up, but is now interested in learning more and understanding more about her culture and her past.

Post-Search: Now What?

The process of searching, like the adoption process is stressful and time consuming. You go on an emotional roller coaster, unsure what the end result will be. The true journey, however, may begin after the search process has ended and the relationship has begun. Some adoptees admit they hadn't thought very carefully about what the next step in the relationship would be.

The Right Time

A search can be successful only if done at the right time. That is, the right time for the adoptee, not when others who are enthusiastic about reunions say it is. It must be something that a person feels in their heart is the right thing to do. The right time for each person will be different, depending on life circumstances. The media and the idea that through the Internet (and through other means) people can be found doesn't mean that you are obligated to search. Each adoptee should make a sound decision based on what is in his or her heart.

The adoptee needs to determine how he or she sees this relationship progressing. For some adoptees, it is the start of a strong new bond; for many, however, where this relationship will lead is ambiguous. Both sides must do some soul searching and evaluate whether this was a one-time meeting to resolve issues and unanswered questions or the start of something more. And if this is the beginning, what are the next steps to take?

Leanne, mentioned above, found that searching led to a new family, and now she is comfortable with the roles both families have in her life:

"I'm working more toward greater integration of my families, having a different configuration of family meetings. I want all of my family to meet. I want to be with everyone. There is a still some sense of being split … being with one family and missing the other. Both families are important to me in their own ways. I'm very glad I searched and found my birth family; it's completed the picture for me."

The stories of searches, like those of the adoption process, are quite diverse. The best adoptive parents can do is help educate and prepare their sons or daughters so that they can proceed carefully and thoughtfully.

Chapter 24
ADOPTION RESOURCES

Here are some of the many places to turn for adoption information. Some are also included elsewhere throughout the book. Many of those listed below provide listings of specific agencies or attorneys, as do many of the web-sites listed in Chapter 21. These listings are provided as a general guide to adoption services.

Adopt America Network
1025 North Reynolds Road
Toledo, OH 43615
419-534-3350
www.adoptamerica.org
Adopt America helps children with special needs (who are freed for adoption) find permanent families.

Adoption Resource Exchange for Single Parents
ARESP
P.O. Box 0645
Rockville, MD 20848-0645
301- 585-5836
http://www.aresp.net

Adoptive Families Magazine
42 West 38th Street
Suite 901
New York, NY 10018
800-372-3300 for subscriptions to this bimonthly adoption

magazine or for answers to your questions.
www.adoptivefamiiesmagazine.com
Their annual Adoption Guide includes the names of adoption agencies and attorneys in state-by-state listings and has useful other listings.

American Academy of Adoption Attorneys (AAAA)
P.O. Box 33053
Washington, D.C. 20033-0053.
202-832-2222
www.adoptionattorneys.org
You can call or write to them for a free directory of member attorneys.

American Academy of Pediatrians
141 Northwest Point Boulevard
Elk Grove Village, IL 60007-1098
847-434-4000
Inquire about members who are part of the provincial section on adoption.

American Adoption Congress
P.O. Box 42730
Washington, D.C. 20015
202-483-3399
www.americanadoptioncongress.org
An organization committed to adoption reform, education, and increasing public awareness.

American Foster Care Resources, Inc.
AFCR
P.O. Box 271
King George, VA 22485
540-775-7410
www.afcr.com
Provides educational training and materials about foster-care adoption.

Child Welfare League of America
440 First St., NW
3rd floor
Washington, D.C. 20001-2085
800-ask-cwla
202-638-2952
www.cwla.org

Children Awaiting Parents (CAP)
595 Blossom Road
Suite 306
Rochester, NY 14610
585-232-5110
www.capbook.org
Promotes adoption for children in the foster-care system.

COLAGE, Children of Lesbians and Gays Everywhere
3543 18th Street, #1
San Francisco, CA 94110, USA
415-861-KIDS

Council on Adoptable Children
589 Eighth Avenue
15th floor
New York, NY 10018
212-714-2788
www.coac.org
Helps parents adopt abused, neglected, and "hard to place"
children.

Families for Russian and Ukrainian Adoption (FRUA)
P.O. Box 2944
Merrifield, VA 22116
730-560-6184
www.frua.org
Support and information for families who have adopted
from Russia or Ukraine.

Immigration and Naturalization Services
1-800-375-5283, *www.ins.usdoj.gov.*
Ask for or look on its web-site for regional field offices. The INS provides all necessary paperwork for international adoptions.

Inter-National Adoption Alliance (IAA)
2441 Q Old Fort Parkway
Murfreesboro, TN 37128
www.i-a-a.org
Organization designed to help provide families formed overseas with cultural resources and help find homes for children who are waiting in countries around the world.

International Concerns for Children, Inc.
911 Cypress Drive
Boulder, CO 80303-2821
303-494-8333
www.ICCadopt.org
Provides information, including an annual report on international adoption.

Joint Council on International Children's Services
Suite 200 1320 19th Street, NW
Washington, D.C. 20036
202-429-0400
www.jcics.org
Member organization for international adoption agencies.

National Adoption Center
1500 Walnut Street
Philadelphia, PA 19102
215–735-9988 or 1-800-TO-ADOPT
www.adopt.org
Presents "Faces of Adoption," America's waiting children photo listings.

National Adoption Information Clearinghouse
P.O. Box 1182
Washington, DC, 20013
888-251-0075
www.calib.com/naic/
Provides a wealth of adoption information.

National Association of Social Workers (NASW)
750 First Street NE
Suite 700
Washington, DC 20002-4241
202-208-4600
www.socialworkers.org

National Center on Permanency for African-American
NCPAAC Children
Howard University School of Social Work—Holy Cross Hall
2900 Van Ness Street NW
Room 328
Washington, DC 20008
202-806-8100 / 202-806-8216

National Council for Single Adoptive Parents. (formerly
The Committee for Single Adoptive Parents)
P.O. Box 44
Wharton, NJ 07885
www.adopting.org/ncsap.html

National Foster Parent Association (NFPA)
P.O. Box 81
Alpha, OH 45301-0081
800-557-5238
E-mail: nfpa@donet.com
www.nfpainc.org

National Resource Center for Special Needs Adoption
(NRC-SNA)
Spaulding for Children

16250 Northland Drive
Suite 120
Southfield, MI 48075
248-443-7080
www.spaulding.org/adoption/NRG-adoption.html

North American Council on Adoptable Children (NACAC)
970 Raymond Avenue
Suite 106
St. Paul, MN 55114
800-470-6665 / 651-644-3036
Information on waiting children in the United States and Canada. You can inquire about a representative in every state who can provide names of parent support groups in your area as well as other information.

Pact, An Adoption Alliance
3315 Sacramento Street
Suite 239
San Francisco, CA 94118
415-221-6957
www.pactadopt.org
Deals with the adoptions of children of color for gay and lesbian couples.

RESOLVE, Inc.
1310 Broadway
Somerville, MA 02144-1731
617-623-0744
www.resolve.org
Main headquarters for the national organization dedicated to providing information about infertility. Inquire about local chapters.

State central adoption offices at the state social-service headquarters. These offices can help you gather information on adopting from the state foster-care system. Here is a phone directory.

Alabama
Alabama Office of Adoption: Department of Human Resources in Montgomery,
205-242-9500.

Alaska
Alaska Division of Family and Youth Services in Juneau
907-265-5080.

Arizona
Arizona Department or Economic Security in Phoenix
602-542-2359.

Arkansas
Arkansas Department of Human Services: Division of Children and Family Services in Little Rock
501-682-8462.

California
California Department of Social Services: Adoptions Branch in Sacramento
916-445-3146.

Colorado
Colorado Department of Social Services in Denver
303-866-3209.

Connecticut
Department of Children and Families in Hartford
203-238-6640.

Delaware
Delaware Division of Child Protective Services in Wilmington
302-633-2655.

District of Columbia
District of Columbia Adoption and Placement Resources
202-724-8602.

Florida
Florida Department of Children and Families in Tallahassee
904-487-2383.

Georgia
Georgia Department of Human Resources, Division of Family and
Child Services in Atlanta
404-657-3560.

Hawaii
Hawaii Department of Human Services in Honolulu
808-586-5698.

Idaho
Department of Health and Welfare, Division of Family and Community Services in Boise
208-334-5700.

Illinois
Department of Children and Family Services in Springfield
217-524-2411.

Indiana
Division of Family and Children, Bureau of Family Protection/Preservation in Indianapolis
888-204-7466.

Iowa
Iowa Department of Human Services in Des Moines
515-281-5358.

Kansas
Kansas Department of Social and Rehabilitation Services in Topeka
913-296-8183.

Kentucky
Kentucky Cabinet for Human Resources in Frankfort
502-564-2147.

Louisiana
Louisiana Department of Social Services: Office of Community Services in Baton Rouge
504-342-2297.

Maine
Department of Human Services in Augusta
297-287-5060.

Maryland
Maryland Department of Human Resources in Baltimore
410-767-7423.

Massachusetts
Massachusetts Department of Social Services in Boston
617-727-0900.

Michigan
Michigan Department of Social Services in Lansing
517-373-4021.

Minnesota
Adoption Unit, Minnesota Department of Human Services in St. Paul
612-296-3740.

Mississippi
Mississippi Department of Social Services in Jackson
601-359-4500.

Missouri
Missouri Division of Family Services in Jefferson City
314-751-2502.

Montana
Montana Department of Public Health and Human Services in Helena
406-444-5919.

Nebraska
Nebraska Department of Social Services in Lincoln
402-471-9331.

New Hampshire
Department of Health and Human Services in Concord
702-486-7650.

Nevada
Office Of Adoption, Nevada Children and Family Services in Las Vegas
702-486-7650.

New Jersey
New Jersey Division of Youth and Family Services in Trenton
609-292-9139.

New Mexico
CYFD/SSD Children's Bureau Placement Services Section in Santa Fe
505-827-8456.

New York
New York State Department of Social Services in Albany
518-474-2868.

North Carolina
North Carolina Department of Human Resources in Raleigh
919-733-3801.

North Dakota
North Dakota Department of Human Services in Bismarck
701-328-4805.

Ohio
Department of Human Services in Columbus
614-466-9274.

Oklahoma
Oklahoma Department of Human Services in Oklahoma City
405-521-2475.

Oregon
Oregon Department of Human Services in Salem
503-945-5944.

Pennsylvania
Department of Public Welfare, Office of Children, Youth and Families
in Harrisburg
717-787-7756.

Rhode Island
Rhode Island Department of Children and Their Families in Mt. Pleasant
401-457-4548.

South Carolina
Department of Social Services in Columbia
803-734-6095.

South Dakota
Department of Social Services in Pierre
605-773-3227.

Tennessee
Tennessee Department of Human Services in Nashville
615-741-5935.

Texas
Texas Department of Private and Regulatory Services in Austin
512-438-3412.

Utah
Department of Human Services: Division of Child and Family Services in Salt Lake City
801-538-4080.

Vermont
Vermont Division of Social Services in Waterbury
802-241-2131.

Virginia
Department of Social Services, Richmond
804-692-1273.

Washington
Department of Social Health and Services, Children's Administration
in Olympia
360-902-7968.

West Virginia
West Virginia Department of Human Services in Charleston
304-558-7980.

Wisconsin
Department of Health and Family Services: Division of Children and
Family Services in Madison
608-266-3595.

Wyoming
Department of Family Services in Cheyenne
307-777-3570.

INDEX